Kathryn Bedard, MA, LCADC, CMS

Compassion and Courage in the Aftermath of Traumatic Loss

Stones in My Heart Forever

More pre-publication
REVIEWS, COMMENTARIES, EVALUATIONS . . .

"**T**his book is a very tough read. It pulls at your heart and soul, as it should. Kathryn Bedard's book—journal, really—of her work at the New Jersey Family Assistance Center after 9/11 allows us to walk with these angels as they escort the families into the hell of Ground Zero and back out again. The wounds of 9/11 are etched into all our minds; this book pushes those wounds and images deeper, into our souls—again, as it should."

Craig Nakken, LICSW, LMFT
Author of *The Addictive Personality: Understanding the Addictive Process and Compulsive Behavior*

The Haworth Press
New York • London • Oxford

Compassion and Courage
in the Aftermath
of Traumatic Loss
Stones in My Heart Forever

THE HAWORTH PRESS

Haworth Series in Family and Consumer Issues in Health
F. Bruce Carruth, PhD, Senior Editor

Addicted and Mentally Ill: Stories of Courage, Hope, and Empowerment by Carol Bucciarelli

Compassion and Courage in the Aftermath of Traumatic Loss: Stones in My Heart Forever by Kathryn Bedard

Other Titles of Related Interest

Healing 9/11: Creative Programming by Occupational Therapists edited by Pat Precin

Surviving 9/11: Impact and Experiences of Occupational Therapy Practitioners edited by Pat Precin

The Trauma of Terrorism: Sharing Knowledge and Shared Care, An International Handbook edited by Yael Danieli, Danny Brom, and Joe Sills

Trauma Practice in the Wake of September 11, 2001 edited by Steven N. Gold and Jan Faust

On the Ground After September 11: Mental Health Responses and Practical Knowledge Gained edited by Yael Danieli and Robert L. Dingman

Compassion and Courage in the Aftermath of Traumatic Loss
Stones in My Heart Forever

Kathryn Bedard

The Haworth Press
New York • London • Oxford

For more information on this book or to order, visit
http://www.haworthpress.com/store/product.asp?sku=5464

or call 1-800-HAWORTH (800-429-6784) in the United States and Canada
or (607) 722-5857 outside the United States and Canada

or contact orders@HaworthPress.com

The Haworth Press, Inc., 10 Alice Street, Binghamton, NY 13904-1580.

PUBLISHER'S NOTES
The development, preparation, and publication of this work has been undertaken with great care. However, the Publisher, employees, editors, and agents of The Haworth Press are not responsible for any errors contained herein or for consequences that may ensue from use of materials or information contained in this work. The Haworth Press is committed to the dissemination of ideas and information according to the highest standards of intellectual freedom and the free exchange of ideas. Statements made and opinions expressed in this publication do not necessarily reflect the views of the Publisher, Directors, management, or staff of The Haworth Press, Inc., or an endorsement by them.

The identities and circumstances of some individuals discussed in this book have been changed to protect confidentiality.

Poem "One" © 2001 by Cheryl B. Sawyer, EdD. Reprinted by permission.

Unless otherwise noted, all photos by Kathryn Bedard.

The 9/11 mural, "America's Heart," was recreated from a painting by Yakov Smirnoff and erected by sixty volunteers from the Sheet Metal Workers Union on a skyscraper at Ground Zero. The painting contains one brushstroke for each victim of the attacks.

Cover design by Marylouise E. Doyle. Cover photos by Kathryn Bedard.

Library of Congress Cataloging-in-Publication Data

Bedard, Kathryn.
    Compassion and courage in the aftermath of traumatic loss : stones in my heart forever / Kathryn Bedard.
        p. cm.
    Written by a mental health clinician volunteer who directed service logistics at the Family Assistance Center, Liberty State Park, Jersey City, N.J.
        ISBN-13: 978-0-7890-2741-2 (hc. alk. paper)
        ISBN-10: 0-7890-2741-0 (hc. alk. paper)
        ISBN-13: 978-0-7890-2742-9 (pbk. alk. paper)
        ISBN-10: 0-7890-2742-9 (pbk. alk. paper)
    1. September 11 Terrorist Attacks, 2001—Personal narratives. 2. World Trade Center (New York, N.Y.) 3. Disaster victims—Services for—New York (State)—New York. 4. Human services personnel—New York (State)—New York—Anecdotes. 5. Disaster relief—New York (State)—New York—Psychological aspects. 6. September 11 Terrorist Attacks, 2001—Psychological as- pects. I. Title.

HV6432.7.B413 2005
155.9'35—dc22

                                                            2005016592

These pages are dedicated to those who were affected by the events of September 11, 2001.

May we find peace.

ABOUT THE AUTHOR

Kathryn Bedard, MA, LCADC, CMS, NCADC, has been in human services since 1972 and has extensive clinical experience, including treatment of individuals with severe and persistent mental illness in psychiatric inpatient hospitals; drug, alcohol, and mental health treatment to individuals in a forensic hospital; behavior modification programming in homes with children who have autism and Down syndrome; and outpatient drug, alcohol, and mental health treatment with a subspecialty in the treatment of anxiety and stress disorders. She also has extensive administrative experience in program development, policy development, implementation, clinical and administrative supervision, and administrative oversight of a statewide initiative that provides for the needs of individuals with mental illness and chemical abuse. She has been instrumental in the development and adoption of a process for the clinical credentialing of staff who work with clients who have the dual disorders of mental illness and chemical abuse, and has been a faculty member of the Rutgers School of Alcohol and Drug Studies, providing day training classes and summer schools. Ms. Bedard has developed numerous courses on anxiety, burnout, and stress management, and has taught meditation and other Eastern arts since 1979.

Prologue

I once attended a training session about spirituality. The presenter drew a horizontal, spiraling line across the chalkboard to represent the cycles of life. He described life as a series of experiences of death and rebirth: never-ending cycles of emotions, decisions, and events that occur as naturally (and are as necessary) as the seasons. Life-altering experiences. Each time we are confronted with one of those events— divorce, death of a loved one, change in career—we must die a little inside in order to move forward and grow emotionally and spiritually. We can choose to remain in the struggle rather than surrender, but we will only perpetuate our difficulty. The part that really grabbed me, though, was the concept that all of these little "deaths" that we experience are actually rehearsals for the ultimate. The trainer completed his description by saying that those of us who surrender many times during our life will have an easier time accepting our ultimate death: we can go in peace because we have practiced it so much. Those of us who resist surrender will go kicking and screaming to our graves. That training session was one of those life-altering experiences for me.

Everyone, at some time in their life, will reach a point where things no longer make sense. Before we die, we all will be faced with an opportunity that brings with it life-changing impact. For some, that may mean making a decision such as marriage, buying a first car, or changing careers. For others, it may mean that life as we knew it can no longer exist. No matter how large or small the event, or how gut-wrenching the decision, we must come to terms with it by taking action. We must allow our former selves to die off, and open our eyes to something new. The journey will always be one that touches our spirit: By "spirit," I mean the spot where our emotions, our true self, and our vulnerability and courage lie. A Chinese saying used in the world of martial arts states, "In every battle, your opponent is always only yourself."

When faced with obstacles we ultimately have a choice. We can run away, shut down, deny or protest, or we can hold our noses and jump in, without thinking about how dark or how deep the water is (or about what lurks in that darkness). These pages are a first-person description of how ordinary people act in extraordinary ways, and what it feels like to hold your nose and jump in. This book was born from my experience in the operations of a disaster relief site.

It is my hope to put into words and pictures the process that occurred as a group of people took a journey every day, walking beside the grieving families of New Jersey victims of the World Trade Center attacks. I want you to see what we saw, feel what we felt, and walk with us each day as a silent participant. I want you to also bear witness to the pain and grief of those who were directly affected by this disaster. I want you to feel the weight of it in your heart. I present these stories to you to honor those who were lost, those who remained behind, and those of us who did whatever we could to try to make it better.

People respond to disasters for many reasons. Some respond because they have chosen a profession to help others—altruism. Some people are voyeurs. The Red Cross Web site says that many responders to horrific events have certain characteristics in common: they are perfectionists who thrive in high stimulation and are very social. Those who helped me by proofreading these pages before they became a manuscript said that I should start by telling readers about myself and my reasons for volunteering as part of the response to the terrorist attacks that took 2,752 lives in New York City.

Like the rest of the world, I was torn by the events of September 11, 2001. I am a clinician by training, with a background and credentials in both psychology and addictions treatment. I have worked in the field of mental health treatment since 1972, and in treating those with addiction since 1985. I have worked with a wide range of people: children, individuals who are labeled "criminally insane," addicts, adults with severe mental illness, college students who have trouble setting goals. During my training and experience, I have frequently walked through the emotionally charged world of others, so I have the professional resources to deal with pain, loss, fear, and upheaval. I am also one of those perfectionists whom the Red Cross describes as being able to thrive in a highly charged and stimulating environment.

My personal motivation to provide assistance at the World Trade Center disaster site came from the following:

- having friends and neighbors who worked in and near the Towers;
- knowing people who regularly stopped in the Towers for morning coffee and breakfast on the way to nearby employment;
- thinking of the thousands of people now traumatized and in crisis,
- having a friend who owned a shop in the mall, which was now buried under tons of rubble; and
- having New York City, with its wonderful Broadway plays, food, shopping, and activity, as my playground.

New Jersey is frequently referred to as a suburb of New York. As a native New Jerseyian, that is just a teeny bit insulting, but in many ways, I accept that as a truth. Part of this Jersey girl has a deep appreciation for that big gleaming city being so close, so accessible, and so full of magical things. I watched the Towers grow as they were being built. I sat in front of the news updates on the progress of the construction and listened to family opinion about the changing skyline of the city. As kids, we used to skip school and go to New York City by train. Something we all did when we first saw the Towers in person was to run up really close to them, looking straight up for what seemed like miles (up against the outer wall with chin almost touching). It made me feel dizzy and I almost fell over backward. The Towers had a personality. *Big* personality.

When I watched the Towers fall, I felt a strong pull inside to offer assistance. It was my backyard; I took it personally. I wanted so badly to turn that ugly thing around, even though I knew it was not possible. But I felt like I had to go . . . it was almost a compulsion, a sense of fate. As time went on that day, and I found (almost all of) my friends one by one, I knew I had to go. I hold inside of me a tremendous amount of gratitude for the fact that those whom I know and love are alive. I wanted so badly to show that gratitude through service. Initially, there were reports of the volume of volunteers being so high that it was causing unsafe and chaotic conditions. Since it was obvious that work would continue with this horrendous event for considerable time, my thoughts turned to providing relief for the initial responders who would soon grow tired. I chewed my fingernails and waited.

Since 1987, I have been involved in the administrative/bureaucratic world of mental health, and over that time I have developed the confidence and bureaucratic alpha dog traits that one needs to oversee statewide initiatives in a large system. My clinical and administrative background, training, and persona were about to be put to work. On September 19, 2001, I went to the Liberty Family Assistance Center (FAC) in Jersey City, New Jersey, for the first time to provide counseling services. My role there soon evolved: I was asked to coordinate visitation to the World Trade Center complex for the families of the New Jersey victims of the World Trade Center attack. From September through December 2001, I dedicated my time every day to taking them to the fractured and tangled seventeen acres within the city that became known as Ground Zero. We also took survivors over to help them come to terms with their nightmares, terror, and grief. That experience will stay locked in my heart and mind forever.

I have never seen or worked in a disaster before. I grew up in suburban middle-class New Jersey, leading a charmed life that contained no violence and very little heartache. In retrospect, I can remember only going to about three funerals before the age of twenty-one, so, obviously life was good. When I arrived at the New Jersey Family Assistance Center location on September 19, I was advised that keeping a journal every night would help me to sort out what I saw and how I felt. I have never kept a journal, or even a diary as an adolescent, so it was not something I did naturally. My clinical training recognized the wisdom of that type of activity, so I was compliant with the advice, for the most part. That journal formed the basis for this book.

Journal pages, being what they are, are filled with personal glimpses, thoughts, and opinions, but not many details. They are raw and unpolished. Unless you were a part of the events contained within, reading journal pages is without context or framework—just a jumble of emotions and reactions, hopes and fears. Hence, to help those of you who were not there to understand the details, I will begin with information on the place and the process to fill in what was not written in the journal. This is Part I of the book. The journal is contained in Part II.

I think most of the families went to the World Trade Center complex to try to find something. Some found peace and acceptance. Others found that their horror multiplied, and they wished they had never gone. Those of us who went with them definitely found something:

> Heavy things.
> Scary things that we will carry with us forever.
> Things that make us want to scream.

I know that most of us who worked with the families also found beauty. Based on listening to the volunteers as we debriefed at the end of each day, I am confident that at least for a time they saw the incredible strength, courage, and compassion of fellow humans. I pray that each of them retained that vision and continue to carry it with them. I know beyond any doubt that the people I am still in touch with saw the best of humanity shining brightly in that place, for they were a part of creating it. I hope that as you read, you also find the beauty and strength that is intermingled with the horror. We should remember the horror forever so that it is never repeated. We should remember the beauty forever so that it *is* repeated.

I am not a professional author but I have a story to share. My goal is to try to bring another piece of this event to life for you—a piece that is known only to those who participated in creating it, because our story never made it to the media. It is an intimate and emotional story that originated through daily interactions between the most amazing people: people who held their noses and jumped into the deep, dark abyss, never thinking for a moment about what they would find. Everyone should meet these people. Once you enter the journal and meet them, and have the opportunity to walk beside them through our many days together, you will (as I do), ever after refer to them as angels . . .

America's Heart

Acknowledgments

A mural painted on a building overlooking Ground Zero bears the following legend:

> The human spirit is not measured by the size of the act, but by the size of the heart.

I would like to express my gratitude to the following people, all of whom share one attribute—the size of their hearts:

Fred Bedard, I don't know what would have happened had you not walked beside me all of those days. I guess that's where the term "soul mates" came from . . .

Bob, thank you, from the bottom of my heart.

Judy, the world is fortunate to hear that laugh of yours.

Rich, you *are* an angel. Thank you for always being there.

George, your smile is a blessing, and your life a testimony that good always conquers evil.

Anthony, thank you for being the first smile I saw, *every* day.

Major Barbara Kelly, you kept me sane, and I bet you didn't even know it.

Jack, the Lord of Equipment—love you! I could never thank you enough.

To my "crew": John, Martha, our EMTs, Ann, Bonnie, Stewart, Lyn, Dom, Laura, *all* of you, so many of you. Thank you!

To Mabel and Beth, my four-footed therapist, and her wonderful owner.

And all of our New Jersey State Troopers, you are the best!

Gail Sheehy, for sending new angels in Port Authority uniforms my way. And for your warm and sensitive words about the families and our work with them at the FAC.

Craig Nakken, for your tears and prayers and for being there.

Chuck and Lee Nussbaum, to Chuck for pushing me. To Lee for pushing *him,* and for your insight.

And thanks to the following people who contributed time, energy, focus, and thoughts to these pages:

> *Peg Marr,* through paper (in more than one context and connotation) I have found another kindred spirit. My heart went out to you for more than one reason as we experienced editing. Thank you!
>
> *Jane Nakken,* in many ways these words are now as much yours as mine.
>
> *Jeanne Hart Convery,* you're a great friend.
>
> *Bruce Carruth,* my editor, for his patience, and for encouraging me more than I can ever express. Thank you!
>
> *And my "readers," Bette Ann, Marcia, Karen, Margaret, Debbie, Lee B., Joy:* Thank you for your honesty, your support, and your red pens.

"How can hearts so big simply stop?" Major Barb simply replied, "When we have accomplished our purpose in our time here, He takes us home."

> *George Donnelly,* We laughed, cried, and talked many nights as the sun set all around us. I know you still watch it, even if it is from above. Rest in peace, brother.
>
> *Major Fred Trask,* Your legacy is in the hearts of those whom you moved with the power of your words. I like to think that when I lay down those stones for the last time that your smiling face will greet me, and you will talk to me just once more.

Part I: Introduction

The Location

In response to the terrorist attacks on the World Trade Center, the state of New Jersey set up the Family Assistance Center at Liberty State Park in Jersey City, New Jersey. We called it the "FAC." It was a spontaneously erected, self-contained microcosm designed to meet the personal and service needs of New Jersey's survivors, victims, and families. Because a state of national emergency had been declared, and to protect the privacy of victims and families, to gain entry to the FAC, one had to be on a list and have two forms of ID, including picture identification. A security checkpoint was manned by the New Jersey Department of Corrections at the entrance to the drive leading up to the area. At this checkpoint individuals presented identification and were cleared for entry. Security was so tight that few pictures were ever taken and published, and very little was ever written about the FAC, so these pages will give readers a rare glimpse of the interior workings of the disaster site.

The FAC was developed in the old railroad terminal building in Liberty State Park. The site is directly across the Hudson River from Battery Park City. In full view of the World Trade Center complex and the Mercantile, it is a seven-minute ferry trip across the river, and a hub for ferry and water taxi trips to Manhattan, the Statue of Liberty, and Ellis Island. The terminal building was constructed circa 1860 and is a beautiful, cavernous old structure with Victorian features including a peaked slate roof and iron scrollwork. The terminal was closed for railroad use in 1967. Signs for local destinations that had not been traveled to since that time were still posted at the old platforms where tracks ran to the end of the terminal and stopped in a field. The platforms became the location of memorial walls (constructed for the families to leave messages and remembrances), the "intake" areas, the dining area for volunteers, and the snack stations set up by the Salvation Army and the Red Cross. Antique railroad cars were parked in the front of the building as a display.

On windy days, the openness of the building and the layout of the grounds caused the wind to whip through the platform area, bringing a chill that could reach your bones in seconds. As winter approached, tents with heaters were erected on the platform area to provide shelter. We wore our jackets indoors much of the time.

The interior of the terminal building had gleaming yellow tile walls, the dust having been recently polished away when the decision was made to use this grand old building as the FAC. If you were to look upward the Victorian scrollwork on the vaulted ceiling supports, you would have to marvel at how they cleaned and polished something that high above the floor. Someone had actually taken a scrub brush to the grout lines of the red tile floor, cleaning away the soil of years. Above the catwalk that ran around the ceiling hung a huge old clock that kept perfect time. American flag buntings were draped on the railings of the catwalk on each side of the square room. Old Glory was displayed from the railing with the stripes hanging vertically. Positioned on the catwalk were large halogen lights, trained upward to reflect off the gleaming tiles, becoming the lighting source for the room. Electricity, phones, and other utilities were all brought in.

Inside the terminal building was a chapel, part of the original building. The room held pews and historical display cases. A table served as an altar, with several different faiths being represented there together: Catholicism, Judaism, Buddhism, any faith that wanted representation. Candles burned throughout the day and plants were brought in to add a softer touch. During the passing of a religious holiday, the symbols for that holiday were displayed. The chapel was used for staff and family briefings, debriefings, meetings of all sorts, for handing out urns and flags, for rest and meditation, for tears, and for prayer. Sometimes during very long days, a few staff took refuge there for short naps. Maybe because our space for all-purpose meetings was a chapel (or maybe just because), prayer occurred during most of the gatherings in that room.

To the rear of the terminal, trailers were brought in and arranged in a circle. The trailers housed services for mental health, legal issues, insurance, completion of death certificates, funding, etc. Outside the circle of service trailers was a double-wide trailer for Administration, where the individuals who directed or oversaw the operations of the FAC were stationed. Landscaping had been brought in: sod, flowers, and small bushes—an effort to make the environment as pleasant as possible. Chrysanthemums in deep fall colors were planted throughout the grounds and indoors in pots.

Immediately after the disaster occurred, and as the FAC was being developed, New York developed its Pier 94, the location where New York families and survivors were to go for information, referrals, and service. New York also began to take the family members of their victims into Ground Zero at the corner of West and Liberty Streets. New Jersey asked for permission to take our families in as well. This became part of the services offered at the FAC in October.

The FAC dealt with a multitude of issues. Clinical staff from agencies who contract with the New Jersey Division of Mental Health Services volunteered their time to work in trailer two, the mental health trailer. In addition to the staff from the state agency system, private practitioners (social workers, psychologists) also arrived to volunteer their services. Victims and family members whose stress levels or symptoms appeared to put them in a potentially precarious situation were assigned a mental health clinician to speak to for assessment, and if needed, referral for clinical services.

My involvement in the mission of the FAC began when I volunteered to go as a mental health clinician, but rapidly changed when I was asked to be the logistics person arranging family visits to New York. This meant that I would coordinate all of the individuals and agencies on both sides of the river who would be involved in the process of registering families to go, and in getting them there and back safely. I went with the families and the many volunteers, whom I called my "crewmembers," every step of the way. In total, more than 3,500 people volunteered to work at the FAC from every state in the nation, France, the United Kingdom, Canada, Mexico, and the Virgin Islands. More than 7,500 individuals received services.

Organizations at the FAC

Many, many organizations arrived to provide services to victims and families. I will only describe a few of them, those that are relevant to text in later pages.

The *Federal Emergency Management Agency (FEMA)*, is an agency that reports to the president, and is in charge of responding to, planning for, and helping people to recover from disasters and events. They also have individual assistance programs that help people and businesses following a disaster. FEMA sent a team who were available on-site, and rotated membership to provide relief for their staff.

The *New Jersey Office of the Attorney General* sent staff (attorneys) who could coordinate the legal aspects of the overall operations of the FAC, as well as the legal issues facing families and survivors. The *New Jersey State Police,* from the Attorney General's Office of Emergency Management, were a presence to coordinate the movement and safety of everyone in this restricted area. The state police also furnished about twelve state troopers per day to be in attendance at the FAC to provide us with security as we took our families to New York.

We had two teams of three emergency medical technicians (EMTs) who alternated days, covering all seven days, including holidays. They provided watch over the medical needs of all who journeyed to New York, and were equipped to provide for just about any emergency.

The *Salvation Army* has a mission, motivated by the love of God, to bring the gospel to people and to meet human needs. In disasters they set up canteens equipped to provide food and drink to those involved in rescue operations. They had set up huge pods in New York to store and dispense food. Inside Ground Zero were Salvation Army tents where the workers could have shelter to rest and a place to eat. At the FAC, the Salvation Army brought in the trailers in which all of the services were housed, and supplied payment for the ferries to bring our families to New York. They gave counseling, spiritual support, financial support, transportation, flowers, and much, much more.

The *Red Cross* responds to all kinds of disasters, from apartment-complex fires in our neighborhoods, to hurricanes, floods, and disasters worldwide. The Red Cross tries to meet emergency needs for clothing and finances. They also feed volunteers and relief workers, set up shelters, and have a team of trained mental health clinicians and chaplains. They call their response to feeding, sheltering, and caring for large groups of people in need "mass care." They provided all of this and more at the FAC. The Red Cross was our main source for the teddy bears we gave to the families. More than once we exhausted the Red Cross teddy bear stock for the East Coast, and out to the Midwest, but they got on the phones and kept finding more. Red Cross teams rotated about every two weeks to provide fresh volunteers.

The *National Organization for Victim Assistance* (NOVA) advocates on behalf of victims for access to services and to preserve victims' rights. NOVA was generally the first organization that one encountered at the FAC. They handled registration of each arriving person and assigned a "companion" who accompanied an individual through any and all of the trailers, services, and activities offered at the FAC. NOVA handled telephone calls to the victims' families to register those interested in going to the Word Trade Center complex. Like the Red Cross, NOVA rotated teams through the FAC about every two weeks.

State of New Jersey, Department of Human Services, Division of Mental Health Services is the state authority for the public system of mental health care. They provided administrative staff to assist in oversight of the whole FAC operation. They also sent out a request to all of the agencies that they contract with for clinical mental health volunteers. These staff were either scheduled to be in trailer two, or accompany those visiting the World Trade Center complex.

State of New Jersey Department of Corrections supplied staff for the check-points at the roadway, which provided access to the terminal building at Liberty State Park. They checked IDs of volunteers, families, and visitors. Over in New York, New Jersey Department of Corrections, Special Operations Group (SOG) staff were stationed to walk with us from the boat to the entrance of the World Trade Center complex. SOGs are the "swat" team members from New Jersey's prison system.

How It Worked

Every family of a deceased New Jersey victim was contacted by telephone by NOVA and offered the opportunity to go to the World Trade Center complex. Families were allowed to bring a total of twelve people. They signed up families on large sheets of paper that were then hung around the room for easy view during the upcoming week. Any special needs were noted, such as health issues or difficulty with ambulation. Any special requests, such as the request for a particular type of clergy to accompany the family were also noted so that I could contact someone to meet those special needs and requests. Each day we took between 100 and 240 people to Ground Zero.

In theory, and in "normal" circumstances, it should be easy to get to New York City from Liberty State Park. On a clear day you can spit and hit Manhattan from the dock. Due to the heightened security, the damage in New York, and restrictions to travel, the spots where the ferries and personal crafts could dock were relocated. It took interagency and interstate cooperation and ingenuity to set up a transportation system that worked. It seemed that nothing was simple: the Circle Line ferry docks and provides the services at Liberty State Park, but that company was unable to accommodate our daily schedule in addition to their responsibility to those still commuting to New York each day. After searching for a company who was willing to adapt to our needs, New York Waterways agreed to take the job, but their ferry did not fit at the Circle Line dock, having about a six-foot difference in height between the dock and the deck of the boat. This situation was unsafe; we couldn't have family members jumping from the dock into a boat, or climbing unstable ladders. We enlisted the help of New Jersey Transit, who sent buses each day to transport our families about 1.5 miles to the New York Waterways dock, located on the other side of the Liberty State Park marina. There, we boarded the ferry each day for a seven-minute ride to the New York side, the dock at the Mercantile, Battery Park City.

As we docked, we were met each day by the New Jersey Department of Corrections, Special Operations Group (SOG) staff. SOGs were part of a security force that surrounded us and served as escorts to help us to get the families through Battery Park, walking us up to the access area to Ground Zero. They had a golf cart available in case anyone had ambulatory difficulties or was unable to walk the distance. The SOGs and the New York State Police would move ahead of the group as we walked, to stand at the barricades that kept the public away from the area as we passed. This provided added privacy to our families.

The construction workers who were clearing the rubble within Ground Zero had built a wooden deck with a railing for the families to stand on to keep them safe and out of harm's way, and to avoid tripping and injury from standing and walking in the rubble. This is the deck that was used for the televised presidential visit on November 11, 2001. The remodeling of the deck that occurred for that event included a memorial wall that was signed and dedicated by President George W. Bush during the television ceremony, along with Secretary General of the United Nations, Kofi Annan.

On the return trip we simply reversed the route, walking through Battery Park to the dock, taking the ferry to the New York Waterways dock on the New Jersey side, and the buses back to the FAC. When we returned, we tried to encourage the families to eat, wait a bit before leaving, apply for benefits to avoid having to make a long trip back, etc. Families frequently used this time to leave messages on the memorial walls that lined the platform area of the terminal. Debriefing was offered for families and staff, providing an opportunity to process the day.

The People-Support Team

To support the families emotionally and to coordinate the flow of activity, a structure was developed. Each family was provided with two "companions" who came from the various agencies that staffed the FAC:

> eight from the Red Cross
> eight from the National Organization for Victim Assistance (NOVA)
> eight from state mental health contract agencies
> eight from the Salvation Army

Two companions were used for each family in case any of the family members decided that they could not go on: one companion could stay with individuals who decided that they did not want to get off the bus or the boat, or wanted to turn around. The other companion continued on. We tried to have extra companions each day because the nature of this work was so difficult that we also had to companion each other.

In addition to the companions provided to the families, our team included others who supported and protected the group:

> three chaplains
> three emergency medical technicians (EMTs)
> twelve New Jersey State Troopers
> three equipment handlers

The first family visit occurred on October 6, 2001, and continued consecutive days until December 2, 2001.

Part II: The Journal

The following pages are from the journal that I kept during the time we took the families into the World Trade Center complex. It was hastily written each night on scraps of paper, and mostly in the format of conversations and scenes. I have never kept a journal. I never thought to go out and buy a notebook or journal book to write in, so I used whatever was handy: napkins, scraps of paper, the back of junk mail. I would sit with paper and pen, and close my eyes and allow the day to run through my head like the replay of a movie. The first event that popped into my head was my starting point. I wrote whatever I could recall about conversations, my thoughts, what I saw, and how it felt. I wrote about things that hurt, things that were funny, things that touched my heart. When the stream of thought ended, I went to bed.

I have changed some of the names. I have left out some parts that may have been hurtful to the people involved. When I closed my eyes and wrote about my day, sometimes anger came out. Some of the strain that eventually crept in between us as we worked together remains here in these pages. Being in an environment of very prolonged and very intense stress, we sometimes got on one another's nerves. We may have interpreted the actions of one another on a more personal level than we would have in another place and time. We sometimes behaved badly toward one another. We struggled. We're human. I hope the reader will see and understand these times as simply the reality of our pain without thinking badly of the people in the situation.

Some days are missing, as I sometimes gave in to a lack of discipline. There may be errors in dates: sometimes at the end of a seventeen-hour day, I may not have had the brain power or the strength to get the date correct. Some of those scraps of paper did not have a date when I went back through them, so I had to make an educated guess based on where they were in the pile. Please be assured that any mistake in the sequence of events is unintentional and without malice. There are inconsistencies in dates. I chose not to change those inconsistencies before presenting them because it is the way it came out of my head. If nothing else, it illustrates very clearly how difficult it was to keep that pace each day. I simply plead exhaustion and attest to the fact that this is the best that I can offer as truth. I offer my journal in raw form, pretty much as it was written.

A Bit of History

One day I was putting materials relating to the FAC into a big box for storage. I still have all of the bookings, the registration and attendance rosters for staff and families, the record of everything I did to arrange what we needed for each day. I'm compulsive that way. I asked a couple of the people who had been in charge of the FAC what I should do with these records, as I thought that someday this information may become important to someone, and I have the originals of everything related to the family visits. With all of the agencies involved, there was really never any central location identified for long-term storage. I was told: "Keep it safe. We know you have it, and we'll find you if we need it." I began the process of packing everything up and decided to throw my journal pages in with it: at least if I wanted it someday, I would know where to look.

I shuffled all of the scraps of my journal together and thought *Someday I may want this—I should have typed it—it's all jumbled together. I should type it* now *before it gets more messed up and scattered . . .*

At that moment, the phone rang. It was a friend of a friend, who was doing some kind of rehearsal for a promotional thing for his business. He wanted people to give him objective critiques about his marketing pitch. I didn't even know the person but I had been warned that he would call. He introduced himself and launched into his speech, which I made polite noises about.

Suddenly, in midsentence, relating to nothing, he said, "Hey, Paul tells me you worked at the World Trade Center. You should write a book!"

It stunned me a bit. I stuttered and looked down at the jumble of my thoughts that were on the scattered papers in my hands. When I found my sensibilities I asked him, "If you were me, what would you write in that book?"

"What I saw, who I talked to, what we said to each other, what we did. Something so that all of us could understand this better. Something that would show us the good and the bad: how it felt to be there every day. You could really give people like me a perspective that we couldn't get anywhere else. You have a very important piece of this puzzle. Don't you get it?"

I looked down at the pages in my hand. I found myself explaining to a stranger on the phone about how throughout my experience at the FAC, people that I didn't know would spontaneously tell me that I should write a book. It was so odd. He laughed and said, "Did you ever think about listening to them?"

"No. I'm not a writer."

"Maybe you don't have to be." And he immediately went back to his marketing pitch.

We hung up. I looked again at the handwritten pages. *Nah . . . I'll just type them up for now. Later I'll think about it . . .*

Once I began to type, I had initially started at the end (simply because it was on top), and began to work backward. Somewhere very early in the process of this typing activity, I decided to go back and fill in from September 11, realizing that memories fade with time and I wanted to remember my thoughts and feelings from that day. After all, it was those thoughts and feelings that compelled me to that place. To get where you're going, you have to start someplace.

It was then that I realized that every end is just a beginning . . .

What was it that Shakespeare said?

"If you have tears, prepare to shed them now."

December 2, 2001

I groan out of the covers to sit up in the dark after not really sleeping. Has it really been more than three months? I am tired to the point that I know I can't do this too much longer. I am beginning to feel my nerves wanting to twitch. I think even my bones are tired. Every day I have left here in the dark. Well past sunset, I am just beginning to think about that long drive back home.

Is it really over? Over means so many things.

Today will not be easy for many reasons. I approach this day with both dread and joy: dread because I don't know what "over" means, and joy because it has been a very long journey.

I think, no, I *feel* in my heart and soul that this will never really be over. Not for any of us . . . and I don't know how to leave it behind.

I run my hands through my hair. 5:00 a.m. I remember when the clock said 3:30. So many nights like this: just lying there with these movies playing in my head. Movies that are either a rehearsal for the day to come, or a replay of the ones that went; I'm never really sure which. Maybe they really never happened at all. . . . Strangely, though, I don't feel as tired as all of those sleepless nights should make me feel. Sometimes I even feel energized after watching those movies running through my brain for hours, as if something about it were healing.

Oh Lord, do I need coffee.

On the drive to New York, as I watch the turnpike traffic I realize I am nervous, wondering how I am going to hold it together today. I feel as though I could just burst into tears at any moment. It isn't the fact that I'm afraid to cry that keeps me from it. It just isn't the time right now. I must hold the flood back until later, simply because it shouldn't be about me: Today isn't my day. Oh, but it is . . .

(Contradictions and extremes: This is the land of contradictions and extremes.) Because I feel the pain coming, I have selfishly made sure that I have surrounded myself with people whom I care about. People who I know are strong. People whom I feel a resonance with. A couple of them are simply kindred spirits. I also wanted many of them back today for *them:* they deserve a way to let it be over, to finalize, to come to terms—just as I know I do. Individually, so many of them have come to me and told me of their frustration and confusion at needing closure and not knowing if it will come. We are all afraid. I know that whatever I do for them will benefit me as well, soothe me too. Help me to discover the meaning of "over," and hopefully I can help them as well, as I search for my own answers. I have planned this day for a long time, scheming, gathering, and enlisting Major Fred to help us with prayer and song.

The routine is the same as always: The predictable traffic jam, a short and sweet conversation with that great guy who is the toll taker at the turnpike exit booth at 14B, the security checkpoint with Ant'ny's cheerful "Hey, how you doin'?" in such a stereotypical Jersey accent, the greetings of sleepy people, the smells of breakfast that typically turn my stomach, and the same walk through the building to the trailers, past the walls where I put on the blinders so I don't have to see . . .

Once outside the back of the terminal, I frown up at the cold, heavy, damp, gloomy day—a day that looks like I feel—and I say a silent prayer for no rain. My mind flashes to the Woodstock chant: *"No rain, no rain, no rain, no rain, no rain!"* Lord, I *am* as old as I feel . . . It is currently spitting and threatening. It has not rained on us yet. I plod up the metal steps into the trailer.

I busy myself with confirming everything one last time—double-checking myself with organizing and cleaning up, gathering and packing, all the while listening to snatches of the conversation of those around me in the administrative trailer. I'm not feeling very chatty. These people will all remain long after today. I feel jealous. Cheated. And for a flash, I think about the strangeness of wanting to stay here so close to Hell. Please, God, just one more? Just one more boat, just one more day?

After a quick glance at the time (Lord, this place is a time warp—it either flies by or drags on!) I see it is 8:30 a.m., so I dash off toward the terminal building. My "crew" begins to arrive. Some are sleepy; some are looking jumpy or apprehensive. I give one a hug: "Hey, love, waz'up? You look like I feel today! You okay to go?" I get a shaky smile, a much too tight and too long a hug for normal, and a "Yeah, sure!" which I can see is a lie. We lie to one another a lot here. Or is it just that "okay" is a term that has different meaning in this time and place than it does for the rest of the world?

Seeing them gathered here together gives me a sensation of safety. A familiarity, a knowledge, a *knowing* runs through this group. Today will run like perfection, no "newbies" to worry or fret over. These are my frequent flyers, those who have volunteered to come for the families more than a dozen times each. Some for as many as twenty-eight times. I can remember when I was told that no one should come to this place more than twice because of the intensity of the stress and the potential impact. . . . Are the little termination rituals that I came up with going to be enough?

One at a time we all greet each other, asking "Has – gotten here yet?" "Have you seen –?" Touching base, trying to build a comfort zone. Yes, I think that my selfish plan to surround myself with wonderful people will work for them as well; they need one another as much as I need them. They are building their self-protection around them before my very eyes: thank you, God! I smile to myself. . . . The routine moves on like clockwork. Being together so much has created a well-oiled machine whose parts work together with what seems to be telepathy. We simply do what needs to be done. No matter what. A many-bodied, one-brained creature. Nothing has ever gotten in the way.

Bustling and busywork is all around me in a huge storeroom filled with bags and boxes, the supplies that sustained us through it all. Chatty conversation and laughter fill this huge place. Anything but quiet and bordering on nervous. *Over* is about two hours away. We all work together to get things ready for the official closing ceremony: bags full of symbolism—Red Cross tissues, and teddies and prayers on paper. Memories in a bag. And soon we will have the *unofficial* closing ceremony. The parting ritual for us. I have a big secret in store for them: a token for each, that only a very few of the others know about. I am *really* enjoying the hell out of the fact that I have a secret.

I look up from my task and have a temporary crisis. "Oh God! Look at it out there; it's going to be dark *really* soon. This light up here fades so fast. We have to do the picture. We have to find Bob and the others." A couple of volunteers run off to locate the missing. We continue for a couple of more minutes of work before going out to collect at the docks and wait for the missing frequent flyers to add to our group photo. We huddle, chat, and make the best of the fact that people are not located yet, and time is drawing close. Ah . . . the best laid plans . . .

Once memorialized on film (not all of us, but most), we're back to the storeroom to finish up the preparations. We begin to finalize our "gifts" for the closing ceremony. There will be two ceremonies:

- One for those whom I have a burning gratitude for—those who came time after time. Those who may not even know that they held me up and kept me going just by being there. I have worked behind the scenes to get them here together, to thank them and show them how special they really are.
- And a closing ceremony for everyone who is here today at the FAC, to say good-bye to this part of the program, now that it's over. We will give them "gifts" as a parting gesture, a way to mark the end. . . .

We are so efficient that we begin to undo everything that we do and we trip over one another. It has become time to just let it be and somehow we all figure that out at the same time. The Major brings out his guitar and begins his tuning as he smiles and asks, "What shall we sing?"

"As long as it isn't 'Kum Ba Ya.'"

"Yeah, that song is pure torture."

"I hated it in summer camp; I sure don't want to sing it *now*."

Laughter. The Major develops a devilish grin, chuckles to himself and strums the notes, and we all join in singing, of course, "Kum Ba Ya"—beautifully, an earnest and solemn rendition. My crew are not only great people, they sing like angels. I smile at their ability and wonder if anyone else realizes what a beautiful sound we have just made—out of this song that only seconds ago we scoffed at. We sing a couple of more tunes from summer camp days. How is it we all know the words to these songs that we never really practice? When was the last time any of us really heard "Michael, Row the Boat Ashore"? Yet it simply falls sweetly out of our mouths.

I ask for the time. "*I have* to find Bob. We need to start our party now if we're going to get done on time for all of the others; they'll be out of their debriefing soon." I dash out the door only to meet Bob head-on in a near collision. As I stop short in his face he is giving me that stern look that tells me I've crossed the line.

"I heard singing."

How can he make those three simple words sound menacing? I hold my breath to brace myself for trouble; he told me not to try to sneak off and have a "special" party, and I really did appreciate the reasoning behind it, but whatever the consequence he chooses to give me, I think it will be worth it. So many of my crew spoke about wondering how to let go. Rituals are so important. Isn't it true that if you do it truly from the heart that you can't go wrong?

Babbling generally works. Bob hates babbling, so I launch in, "I know. It was us; we're practicing. You know, warming up. I was just coming to get you. We sent people out to look for you before, and see, here you are! Come on in; we're getting ready for the closing ceremony, and we decided to do a run-through with the singing to get it right. Come on in and sing with us. . . ." I grab his arm as I babble and pull him through the door into the storeroom. He's giving me that impatient wave of his hand and head nodding that says "Will you just shut up already?" I give the Major a nod and he begins with his booming preacher voice to gather us together in a circle. I hand Judy a bag, and with a nod, we divide the circle between us. Judy and I know our cues, because we schemed together and discussed it in advance. The Major gave us a copy of his sermon and we timed our actions to his words to make it meaningful for everyone.

I try with all of my might to listen to the Major as he introduces our reason for collecting here: to bring closure, to bury our ghosts, to pray. But my mind diffuses. *Over* has become *now*.

There will not be *one more*.

I practice all that I know about abdominal breathing. I have been trained in meditation and other Eastern techniques, which were all invaluable in helping to preserve my stamina during these long days. They aren't working for me now. My emotions have gone into overdrive and I have crossed over into the land of no rational behavior. I bite my lip. My hands ball up into fists. I look at my feet. I have a lump in my throat that will not leave, and I know that if I do listen to the Major's words I will cry. *Please, God, take this feeling from me. Let me do this with dignity and grace and just get through it: I can't cry until it's* OVER.

I realize the irony; magically it will not end as long as I don't cry? Partly. Mostly I'm too vain. I just can't cry cute. I feel crappy when I cry. I don't want to feel that yet. The drive home is a better place to feel crappy. *Now* is for enjoying *them* one last time . . . for singing, praying together, giving, hugging, celebrating, mourning . . . and saying good-bye. Crappy can wait.

. . . and it has been a *long* time. I am tired and really want to just pull the covers over my head and cry forever. Now is *not* the time to start that, so I bring my mind back to the room to hear the Major's sermon begin:

> September 11, 2001, is going to be one of those special dates in history. Everyone will recall where they were between the hours of 8:30 and 11 a.m. At 8:30 Inspector Anthony Infante was driving on the Boulevard in Jersey City. It was going to be just another day of meetings for the commanding officer of the Port Authority Forces . . .

September 11, 2001

My husband, Fred, and I had participated in a very successful neighborhood fundraising event this past weekend, and were looking forward to rest and relaxation, a week ahead of us for vacation. We made plans for day trips for the week—today into New York City for shopping and lunch at Windows on the World—the restaurant at the top of Tower One of the World Trade Center. Later in the week we planned to go to the Pocono Mountains and the Philadelphia Zoo. We are leisurely lounging on the bed; watching the morning TV, drinking coffee, and having nothing to really rush for, except the perfect sunshine, perfect temperature, perfect day, just waiting for us to come out and play. We don't have to leave this early to go to the city. Lunch is hours away; we can be there in forty-five minutes, and it's always better to let rush hour on the New Jersey Turnpike take its course.

"Hey, babe, you know it's *really* beautiful out today. Maybe we should go to the Poconos today instead. It's supposed to rain tomorrow. We can go to New York tomorrow and stomp around Canal Street in the rain. I've always wanted to eat lunch in that Windows on the World place in the Towers, so—what do you think?"

"Yeah, okay—better to duck in and out of stores in the rain. It is really beautiful today. I just have to brush my teeth and I'll be ready." I wander down the hall to the bathroom and begin brushing. From the bathroom I can hear the morning show still on. Then, that special crisis-oriented music that they play for *Breaking News* . . .

"Hey, come here, *quick!* The World Trade Center is on fire!" My brain says *No way. We were just talking about being there.* For a second I just stand there. He has to be making a joke. . . . "Really, you have to come see this!" Okay—no joke? I come down the hall with my toothbrush still in my hand, still brushing, my mouth full of bubbles, and stand before the television. "I had my finger on the button to turn it off when I saw the bulletin come on, so I waited. I don't believe it."

I look at him and listen to the report of a small plane hitting the North Tower.

I look at the hole.

My suddenly nervous brain begins to chatter with itself: *Please, God, take care of those poor people in there. Someone must be hurt, even if it was a small plane. It looks like such a big hole for a little plane. . . . What kind of an asshole hits the World Trade Center anyway? Like, how do you miss seeing something that* big? *He must have had a heart attack, been drunk. Wait. This is a no-fly zone. What would a little plane be* doing *there?* How can you hit something that big? *Those poor people in there must be terrified. Please, God, don't let it be too bad . . . please protect them, keep them safe. . . .* And my brain is interrupted in its self-discussion by a *huge* airliner coming from the right side of the screen.

Something unspoken frizzles through my brain, because I know that the plane should not be there—it's wrong, but I don't process it. I watch as the plane appears to go behind the South Tower. A huge fireball erupts, yet I still cannot believe what my eyes have seen. I refuse to recognize that that plane was simply absorbed into the building. It never passed by. And the internal chatter begins again as tears well up in my eyes: *Oh God, that was a* passenger *plane. It was* huge, *and it never came out the other side. It has to be on* purpose. NO! NO! *A pilot error, a heart attack*—but there are two *holes. How could it be an accident if there are two holes? A computer malfunction, static electricity. Something* must *be overriding the planes. American pilots would never do that—they would never kill innocent people. How could two planes hit on purpose? Oh God, anything but on purpose!* The news commentator is talking about a deliberate act;

they have no confirmation, looks like terrorism . . . Somewhere in the recesses of my mind I also hear the sounds of my husband sitting next to me praying. Out loud.

I sit down on the edge of the bed. I swallow my toothpaste and simply sit. My brain has short-circuited to the point that I have frozen. The tears in my eyes run back through my sinuses. I can't even cry right. Something very heavy, dark, and ugly has found my insides. I began to pray that the human damage would be small. . . .

I don't know how long I sit. Fred looks at me and says, "I can't look. I have to go outside in the sun." I nod. My brain simply says to itself, *I can't move.* Almost to the second, the front door closes and the bulletin comes back on with the news that the Pentagon has been hit. Now the tears come. I am alone in the house and the entire world has fallen apart. *No, No more hurt people. No more, please, God. How many more? No more!*

I am a child of the 1950s. I remember bomb shelters and air raid drills. I was raised on a steady diet of "Don't worry. They wouldn't *dare* attack on American soil. We're the greatest country in the world; they would never come here!" My brain woke up and screamed, *"You promised—you said we were safe!"*

I realized that I have never been so angry, outraged, and terrified all at once. I became at that moment a thinking and feeling person once more. I still had my toothbrush in my hand, which I looked at stupidly as I cried, feeling for all the world like a lonely and cold five-year-old lost in the woods full of monsters. The front door opens as Fred comes back in. I wipe my eyes and run to the hall leaning over the stairwell railing.

"They've hit the Pentagon too."

"Oh God, no."

Fred comes back upstairs and says, "Come on, let's go downstairs." He holds out his hand to me and I follow like a child needing help to cross the street. We sit and watch, like so many others must be doing. Outside the beautiful day rages on with brilliant sun. And people are dying. Lots of them. *No more! No more! No more!*

The South Tower begins to fall. My brain feels like it will explode. I'm staring with my hand over my mouth, and my ears hear "Holy shit, *no!*" I'm guessing Fred said it. Sirens begin. We are so close to the city. It must be ambulances, EMTs, doctors going to help. The sirens scream from all around, every direction. I realize that I am actually terrified. The sirens continue. I want to scream with them. Dogs are howling. Yes, it is time to call the pack together; something evil, sick, and twisted has come to kill us.

Then the North Tower turns to dust. I am trying very hard not to think about what has happened to all of the people that I know who work and live in that area, because I know that the phones aren't working. I know I have to wait. I can't call; I can't ask. The news reports are beginning to say that these twisted demons did it for their God. I don't know much about their God, but I do know that their God would not approve. If I were their God I would come down to personally deliver them to the worst hell that I could invent.

We turn off the TV for a while. Later we learn of the horror of United Flight 93, and the courageous act of the passengers who fought to overcome the hijackers before their plane crashed in Shanksville, Pennsylvania. Please let this be over.

The newscasters are telling us to go outside this evening and light candles as a show of unity. We let a neighbor with two small daughters know that we will go to the city to get her husband, no matter where, no matter what time, as soon as she hears from him we will go. (Never thinking he could be in that cloud of dust.) The phone calls begin, and one by one we give sighs of relief instead of more tears to shed. Speaking to neighbors and friends, reaching out to someone for comfort, everyone, universally, wants to stay inside and huddle.

At 7 p.m. we obediently go outside with our candles, as we were asked to do by the media. If it would do anything like turn back time to yesterday, I'd burn the house down. All along the street, people emerge from their houses with candles and matches. I barefoot my way up the street to exchange hugs with about ten of my neighbors who are already huddled in a group. We don't talk much, just letting the pain and the little twinkles from our candlelight be the bond between us. We donate candles to a new neighbor who has not yet moved in but is there remodeling.

September 12

Again the sky is blue enough to break your heart. The weather is perfect. The world is deadly quiet. You never know how much noise there is until there isn't any, and then the silence becomes overwhelming. Morning coffee on this vacation day doesn't feel quite right: no happy planning, no excitement about running off somewhere. We may have our faults as a couple, but we can laugh and play like children. We agree that we should go out, even if just for a little while. Where? The zoo. We discuss the bizarreness of going to the zoo in the face of such devastation. We discuss the fact that it seems sacrilegious, but we decide to go as a distraction, as medication. Ice cream, hot dogs, and animals. A return to innocence.

I don't bring up the fact that I have this nagging thought that has been in the back of my head: I need to *go there*. The thought, actually, is almost a premonition; I know I will end up there. I want to help. I have found many of my friends and neighbors (but not yet all of them) from the World Trade Center area, and am feeling indebted for this good fortune. The reports were saying that volunteers shouldn't just arrive, because there are so many volunteers that it has become chaotic. I know the ones who went already will soon become tired and need relief, so I decide to wait. This will go on. Next week, or soon thereafter, I will find my role and offer my strength as a replacement for someone who is tired.

The hospital staffs are concerned because they have no people to treat. I hear that the diggers are disheartened because they are not finding victims. The magnitude of it is beyond understanding. . . . They are all praying for just one more live person to bring home, someone to help—frantically searching for just one more . . .

Being at the zoo on this day is beyond bizarre; the zoo is actually open. The world persists in being silent; there is no traffic, no bustle, no planes, no people, no sounds. Spooky quiet. All the way to Philadelphia on the highway we passed maybe ten cars. When we arrive, we see five other cars in the parking lot. As we wander through empty exhibit areas we hear the static of staff radios followed by, "You can go home if you want; we're really overstaffed today." No lines. No waiting. Polite staff want to talk to us. We share our disgust and anger about the terrorist attacks with one another. We buy hot dogs and sit in front of the fountain, hissing at pigeons. "This is just not right, sitting here. Do you know how bizarre this is? We're under full federal military alert, we've been attacked, people are dead, and we're *at the zoo*. What is wrong with us?"

Military planes buzz overhead with their distinctive low rumble. We both look up, and Fred answers my tirade with, "You never know how many planes there are until they're gone."

"Or how much noise they make. It's creepy quiet. Everywhere. I don't like it. I think the animals knew; remember how all of the dogs in the neighborhood were howling for the past couple of weeks? Like before earthquakes. They have been restless and edgy. Animals know when things are not right, when there is evil afoot."

We hold hands as we stroll through the silence back toward the empty streets. My hair stands up. Seeing the Twin Towers fall and hearing about Shanksville and the Pentagon have hurt me somewhere so very deep. I think about the arrogance and stubbornness of Americans; we have been that way as a people for so long that fierce pride and determination have to be genetic by now. We escaped our mother countries for freedom, and made our own rules when we didn't like the rules of others. I am second generation American. My family came through Ellis Island for a better life in this great land. My grandparents (on both sides) never lost an opportunity to remind us of how wonderful freedom and privilege are. They would be outraged to see someone do this to a land and a people that they held in such high esteem. I think that the pain that I feel now is just as genetic as that stubborn pride must be. It runs somewhere down inside where my soul lives, part of my internal program. My DNA is hurting and screaming. And it is very, very angry.

Since my employers are the ones in charge of the mental health system, I know that they will have some plan for dealing with this. I return to work and check on what my office is doing as a response. I offer to lend assistance and my supervisor readily agrees to allow me to go. I'm told who to speak to, to go to the FAC to provide counseling and clinical support.

September 19

I am armed with papers from my office to deliver, and a list of things to pick up and bring back. Since I am not directly assigned as staff to the FAC yet, I am told that arriving about 9 a.m. is okay. I plan to arrive about 8 a.m. anyway.

Driving up the New Jersey Turnpike is never fun during rush hour. If it serves no other purpose, at least driving like an idiot that early does give time for the mind to wander. As I approach the vicinity of the airport, I think of all of the times that I would race the planes in the southbound lanes on my way home from somewhere. Who would ever think to build runways so close to the turnpike that the planes look like they're in the next lane, let alone have the runway parallel to the highway? To whoever developed that design—thank you! . . . for so many opportunities to return to childhood delight, getting goose bumps at the beauty of flight with the big planes zooming in so closely. And here on the turnpike we have the opportunity to race them down the runway if the traffic patterns in the southbound lanes offer enough of an opening. Try as I may, I have never yet won the race.

Today I know that limited air traffic is beginning. I have seen the first of the planes allowed up, and my thoughts turn to how strange it was—first that the planes had gone . . . and then when they came back—chilling. I would look up without any more childish thrill at these big birds looking suspended in midair—looking as if they are moving so slowly. Now the goose bumps are for an entirely different reason.

At the bridge right before the airport, a plane looms up from behind the abutments. Huge. A sight that usually would transport me to age five, wanting to squeak with delight, I hear myself gasp. Suddenly I'm wide awake. My heart skips. I realize that I'm actually having a panic response; in a split second my hands are already sweating. The adrenaline rushes through me. My brain stops, and my foot goes to the brakes as I become aware that every car around me has suddenly lit up with red lights. A collective panic attack—a turnpike of people frozen for a split second in time—just long enough to say *holy shit!* before that big bird blasts off over our heads to the south. So close, so low. I can only think what it must have been like for anyone who saw those planes hit the Towers. . . . Even though we are once again driving like rush-hour idiots, I can't get the image of that low-flying plane from my mind; how terribly huge it must have looked to those who saw . . . the Towers . . . the people . . . Will we ever look at an airplane the same way again? Will it heal? Ever?

As I near the exit for Liberty State Park, I avoid the view of the New York skyline, which is plainly visible from here. I don't want to see. I don't think about how I must eventually see. This is our playground where friends live and work. Our shopping, theater, lunches. *It's supposed to be beautiful!*

I still have a dear friend who is missing . . .

My mind flashes to parental conversations about the Towers as they were being built: "They're ugly. How dare they deface our beautiful old skyline."

"No one will ever move in there. They just aren't right. Spending all of that money on things that don't blend in. . . ." Change is so hard. . . .

I succeed in not looking until I go over the bridge. *Ooooh no.* Tears are coming. *No!* I avoid looking. As I enter the Liberty Island area, I can smell it. I shut it out again and practice denial with all my might until I pull into the parking lot in front of the terminal building. I open the car door, get out, and want to throw up; in front of me is that smoking hole in the skyline. It is so close I could spit and hit it. No more denial. Cranes are moving. I want very much to throw up. I hold onto the window of my car door without closing it and look, never realizing that a group of people are standing about five feet from me in Red Cross vests until I hear a soft voice: "Are you all right?"

What? I don't answer out loud.

"Would you rather throw up or pass out?"

I'm not sure. Still with no voice.

An arm goes around my shoulder, and Mary says to me, "Let me give you four of the unofficial Red Cross rules:

One: Always carry tissues."
    (She hands me a pack of Red Cross tissues.)
Two: Wear waterproof mascara.
Three: Keep a journal. Write in it every night. It will keep you sane.
Four: Only cry for one minute at a time. More than that is counter-
    productive and only makes you feel and look like shit.

"Now come with me. Who do you belong to?"

I don't know anymore whom I belong to.

She walks me into the terminal building and answers my questions as we go and I begin to locate some of my sensibilities. I see that a city has literally been built in this place overnight: tents hold food and supplies and everywhere people are working at something.

NOVA are the blue-shirted people assigned as companions. I watch as a family who enters the building before us is intercepted, and the NOVA people simply fold themselves around the family, absorbing them and guiding them in, offering coffee and a chair to begin paperwork.

The Red Cross is providing food, clothing, and is tending to basic needs. Medical areas are available. Down the breezeway that runs off the platform are little tented-off areas filled with people who have brochures, forms, and tissues. Tissues with the Red Cross insignia are everywhere.

The Salvation Army has put up tents and trailers for all kinds of services. As we pass through the building to the outside, we walk toward the trailers in the back. I see that sod has been laid, flowers planted, and paving stones placed as a walkway. I am amazed at the detail, the speed of everything arriving here so fast. I walk along the paving stones and wonder what kind of person placed them there. They conform to no comfortable human walking pattern: the spacing is all wrong. Hey, can't have everything . . .

"So, who did you say you were to report to?"

Actually, I don't think I said anything . . . "Susan."

"Where does she work? In what agency?"

"She's a consultant. I was told to find mental health and ask for her to deliver this pile of forms."

"Then you're in trailer number two. Right here. If you think you can take it from here, I'm going back to the terminal."

"Thank you so much."

I enter trailer two, clutching my papers to deliver, and find about ten people sitting inside in a miserable-looking little circle. They all look up as I enter.

"Hi. Is Susan here?" they all look at one another and back at me—saying nothing. Am I speaking the wrong language? Missing my clothes? Do I look as bad as I feel right now? *What?!*

I try again: "Is there somebody here named Susan?"

"Somewhere, but she isn't here. She's supposed to be our supervisor but she hasn't been here and we don't know where she is."

"Okay, where are you all from? Do you work for mental health agencies?" They all nod at me. Good—I'm at least in the right place. . . .

"So what are we supposed to do?"

"Wait."

"For what?"

They don't know. I deposit my papers on a desk and leave.

I have gone to the front door of the terminal building looking partly for direction, from where I don't know, and a place to decide how to make sense of this scene, and I find that I want air and sun. Just as I just reach the front door, an amazingly pregnant young woman gets out of her car, looks at that smoking spot on the skyline and falls screaming to the pavement. NOVA staff near the edge of the sidewalk run to her, sending one back for a chair. They gently soothe and lift her into the chair—she is sobbing so hard. I thank God that they were so close and marvel at where they learned to respond like that. Am I in the right place? I don't think I can respond like that. I feel numb and stupid. I want to scream too. I am dimly aware that I have become as nonverbal as the staff I met back in the trailer. For the second time.

A Red Cross worker is smoking her cigarette near me at the doorway and must have read my thoughts: "They have her; there's plenty of them. Let this one go. She's in good hands." The young woman begins delivery breathing: panting, blowing, and holding her belly as they carry her, in a chair, into the building. Dear God, don't let that baby be born here. . . .

"Is this your first disaster?"

What? I hear in my brain. *What kind of thing is that to say?* Apparently I don't answer her. Apparently I don't *need* to answer, because she continues: "Yeah, I thought so. After the first you get used to it; that was your first. Next time you'll be the one running to carry, or lift, or wipe tears. Get your hugging muscles ready! How long have you been here?" I'm still staring at the skyline. Somewhere deep in my brain I realize that I have definitely become nonverbal since I arrived here and I don't know how to reverse the condition. . . . I can hear, I can think—but it stops there. She grabs my arm and whispers "Walk with me." I am being pulled around the side of the building and I follow like a robot. Apparently moving helps to unfreeze the brain. "Everyone here is so compassionate, so caring, so able to anticipate everything. They always do the right thing. How?"

"Disasters are what we do." I really look at her for the first time: I see a great smile, a sweet spirit, and a gravelly voice—too many smokes. She takes my arm, and I realize that she is leading me back inside, toward the memory boards that line the side of the platform: large blank walls built from 4-by-8-foot sheets of plywood and Sheetrock for the families to leave messages. One side of the terminal has sections in a zigzag line; these were built first and very quickly were filled with flowers, notes, and pictures. Other memory boards have been constructed as free-standing cubes that are placed in the open spaces of the terminal platform. I am steered to one memory board and told a story:

> This one we did for the poor park people. Poor sad people. Please write to them: They need to know that others know how bad it was for them too. They pulled those poor hurt, burned people from the river. One of the park staff told me that he reached down from a boat to pull a man from the water and the man refused his hand—told him "No. Take this instead" and undid a jacket that he had tied around his neck. He threw the lumpy jacket into the park man's arms. The jacket moved.
>
> Park man says to the person, "What is it?"
>
> "A baby," the guy says. "Take care of the baby."
>
> "Where are the parents?"
>
> The guy tells him, "I don't know; I found it floating. Take care of the baby."
>
> This man had jumped in the river in his suit, saw this poor baby, took off his jacket in the water, and tied the baby around his neck to keep it above water.
>
> These park people were outside when it happened; they saw the planes hit, the Towers fall, and the people running so terrified that they simply ran into the river to get away. And they

knew that every one of them would drown. It's too deep, too cold, too far to swim to New Jersey. They were just so panicked they thought only about running. And then the park service staff were up all night with the people: pulling them from the river for hours, giving them blankets, holding them, caring for them, giving them coffee and soup. These park people are heroes too. Write to them.

She hands me a marker and a sweet smile. I wipe my tears and write a thank-you note. She again takes my arm and steers me through the walls: "READ." I read. I cry. I listen to another story:

One girl out there is a twin. She's the one you'll see sweeping and crying. Her grandfather was one of the engineers or something with the Towers as they were being built. He came home one night when she was five and said that he was going to work on the most beautiful buildings in the world, buildings that everyone would look at in amazement. There would be two buildings, one for each of his girls. They would be twin towers shining for all of the world to see and admire. Very special and important: the biggest most beautiful buildings ever. And the buildings would belong to the twins, one tower for each girl. As the project went on, each girl would be given a hard hat and would visit the building site to see their buildings. She grew up with "HER TOWER," and her Tower was Tower Two. Every morning she would stop and watch her Tower in the morning light with her coffee. And she took a job where she could be with her Tower. Guess where she was when her Tower was murdered? . . . she watched it being born, and she watched it die. And part of her died with it. She is so sad, so broken up. How do we ever heal from this?"

I cry harder.
"Now you are ready for this place. Promise that you won't let them forget the park people."
I promise. Red Cross tissues are pushed into my hands.
"Dry those beautiful eyes. You look like hell."
I laugh. After a well-placed bear hug, I laugh harder.

"We need you here, love. We need for you to give until you have nothing more left, and then some. There are so many hurt people. We can get to them just one at a time. And after we think that we can't give any more, we will find room in our hearts for just one more. . . . There's *always* room for *just one more.* Come now, let me buy you some coffee."

"I thought it was free. . . ."

"Okay. You aren't smart, you have no sense of humor, but you give decent hugs. You'll do okay. . . ."

September 21

I am trying to bring order to chaos and structure to nothing. Again as I arrive there is no one apparent to tell the staff in the mental health trailer what to do or where to go. As staff begin to arrive, I try to enlist someone to explore with me to find someone in charge. No takers.

"We were told by our agencies to come to this trailer and wait. If we go out they won't know where we are. The families might come."

"But aren't the families over in the terminal building?"

"We were told to wait."

"*You're just going to sit here?*"

"They told us to *wait.*"

"Does anybody want to go over to the administration trailer with me? Maybe we can straighten this out there."

"We aren't allowed there. They told us not to go in there. We're supposed to wait here."

"Who really told you that?" No answer. "Okay, you all stay. If anybody wants me for anything I'll be in the terminal building looking for something to do. This is a huge ugly thing. I can't just sit in here and wait. I'll go nuts." I wander to the terminal building; it is quiet, I guess because it's so early we have no families here yet, so I begin to read the memory boards.

Low to the ground are the scribbles of very tiny people. No words, no real pictures. One scribble batch goes on forever. The little one had much to say, and took great pains to be deliberate and exact. Too small to write and form words, too tiny to draw, but they go on and on, in a language that only they know. In ten years, will they remember what they said to Daddy? One has marked in very deliberate and defined rows, an imitation of adult paragraphs. I squat down and lay my hand on the scribbles, and wonder about the pain that this little one expressed for the parent that will never come home again. And again the tears come. A wall ahead of me is still starkly blank, but just above my eye level I see a very tiny message. I wander closer and have to get almost on top of the board to read I MISS YOU SO MUCH.

I have to bite my finger to keep from screaming. I can't read these anymore.

"It's the babies that kill me, too" says that gravelly voice behind me, my Red Cross Angel from yesterday. I wrap my arms around her neck like she's a long lost friend.

"I'm looking for something to do. No one in my trailer knows what to do. I was given a name of someone to report to. The people in our trailer say they don't know that person. It's been two days. What should I do?"

She laughs and gives me an education about how disaster sites work, about NOVA companions, the Red Cross, and a recommendation to see the Red Cross supervisor and the NOVA supervisor to coordinate myself. I am introduced to too many people to count. I am confident that I can make some sense out of this, so I go back to the trailer with news.

"The families are over there; they don't come here because nobody in the terminal building knows to get us. Let's go over there."

"We were told to wait."

This is getting *really* old. "You've been waiting for two days. The person who we are told is in charge has not been here yet, right? We called the cell phone number they gave us, and got no answer. So until somebody in charge shows up, *I'm in charge, okay?*"

I get a couple of snickers, and mostly looks of *whatthehell?* Some of them want to join, so I explain to them what I've learned about the place. We wander around the terminal and make friends with the Red Cross and NOVA. Now the other agencies know who we are and where we are. We negotiate how to work together. We find the families. We have a system to really get to work.

September 22

First thing in the morning I run into someone I know from our Department of Human Services. Nice to see a face that I know. He's one of our administrative types—he'll be in charge: "Hey, Lou, need any help with anything—is there anything I can do?"

"Yeah, go check the toilet paper in the women's rooms for me and replace it when it gets low, okay?" Not really the answer I was expecting, but, yup. I help as he checks the men's, and we move on through the group of Port-a-Potties playing toilet paper Santa.

A tiny woman arrives at the trailer with a face as white as her T-shirt, which says I ♥ NY. On her shirt is the New York skyline: the *old* skyline with the Towers. Her family is holding her arms and legs, and have literally dragged her in: she had been hit in the head by shrapnel in Tower Two as she was running down the last ten flights to the ground. She has not had medical attention and has been hiding in her room and crying, not eating. The family fears for her and they speak very little English. She is screaming, crying, and shaking. She screams, cries, and shakes for six hours. One of the counselors who is closest to the door takes charge of them immediately, and scurries away with her and the family. She is given a teddy bear to hold. I take some of the rest of the staff, and we go to the terminal to give them privacy and to see what is needed elsewhere.

Our little lady has lost her immigration papers. A sweet female FBI agent, soft-spoken and gentle, comes in and resolves the issue, providing a temporary visa until the papers can be straightened out. We talk in hushed tones about our rage at this thing. The Liberty Science Center, which is at the end of the drive, has agreed to provide temporary photo IDs for individuals such as this person, who may have lost their identification. Some of the victims are aliens who are in the United States on work visas, so these types of IDs and paperwork are especially vital in helping them to straighten out any missing documents.

Medical attention is sought to determine if there are any complications to the head injury, appointments are made, and our tiny lady leaves with trauma-blank eyes, pale and still shaking, clearly exhausted, but cried out for now. She is still holding the teddy bear close to her chest.

How does a person deal with this? My family would find me under my bed screaming too. For an eternity.

September 23

I go to the FAC today with a co-worker to work in the trailer. She concerns herself with trying to organize the data collection, what to do with paperwork, and the forms that are supposed to be going back and forth but aren't doing so consistently. It seems that expecting any type of order when so many different people are coming and going is difficult at best. I concern myself with trying to sort out operations: trying to get counselors to families, and to network them with the other agencies on grounds with some semblance of order. Each day brings new volunteer faces, and the operations must be explained and reinforced all over again. There are outside, independent consultants who have apparently been hired as clinical supervisors to the staff who have come here from agencies throughout the state to provide mental health services. According to the trailer staff, the consultant still has not appeared. I go to the administrative trailer to try to find out what to do about this. I am given a number to call. The person I call tells me that she spoke to this consultant on her cell phone, and she is on grounds and has been all along. "Trust me, the place is not *that big;* she isn't here or I would have seen her." I'm told in not-so-few words I'm a trouble-maker. Okay. So I decide to just give up and handle it myself. . . .

My co-worker and I also arrange a couple of impromptu meetings with the individuals in charge of coordinating large groups of volunteers within NOVA and the Red Cross. We decide who will cover what details, and how to catch up with one another regularly to see that things run smoothly. Later in the day the fruits of our labor become apparent: the Red Cross mental health staff, and some of the Red Cross chaplains have begun moving into our trailer with us. I invited them in with "Come on in, we have room. There are phones no one is using, chairs, cubicles. If anybody has a problem with it, I'll plead insanity and take the blame." They bring with them teddy bears, Beanie Babies, phone cards, and lots of smiles, setting up camp in the back two cubicles of the trailer where they can see families along with us. NOVA is showing up now with families, pamphlets, and kids' books. They wait inside to chat while families and victims receive services. People are poking their heads in to use the copy machine, say hi, use our fax machine, and hang out to get acquainted when it becomes a bit slow.

It seems that things are a bit slow; many of our families are going to New York—they are following the ads on the major networks to see the staff at the Pier 94 Family Center. Even though the FAC has run ads as well, the air time that Pier 94 gets is much greater, so New Jersey people have become confused about what to do. Also, the factor that occurs with sudden and devastating loss is that people want to be where their loved one was last. Their loved ones were last in New York, so it is natural for them to gravitate there. I volunteer to go to Pier 94 with a big sign saying NJ PEOPLE FOLLOW ME.

As staff, though, we are beginning to find our niche in the operation and are being consulted and included in the overall FAC activities. We are now seeing the families regularly when they arrive. Order can be found in chaos.

So can interesting people: Mary from LA is a sweet, soft-spoken social worker who is quick to hug and smile. She is tall, with an open, wonderful face that has aged in compassion. She is a veteran at disaster work, and was the person who intercepted me in the parking lot when I arrived. She is beautiful and gentle and I love her immediately. She has a dry sense of humor, and deep, wise eyes that have obviously seen the best and worst of life. She is one of the Red Cross Mental Health team.

At lunch I meet some of the Red Cross nurses, who ask me to take their photos in front of the memory boards. I comply, taking pictures with all three of their cameras. Photos are forbidden at the FAC, except for the hours between midnight and 7 a.m., to protect the privacy of families and victims. We decide that we will look closely for people in the area, and sneak the shots because they have to depart so soon. No one is in the area of the memory walls. One nurse grabs my hand and pulls me over to look at a certain angle: "Look there at those two chairs, alone and empty in front of those walls. Take that picture—it's amazing."

Over lunch, they tell a story about how we came to have therapy dogs: On September 12 someone said that therapy dogs would be a good idea; people like therapy dogs. A volunteer goes to the phone book and after finding a number, calls with the innocent request "We'd like some therapy dogs."

How many?

"As many as you can get here."

How soon?

"As soon as possible." Within a couple of hours there are over 100 therapy dogs. They arrive in vans, cars, and from as far away as Connecticut. A couple of them commence to fighting on the lawn. The shrugged response to this good fortune was "How was I to know? I never heard of therapy dogs before." I thought, *What, were there like ten in the world or something?"*

Thank you to whoever came up with that idea! These pups are definitely a source of comfort to me. I can't resist ruffling a little fur as I pass them. I know that they must also have that effect on others.

I keep thinking of all of the pups that live in New York in the areas where the neighborhoods have been emptied, with no owners being allowed to go into their homes get to them. I have dogs at home, and can only think of how it would be to not be able to get home to feed them and take them with me. I have heard that people have volunteered to go in and get them all, and care for them until their owners are located, or until they can return to their homes again. Hope so . . . the thought of them pacing, and being so scared, hungry, and alone is so sad.

I also think of the pups over there working in the debris. I hear that they are searching and looking, often cutting their feet on the sharp metal. And they are becoming depressed because they are not able to rescue people, so their humans have to stage periodic "rescues" just to keep them going. They work so hard for their people. Bless them. I really want to go there and help—do something to make a difference. I don't feel like I'm contributing enough. *God,* this is frustrating.

We have begun to issue death certificates, so families are now coming more often. But still, everyone keeps saying the numbers of people coming should be higher. . . .

I am on the phone having a routine discussion. I hear an *"Ohmygodlook!"* from the Red Cross section in the back of the trailer, and stand up to look over the cubicle walls. They all begin running to the trailer door, and pointing to the water. I look out the tiny window behind me and involuntarily say *"Ohshit!"* a comment that the person on the other end of the phone ignores. In the harbor is the biggest boat I have ever seen in my life. The hospital warship, the Hope, is cruising through the harbor, with her water cannons at full blast. Big red crosses on the sides, guns in the turrets. What an amazing site. I grab my camera. The impatience in my voice is not apparent, I guess, because there continue to be questions and conversation in my ear. "I really need to go . . ."

—ho, but one more thing . . . buzzzzzz . . .

"No, sorry, I have to go. I'll call you back in a couple of minutes, *please*." I all but hang up on the person, and then dash out the door, thinking, *When someone at a disaster site says "Oh shit, I have to go" in your ear, why do you keep asking questions?* No matter . . . just a big old boat, right?

By the time I arrive outside at the dock, the ship is so far away, almost to the Verrazano Narrows Bridge. I need the 150 zoom to catch it, even as a tiny thing. They just don't move *that* fast. Damn. Probably won't come out, but there are some great people on the dock just waiting to be photographed. We talk and comment about the size of that ship—(it blotted out all of Manhattan Island on the way by), and the beauty of the water cannons giving a full salute. After hanging out for about ten precious minutes, we go back inside. Where on earth did they dock that thing that you couldn't see it from where we were? How do you hide a warship in New York Harbor? David Copperfield?

Already the first wave of volunteers are pulling out to be relieved by new teams. Seems like the numbers of volunteers on-site are going down too. New faces are arriving, the changing of the guard. My lunchtime nurses are among those to ship out. My angel, who rescued me during those first days is leaving and I feel sad, like part of me is going, or an old friend is moving away. I am surprised at the level of grief that I feel over her departure. Strange to feel so strongly about someone that I don't even know, except as a kindred spirit and a recipient of her compassion. I think that no one has shown me compassion like that. Ever. That is the connection I mourn. I give my angel a long tearful hug good-bye and my e-mail address. "I don't know how long I'll be here. Send me a note when you get home so I can find you again someday." We hug again for a long time, and I walk with her to her ride out, carrying her suitcase and thanking her for her kindness. As the van pulls off I think of battlefield friendships, bonding through intensity. . . . Robyn, the site supervisor from NOVA, who has the best smile I had ever seen, is replaced also—by Karen from Ontario.

They are coming from foreign countries even!

September 28

Back to office life for today—I have to meet with one of our agencies to discuss how to resolve some issues they are having in their program. At least I can spend the day on the road and not behind a computer screen in a cubicle.

The agency director and I discuss one of their staff, their clinical director, who is apparently in a mind-set lately of sweating the small stuff and making everyone crazy with details. Staff complain that he needs gratitude. We discuss a couple of options to help him to lay back a bit. Then an idea comes to me—I'll take him with me to work at the FAC: "Give him to me. I have a place that will make anyone understand how insignificant this stuff is. . . ."

I feel so abnormal in normal work; I can't listen, I feel like falling asleep, and I can't sit still. I can't seem to find a niche that feels like the right pace. My brain is racing at full speed, but physically I feel slow and sluggish. I'm trying to act like it's a normal work day and a normal meeting, but my self is half here and half somewhere else. Stress symptoms already?

September 30

I know I was "told" to write every day to keep my sanity. I'm too tired. Never was known for my sanity anyway, so the hell with this. I missed days already, so what's the big deal? I will probably never pick this up again. I want to come home and sleep, not write. I don't have anything important to say anyway—diaries seem to be nothing but self-serving . . . okay, I guess that's the point. It's supposed to be self-serving. But how can writing be the cure all for this? I can't write. I just can't.

Okay, I lied. It's now an hour later, and I can't stop the feeling that something is chewing up my insides. I'm pacing. I typically fidget all the time, but this is raw nervous energy. Fidgeting is not enough—I'd rather explode, combust, break things. My head is spinning and filled with stuff that wants to come out and go *somewhere*. And I can't get my mouth to open to talk about it—what do I say? Do I sit my husband down and tell him that some nameless, unknown thing is eating me up inside, and I want to scream for no identifiable reason? Fred is looking at me out if the corner of his eye like he believes me to be morphing into some kind of altered state. He's a hairdresser—he owns a hair salon. Can I ever expect him to understand what it feels like to look at those people who survived such a terrible thing and hear their stories? How do I tell him about the smell? About the empty hole in the skyline—yeah, it's been on the news—but in person it's a whole different thing. How can I explain to him what I can't explain to myself?

It certainly feels like I'm turning into *something* . . . and it ain't pretty.

I'm a mental health clinician. I know the symptoms of exposure to trauma and high stress: difficulty communicating, memory problems, being out of balance, short attention span, low impulse control, lack of problem solving . . . *okay, I have them all* . . . and then some.

I have decided that Red Cross Mary was right: I need to write to be sane. I never journal, so it seems silly. One of the reasons I never journal is because I never know what to write, and never thought I had anything important enough to say. I'll just close my eyes from now on and describe the first scene that comes, and finish when it stops . . .

I am pacing and my thoughts are unsettled.

I have been working in the land of no time. At the FAC, time is different. Time warps into minutes that are years, and seconds that are eternal. I have many times looked at the clock to find that an hour has gone by, yet I would swear it was just a few minutes. And other times I have been shocked to learn that only five minutes has passed. They felt like two hours. I don't get it; it has nothing to do with activity or lack thereof. There is just some type of horror movie time warp that I fall into when my car pulls into the parking lot. Hours go by before I can blink. What is it about that place? I am told by the veteran disaster workers that disasters are like that—the stress and the pace of work causes time to be experienced differently. It must be why I can work seventeen-hour days (not counting the commute) and not think anything of it. When I do get home again, I am only there long enough to sleep. . . .

And there is also the factor of extremes: things are great or horrible. And they flip-flop in a heartbeat. Emotions swing. As soon as things get really depressing and black, something amazing and wonderful happens. No moderation, no gray areas—just extremes. And no rules. The land of extremes, and no time. It has a hold on me that feels strange but not unpleasant.

It is also the land of purpose.

I saw a familiar little lady out back at the railing today, gazing out at the water and skyline of Manhattan. Our tiny, scared lady with the I ♥ NY T-shirt. I wondered as I spotted her if she was okay there alone—looking at what used to be.

I walk up to her and say hello, asking how she is feeling. Limited English is not an issue when she gives me a great, dazzling smile of recognition and says, "Better." Good color in her cheeks—and a smile. I believe her.

"Great. So good to see you smile, be able to be outside alone. I'm glad." She nods, smiles broader, and thanks me. I give her a little hug and tell her to be sure to come around if she needs us. She nods and smiles again, turning back to the railing and her view of the fractured New York skyline. I say a little prayer for her as I walk to the trailer.

Tonight I came home to a wonderful message on the answering machine—my last New York resident has been found! I have called her almost every night, sometimes at the most god-awful late hours, and left a message on her machine. (At least she still *had* an answering machine. I found that, at least, comforting.) Her shaking, tear-filled voice simply said "I love you too. I'm okay." *Thank you, God!* Despite the fact that it was after 10 p.m., I called. She had simply gone to work that morning at St Vincent's Hospital and never went home until Sunday. That night she wandered the streets, crying. She sat on the curb in Manhattan with other New Yorkers, crying at midnight and wandering, then went back to work because she couldn't be alone, and never returned home until tonight. We promise to try to keep in touch through the next few days.

October 1

I'm in my office again today. I find that I can't sit there—not that I ever could—but *now* I really can't stand sitting and doing computer work and paper pushing. I am hyper and restless and wanting to fall asleep at any moment—and that doesn't even make sense; it's both ends of the spectrum. I am becoming as extreme as that place.

Last Friday, when I met with the director of one of our contract agencies, I asked his permission to "borrow" his clinical director, John. John seems to have lost touch with some of the things in life that are important: his staff have complained that he spends too much time sweating the small stuff. He worries about little things and fusses. If the FAC is good for anything, it's a healthy dose of gratitude for what is, and *was,* and could be. I'm hoping that he will be able to put things into perspective after spending a day or two serving the families. When he arrives tomorrow, we'll see . . .

My office asked me today if I would be willing to work on coordinating the boat trips to Ground Zero. New York is taking their families in. We asked if we could have the same right and New York agreed, but a person is needed to make all of the arrangements. When I asked why they chose me, they didn't answer. I don't know if I feel more honored or terrified. Both. I hear that there are still body parts everywhere. I can't imagine . . . don't want to.

I'm told to ask for Bob, a person who, according to my office, has a reputation for being hard to work with. He sounds as though he can be somewhat of a beast. My office is apologizing to me, mostly for my assignment to him. (How bad can one person be?)

They are telling me not to go over there with the families on the boat. It isn't good for me—"Don't subject yourself to that." How can I do it *right* if I don't know what happens, don't see it working? I don't understand how I can accomplish this task without seeing it, being part of it. I don't know why it is okay to subject families and volunteers to this but not me. . . . I don't know a lot right now except the old "be careful what you ask for; you just might get it." I wanted to really do something, to make a difference. Now is my chance.

I allow the words in my ears to blur and just let go—

". . . we don't know how long this will take . . ."

I begin to mentally conjure up who and what I have to clear from my calendar.

". . . don't know what long-term exposure will do . . ."

Who cares? People are *dead!*

No matter what happens, I am currently far luckier than any of those families or victims, so what do I have to worry about? God takes care of fools and drunks. I've been both. Several times. If I walk into this, what's the worst that could happen? Fear is a lack of faith. Slogans can help.

I interrupt: "It doesn't matter. It's okay. Don't worry about it."

"You don't understand . . ."

"I'll be all right. I'll do it. Just tell me what to do next."

October 2

Back at the FAC, John arrives today, and I see him smile for the first time in a long time. Is it that easy? He tells me how grateful he is for my request for help. I talk to him a bit, and he seems able to be at peace here and able to just dive in. I leave him in trailer two with the mental health agency staff, and go in search of the infamous Bob, who resides in the forbidden administrative trailer. I have a bit of a knot in my stomach because I've been told that he is hard to deal with. I wonder why he would be in charge of a disaster site if he were so difficult, and I'm determined to see for myself. But instead of looking for Bob right away, I sidetrack myself by becoming involved with those who are arriving at the front door.

Again I have that sense of suspended animation: the world has no date, no time, no purpose other than to care for the hurt. And the injured ones are now coming—with staples and stitches and casts and bruises and burns. I come through the terminal toward the front and see the victims of this attack as they arrive. Walking with crutches, empty sad eyes, and shaking hands. The living cry. The families cry. The survivors cry. We cry.

They talk of guilt for escaping, anger, fear of living their lives, fear for the future, loss of friends and co-workers. So many, turned to dust. I think about spirits, souls being of energy. And of that giant fireball. Energy. I listen to their stories of nightmares and screaming and darkness. I hold hands, hug, and wipe tears. I run for coffee, help them fill out forms when they can't write, and try to offer soothing, soft words. I want to kiss it and make it better.

I can't.

The memory boards are rapidly filling with poetry, flowers, photos. Still they refer to those that they love as "missing." The workers over there have not found anyone for days—not even bodies. My heart breaks, and I wonder if I'll ever go a full hour without crying again. I find myself standing before a memory board, crying. A young NOVA worker comes up to me and tries to do an intervention:

"You okay, sweetie?"

"Yeah, I just work here."

She laughs and says, "I'm new." I tell her I'm beginning to feel old and thank her for caring. She smiles—a big toothy one. We hug and part ways.

I go out of the back door toward the administrative trailer, and ask for the "ogre" they call Bob. Bob works for the Human Services Administration in facilities management, so he has been sent here to oversee operations and setup of the facility. I guess I can see why he might leave a person with the impression that he's difficult. He has a scary look, heavy brows, and wears what looks like a frown. Seems to have perfected frowning, actually. Those dark eyes have a way of looking at you out of the side of his face as they size you up. . . . He doesn't waste words. And I can't quite figure out if he's grumpy and mean or just big and quiet. But as I talk to him and watch him with others, he seems quick to laugh. I settle on big and quiet. I soon learn that Bob is a man who throws his heart and soul into whatever he does. His whole aura tells me that he also expects the same of those around him. He at least seems to want the best that you can give. So this difficult way with others is just perfectionism. . . . I think this man is about to put a lot of faith in me. Even though he isn't threatening, something about him tells me that staying on his good side should become my mission in life. As a fellow perfectionist, I promise myself that he will never have to show me a difficult side—this work is too important to not do perfectly.

Feeling as scattered and crazed as I do in this time-warped place, I hope I can hold up under this . . .

October 4

Now being Bob's "property," I follow him around like a good puppy all day, smiling and nodding and being introduced to more people than I can ever think of remembering. I have paper, and try to write down what I'm supposed to remember. I ask Bob if there are any rules. He stops walking, turns to face me, and gives me a look with one arched eyebrow:

"You want rules? Rule number one: there are no rules. Rule number two: if you're dumb enough to make rules they will change within five minutes. Disasters don't follow rules."

He walks away, saying "You coming?" over his shoulder. I'm beginning to realize very quickly that Bob is in no way a beast. He casually hands me a listing on legal-size paper. It's a page of phone numbers, names, and fax numbers—two columns of them in the smallest type I've ever seen—the only thing I have to begin my task. It appears that this page has the phone number of every person who lives on the East Coast. . . .

Apparently my job is to coordinate the Red Cross, chaplains, NOVA, Salvation Army, hard hats, goggles, masks, food, flowers, teddy bears, Division of Mental Health staff, state police, family members, buses, ferry boats, Port Authority, New Jersey Department of Corrections, medical staff, and *everybody* on the New York side. I take it back. I can't do this. I also realize that no system is in place for this to happen. *I am* the system. But I have phone numbers! Saturday the sixth is our first trip over and everything must be done by then. *What's* today's date????

God help me.

As I follow in my happy puppy role, Bob supplies even more phone numbers and information. We have little mini meetings about how to coordinate, especially with the state police, who of course will not be coordinated. At least not by a silly female with no rank. We meet with the New Jersey State Police on the second floor in an office with beautiful windows facing Manhattan. There are enormous FEMA posters: aerial, satellite views of the damage that are simply too unreal to be accepted. The posters are so big; I have never seen paper so big. Tiny fire trucks lay on their sides near the damage, blown over like Tonka Toys just flicked by an evil giant kid. My stomach turns. I stand before a poster and trace my finger over the streets, across the rubble where streets should have been, as if my finger can erase this or something. . . . Trying to orient myself to what I knew was (should be) there. Trying to figure out where things went. . . . It's a *hole*. How can there be a hole? I search the map for the benches in the open spaces by the gold ball that represented the world: where I used to stretch out flat— looking skyward along the lines of the Towers, squinting up at the sun. . . . No more. A state trooper comes to my shoulder, and softly explains the route we will take in, the access points by referencing the map, tracing our path with a businesslike and authoritarian finger. I can feel his voice calming the scared little kid inside me.

We are to take a ferryboat to dock at the area in front of the Mercantile. We will walk through Battery Park City to the entrance at West Street. Currently there is extremely heavy security: the National Guard remains on full alert, as does the New York State Police. The area of damage is completely surrounded by a chain-link fence. They will escort us through to the area inside the damage zone, and then to an area where the families can leave tokens to the people whom they have lost. We can remain in each spot for fifteen minutes. It is so regimented, so controlled. How can this be of value? The families deserve more—they have lost so much! Only fifteen minutes! But we are not the only group . . .

NOVA is also stationed upstairs, across from the state police, where they are beginning the process of sorting families through a schedule for the boat visits. They are calling families of all of the New Jersey residents who are listed as missing or dead. Each family can bring up to twelve people. NOVA already has everything for the first week of visits color-coded, alphabetized, and in folders, with special needs flagged and waiting for me to fulfill. They are posting the rosters for the days to come on huge flip-chart paper, hung on the walls all around the room. The first week is apparently booked completely already, and they are working on week two. Special needs are noted and in contrasting colors. These people are so efficient, they're scary.

I meet Karen from Ontario, a NOVA site supervisor who is quiet and serious. She has a very strong presence, but at the same time she is quiet and soft in her mannerisms. As I meet her, she launches into a complicated list of everything that they have done, as if I knew what she was talking about and what to do with it. I am drowning in detail and can hear no more, so as soon as she takes a breath I ask, "Have you done this before?"

The question obviously being unrelated and out of context, she looks at me as if I have two heads and says, "No."

"Then how do you know how?"

Karen tilts her head to the side, and looks at me as if everybody should know how to do this, and she can't imagine anyone not knowing how. I laugh at the look on her face, and tell her that she's amazingly wonderful. She becomes clearly embarrassed and tries to undo my compliment.

"No, really. You are amazing. You've done everything, thought of everything. I am in the presence of greatness. What are you, military?" She smiles this time.

"No, I'm Canadian."

God has sent this woman here because she has this special talent of color-coding, and making the hopelessly complicated sensible. I just feel it in my bones.

Bob finds me and with urgency in his voice says, "Come with me." I grab my pad of paper and run after him. He brings me to two men in the chapel and introduces me, telling me that they are people I really should get to know. I shake hands and begin with the pen and paper ready, ever the good notetaker. I begin to jot them down so I can be sure to deal with them during my important coordination stuff. He laughs and says, "They're chiropractors. Donating services. Take a few minutes. Enjoy yourself." He leaves me there with my mouth open. No. Bob is definitely not a beast. I decline their offer for an adjustment and head for the mental health trailer. I'm worried about the staff there and want to check in.

I suggest to Bob that he let me train a replacement—in case I get hit by a car on the way home and die on the turnpike, or need a day off—since this looks like it will be a long haul. It's never a good idea to have a one-person system, especially when there are so many details. He agrees.

I begin to make my phone calls and lists, and check them twice. I stop for a second when I realize that every muscle in my body is tight. I'm not looking forward to this. I have enough trouble holding myself together without seeing it in person—all of that evil suspended in all of its glory. I take a deep breath and pray for strength, realizing that I have suddenly, in this place, found a need to pray a lot. I shut down the need to be afraid, and concentrate on relaxation breathing and faxing. It's getting dark out there . . .

When I get home, I have a conversation with a friend, telling him why I will not be around for a while. He is very upset with me about volunteering at the FAC, but when he hears that I will be the logistics person for the family visits, he really goes off on me. He was in Viet Nam. He tells me about dealing with the emotional impact of a place that has been bombed out, the stress that will occur from exposure to so many people in trauma. In his opinion, "civilians" shouldn't be in areas like that—the military should be. He gives me a long tirade of hard-headed loving concern. After he goes on for a while about how I can't do that to myself and he runs out of steam for a second, I tell him, "But there's a difference. When you went to war, you made the mess. I'm going to clean it up. I'm not sure about this, but I think that has a different impact, no?"

"Oh. *But I'm still worried about you!*"

October 5

There is a New Jersey State Trooper here named Sam. He is probably somewhere around my age, but a bit younger. He is one of the state police who will oversee and coordinate the troopers who go with us each day. He is a trooper, meaning that he doesn't have rank to give orders, but he is coordinating the troopers who will go to New York. Sam will also go with us on many days, as the lead person for security. Many of the state police who go with us will be above him in rank. Interesting . . . I wonder how cops will take being told what to do by someone of lesser rank—maybe they're not as military as I thought? Sam seems to be serious, but behind the scenes after meetings I see him joking with others. He has an older-brother quality about him.

Yesterday Sam came in wearing dress blues. Over lunch I was teasing him by stealing his trooper hat, which he had left on the table when he got up to get something. I hid it behind my back, shushed the FEMA guys and other state police who were at the table, and gave him innocent eyes when he looked at me asking where his hat was.

They played along and teased him about taking better care of his belongings. I gave it up when he started to look uncomfortable about being the subject of teasing.

Today he came in for morning meeting in field uniform—which is the baseball hat and the tight pants tucked into boots. He left his hat on the desk behind me. I lifted his hat and put it on my head. After morning meeting, he looked on the desk for it—not there. He got up and walked around the trailer looking everywhere he had been, or thought he had been. I sat quietly by, numbering companion stickers, watching. He sat and scratched his head. Looking around again—his trained cop eyes were saying, "*I know* I had it here somewhere." I watched and had a hard time not laughing. "What's wrong, Sam?" I attempted to get him to look up, but he was troubled and busy with searching his mind and the room.

"Nothin'."

"Are you sure? You look concerned about something."

"No." He still doesn't look at me. He is really frowning now. *Finally,* he looks up. I just grin.

"Let me have my hat."

"What if I say no?"

"Come on. Just give it to me." I hand it over.

"Brat."

I meet a wonderful laughing man, Major Fred, the site supervisor for the Salvation Army. He actually lives about five minutes from me. He is a big guy who probably looks even bigger in that uniform. Major Fred is like Santa Claus: jolly, laughing, silly, sweet. But if you really look, there is a sadness about him—the same sadness that the others who have seen too much pain also carry. The Major has a huge heart and is able to tell silly jokes to make you laugh, or turn it around and have a serious philosophical discussion, a man of extremes in this land of extremes. He has a very commanding and confident presence that comes from standing before many congregations, and as light-hearted as he wants to seem, he is obviously capable.

We have a man named Wendy from the Red Cross who has taken over the role of orientation; he hangs up the date everywhere, every day, with a note on the bottom—a kind of Zen meditation.

"Who orients you?" I ask.

"The day before. I take that one down and hold onto it until I make the new one."

"Bless your soul—I'd be lost without you!"

"Yeah. You can lose track of time in a place like this."

Today's thought is IF YOU GAZE INTO MUDDY WATER LONG ENOUGH IT BECOMES CLEAR.

I steal one of his signs so I can remember it—it strikes me as so appropriately strange for today. Wendy gives everyone Hershey's Kisses. Ya gotta love a man that feeds you chocolate for no reason, for breakfast. He is another of those souls who has infectious cheer; it precedes him actually, everywhere he goes. He oozes giving and warmth.

Over lunch, Major Fred and I talk about the pending ferry visits. He offers words of wisdom for me to ponder to ease my concerns. He has an honest and direct way of saying things, and it makes me think. He is obviously wise. We talk about the fact that the families aren't allowed to take any rubble: New York had stressed that as being so important because it is a crime scene. But that seems to be such a normal act—to collect things from places where we go—a rock or dried flower or object brings us back to the places we have gone. Maybe the stones that they find over there could bring them back to their lost person. A shame . . . I think about a recent trip to Colorado with my husband. In the airport, when we came home, as they checked our bags the woman looked up at me and asked: "How many rocks do you have?" I was amazed, and cracked up.

"How did you know?"

"Everyone does it!" she answered.

I have always collected stones or leaves or something from spots I visited—nature has a way of tying us to the places we go. . . . The rocks over there may not be from nature, but they are still a tangible connection.

Major Fred asks me if I know a story from the Bible: Joshua. At first I think: *Oh, no—I'm about to be preached at by the Salvation Army* . . . but curiosity gets the best of me, and I ask him to tell it to me. In the story, God parts the river and tells Joshua to round up twelve people, one from each tribe in Israel. Joshua is to take the tribesmen with him across the river, and direct them to pick up one stone each from the riverbed. They are supposed to take the stones back to their camp and build a memorial to the people to prove God's ability to part the river—a testament to His strength.

Is it me, or are there some strange parallels here? For the rest of the day, I keep thinking about that memorial: letting families have stones could be their only memorial. Apparently New York will send over urns for our families. The urns will be filled with ash from the World Trade Center. They will get their memorial.

I find that one of my "jobs" (unofficially) is to watch out for Bob's food intake. He's diabetic, and being driven as he is, he gets involved in things, forgetting the time and forgetting to eat. I feel compelled to remind and mother him into caring for himself. I run to find him, and remind him about lunch. On my way to find him, I see people toting supplies and stop there for a while to lend a hand. I pray.

I run into Red Cross Mary, who asks me how I've been sleeping. "No problem. Why?"

"Because you're the only one here that sleeps, if that's the case!"

"What do you mean?"

"Stress levels—being exposed to this type of environment. It's common for people at disasters to have trouble sleeping. So keep your eyes open, and care for yourself."

Generally I can sleep through anything . . .

New York mandates tight security for us. I have to put stickers on companions (yellow) and families (green). All stickers must be dated and numbered sequentially and be worn on the outside of clothing. I must fax the head count to the bus company to get us to the docks comfortably because there are different-sized buses and different seating arrangements inside the buses—"How *many* buses do I want?" *Whothehellknows!*

Faxes have to go to New York with head count and identified special needs; they have a golf cart available for us if anyone feels unable to walk. Every afternoon, someone from my office will fax me the listing of the staff who will be arriving for duty the next morning. Staff who are coming in for the day to volunteer must be listed with the state police upstairs, and the checkpoint at the front gate. I have about twelve volunteers coming in from the outside.

New York wants control over everything that the families leave behind in the area designated as the Wall of Remembrance—nothing can be left but what we furnish them: flowers and teddy bears. The Salvation Army has taken over flower duty and will ensure that we have red, white, and blue carnations each morning. The Red Cross gives us access to the storeroom behind mass care so that we can take teddy bears for families. Boxes of teddy bears are piled high. Hard hats and goggles are being assembled with dust masks and loaded into boxes by some of the NOVA people who are doing night shift. We have a van for equipment that will go to the ferryboat early. Details . . .

Another friendly face and old friend, Jack, wanders into the trailer, giving me a big grin. Jack is a huge bear of a guy with a wonderful graying beard. He works for the Division of Addictions Services. Jack has a Barry White kind of a voice and is friendly, outgoing, and confident. He had been up here checking on his staff from Addictions Services, who are helping out in the Department of Health trailer. I have known Jack for years, and although I have never worked with him directly, I have always known him to be supportive but a no-nonsense kind of person. I knew him forever the first time that we spoke. From the day we met, he has always called me "baby." Strange behavior between bureaucrats, but Jack can get away with that kind of thing. I never thought it was strange, but many around us did. Over the years I have heard occasional astonished whispers in my ear during meetings: "Did he just call you *baby?*" He has that kind of a way with people, especially women. Jack can call a stranger "baby" without being offensive. Jack was born to be a teddy bear, and he knows it.

We have catching-up conversation, and he volunteers: "Baby, do you need any help with anything?" *Oh,* if he would just be willing to take over equipment—that would *really* free me up from a lot. . . . But it's such a BIG job. . . . So I venture to ask. . . . "Hey, baby, anything you need. No problem. Let me check my calendar and I'll be there for you when I can." Thank you, God! I breathe a sigh of relief.

Darkness has come quite a while ago. I was outside and caught the sun going down, and stopped to breathe it in for just a bit. Amazing reds and purples surround the big green Lady in the harbor. I snap a picture that will probably not come out. I go back into the administrative trailer to wrap things up and to see if anything is needed before I go. I meet with Bob for a few minutes, compulsively running through everything that I've done—to gain his assurance that I've covered all bases.

"Did I forget anything, you think?" He shakes his head no.

"Anything else you need me to do?" He shakes his head no again.

"Are you as tired as you look?" He nods and tells me to go home.

"You too, buddy. See you in the morning. And thanks for your help."

(Wait a minute—was that a smile?) He waves his hand at me like I'm a mosquito, but it somehow comes out almost like an affectionate gesture. This is a really nice guy; I don't care what anybody says.

October 6

Today we are to take 104 people to New York City. Last night I didn't sleep. Did Red Cross Mary jinx me with that remark, or what? I think that I laid there with my eyes closed and my brain racing all night. It was as if I were watching movies—not asleep, not really awake, pictures and conversations running through my head, looking not like dreams, but like movies. I am awake—I can open my eyes at any time, yet these vibrant visual scenes, complete with surround sound, are running all night as soon as my eyes close. If I open my eyes and close them again, the movie picks up where it left off. Through it all I couldn't figure out: Did the things in the movies in my head really happen? It was all about the FAC and the people—but was it real? Was it past or made up? Can a person dream while awake? If so, these are the most realistic dreams I have ever had. And why can't I tell if they are real or not—what's up with this? *Weird*. I did nothing but remember to breathe deep, and occasionally open my eyes to prove to myself that I was not asleep. Even though I didn't sleep, I don't feel tired. Running on adrenaline? I haven't had a day off yet since the twentieth of September, so I guess nervous energy is taking over. *Please, God*, let this thing come together today!

By 9:30 a.m. things are happening like lightning. Staff are arriving for orientation in the chapel. Orientation began by finding out where individuals came from. Those from out of state, which most were,

were given a round of applause for coming to help New Jersey. They responded to the applause by looking shocked.

Orientation for staff was to give information and direction:

> Companions will be identified by yellow stickers. Families by green. We occasionally have visitors or administrators from agencies such as FEMA (the Federal Emergency Management Agency). They will be identified by blue stickers that say "official." We are not providing companions to individuals with "official" stickers. This is a high-security area, so New York has asked us to wear the stickers in a highly visible spot on the outside of our coats and jackets.
>
> Each family will have two companions in case one of the family members cannot go on, or wants to leave the area. If that happens, see me and I will get one of the Department of Corrections staff—the Special Operations Group—or someone else to go with you so that we do not upset the security of the area. If anyone wants to go on but feels unable to walk, *we will carry you.* If *you* feel like you can't go on, let someone know. This is a very hard thing to do, and there is no shame in not being able to do it. If you become upset, let someone know; we are here for one another as much as we are here for the families.
>
> We will board the buses out front (pointing) and leave by 1 p.m. for a short ride to the dock, where we will board the ferry. Please be sure that the families get a bite to eat before they go. All of the equipment that we will need will be on board. The ride to New York takes about seven minutes. Please do not allow anyone to move around on the ferry; it can be rough in the water and we don't want any injuries. We will let you know every step of the way when to move.
>
> There are many tripping hazards. It will be a natural inclination for people to look up as they leave the dock: immediately you can see damage to the buildings. Go to the hazards when you see them and stretch out your arms to form a barrier.
>
> Everyone will have a map. We will be on a platform at the corner of West and Liberty that looks diagonally across the World Trade Center complex toward building number four. (We used a

map from the CNN Web site that had all of the complex buildings numbered.) Many people find it disorienting once they are inside the damage zone. Help them to locate which building is which. Tower One was on the left as you look at it, Tower Two on the right. If you have questions about any other buildings let us know.

We will have about fifteen minutes on the platform. You will know it is time to go when we ask for our closing prayer. At that time, begin to herd the families together. The movement will help to bring them back and refocus; in their grief, they may become stuck there, just watching. Following the prayer, we will go to an area called the Wall of Remembrance, where they can leave flowers and teddies. If they bring any cards or papers from home, check to be sure that there are no identifiers on the papers. Be their eyes. Think for them. Let this be their time to not have to think or worry about how or what to do. Protect them.

Families are arriving now at the intake tent in the back of the terminal (point). After this meeting we want you to wander to the back and first pair up with another companion. Once you have companioned yourselves, and as you see a family being signed in, approach them and introduce yourself. Bring them into the eating area and help them get settled. These are grieving families, so keep your distance. Let them know where you will be, and check back if you think you need to. Let them have space, as you would want to have; no one wants a stranger around at a time like this. Ask your family if they have any special needs or any physical problems. Introduce them to an EMT right away if they do have any problems, so that we can keep an eye on them.

Be sure that you eat. If you are not strong, you can't be there for others. Be back for family orientation in this room at 12:30. We will return by about 3 p.m. Staff debriefing is at 3:30. If you are still with a family we will arrange to debrief you separately. It is *strongly advised* that you debrief.

Stay with your family until they are ready to leave. If you are worried about them driving because they are upset, if you need to, find someone to help you to convince them to stay. We are all here for one another. Don't do anything alone if you don't feel right about it.

At both ends of the terminal building is a huge doorway. At the rear entrance, NOVA has set up a blue tent and table for "family intake." The families were told to enter this area and present their paperwork to sign in. By 10 a.m. the families begin arriving out back, and are being registered and given prenumbered stickers with the date: 6 (for October 6), and a number indicating the order of their arrival. They look visibly frightened, nervous, sad, tearful, quiet, dazed. They wander, looking at the memory boards, writing, leaving memories, eating little, if anything.

At 12:30 there is a somber orientation for families, who become visibly tearful as they file into the chapel and sit down in rows:

> Everyone will be given a hard hat, goggles, and a dust mask. Debris is still falling from the buildings and it is a dangerous area, so hard hats must be worn. If you have sensitive eyes, or wear contact lenses, and have sensitivity to dust you may want to leave your goggles and dust masks on.

Bob tries to relieve fears by describing what everyone says is the worst thing—the first thing to hit you is the impact of seeing an ash-covered world:

> Everything there is in color at first, then as you turn the corner, it will become gray. Everything goes from color to gray.

We have a list of things to mention, to give them a buffer so that they know what to expect. Bob introduces me as "captain." We hand out the maps and reminders to use the bathroom. Families are told that workers are still searching for victims, that even though it appears to be a construction zone, they have searched all areas before any of the heavy equipment is brought in.

> At the request of New York, there are to be no pictures taken. This is considered a crime scene, and photographs are not permitted. They will confiscate cameras, and it is our understanding

that they will not be returned.

We have other people traveling with us as well: (point to, and they stand) clergy, state troopers, EMTs. If you feel faint, short of breath, or have any physical problems, let us know. Our EMTs are equipped to handle anything.

You have already met your companions. Please consider all of us to be your companions. We are all here for you. If you need anything, please feel free to ask whoever is closest to you.

We will surround you as we walk and protect you from any tripping hazards. We will be your eyes and ears. You should not have to worry about anything but what you came here for. If at any point in this process you do not want to go on, we will stay with you or take you to another area. We have enough people to accommodate your needs. I have asked the companions to let me know if this happens, and I will get one of the corrections officers in New York, who are dressed all in black, to stay with you or accompany you to another spot where you will be more comfortable. This is because the security in New York is very tight at the moment. If you feel unable to walk but still want to continue on, don't worry—we will carry you.

The buses arrived out front at 11:00 a.m. The troopers would wait for them to arrive and check the luggage and engine compartments as well as the interiors for bombs. They would then remain with the bus to keep the area secure until we boarded.

By 12:30 our three equipment people would have already taken the teddy bears, hard hats, goggles, masks, flowers, and coolers of juice, water, and snacks to the boat. A few of the troopers would go with them to the dock, and do a bomb sweep of the boat before we arrived, checking under seats and the engine compartments.

We had seven minutes during the ferry ride to fit everyone in a hard hat and distribute teddy bears. We discovered on the boat today that the linings for hard hats must be assembled—the plastic lining has clips to secure it to the hat. *(Oooops!)* Volunteers frantically popped liners into hard hats as we passed them out and fit them to many heads, including our own. We also had people carrying teddy bears up and down the aisles of the boat, handing them to families.

The Salvation Army positioned themselves at the front of the boat and handed out red, white, and blue carnations to family members as we disembarked.

We assembled as a group in front of the Mercantile, having been met by three of the SOGs (Special Operations Group from the prisons) one of whom drove the golf cart for those unable to walk.

We form a protective cocoon around the families as we enter the dock area. To the left, the Winter Garden sits before us, fractured and burned. Ribs are poking out of the American Express building: the steel framing of Tower One that sliced into the building when the Tower fell. Glass is glazed from fire, and broken. Asphalt safety ramps are built over the top of the wires and hoses that run through the street so that they can be easily crossed.

Our SOGs begin the escort. Huge boys from the New York State Police, dressed in leathers, stand along the sidewalk at parade rest with tears running down their faces. It seems like hundreds of them—flanking the sidewalk on either side—a human fence of pain. Painfully young. Silent. I want to hug them but I can't. I want to bury my face in one of those leather jackets and cry with them but I choke it back. I don't want to look, I don't want to breathe in this smell, and I don't want to see these big, strong, beautiful men crying and in such pain. As I look at my feet I see wide cracks in the pink granite inlay of the sidewalk; like an earthquake has hit. Solid granite, thick as can be—cracked like a potato chip. I vaguely wonder if it is safe to stand on; it now looks so fragile.

We begin walking past the Winter Garden through Battery Park City. Family members gasp. They shield their eyes from the sun and look up, staring at the damage as they walk. A young woman cries very hard, comforted by her husband. I hand her a tissue.

We round the corner toward Liberty Street and the world does turn to gray—ash covered and bland. Sidewalks, streets, buildings. Gray. Nets cover some of the buildings to keep the papers and debris inside. Papers and many different types of debris are still in the trees, things are hanging in the branches. Gray leaves. The covered walkway that crosses over Liberty Street is fractured and broken, burned. Windows gone. Smoke rises from the still-burning fires—and the smell is death, plastic, ozone, burning metal, chemical, petroleum, and rain on hot cement all rolled into one. I breathe deep to choke back the tears, and wish I hadn't.

As we move slowly along, we pass men in a hazmat decontamination tent on our left, and other workers on the street. They remove their hard hats and place them over their hearts. They stand this way as we pass. Many of them—most—are crying. Now I can hold it back no more—I swallow the lump in my throat, but let the tears run. Oh, God, I don't want to go in there! The silence here is deafening. I keep wondering *Where is the noise?* People, vehicles, activity everywhere, but not a sound. It's like the hush of a really deep snowfall at night. Just a whisper, if anything. I look at a small group of diggers standing with their construction helmets over their hearts, covered in dirt, hands bandaged, bloody, crying. My heart swells with American pride, and breaks all at the same time. Somehow this world becomes even grayer with every step . . . and we aren't even inside yet . . .

We walk up to the area surrounding Ground Zero. To get to the fenced-in portion under guard was a short eighth of a mile of eternal pavement that took what seemed like hours to cross. Military are everywhere to protect and secure the location. As we approach the gate, the national guardsmen, who are surrounding the area, snap to full attention and salute the families as they pass—a salute fit for presidential review. Can the families even see this—what these men are giving them—or are they so caught in their own world of pain that they don't see anything anymore? Behind the gate I see the biggest crane in the world rising up. Once the entire group was assembled, the gate opened and we parted the ranks to allow the families to file up onto the platform. We go in behind them to stand to the rear, allowing them the best vantage point. Companions watched their families from about an arm's length, waiting for a question, a need for tissues.

There is no way in hell you are ever going to convince me that this is New York City. My playground cannot look like this. *Goddamn it, this can't be New York City. It can't be America.* I have heard the phrase: " . . . words cannot express . . ." from so many who have been here.

There

are

no

words

No description. No explanation. No words. Nothing. It is just too big. Too ugly. Too evil. Too terrible.

Oh God, I can feel the weight of all of those souls, so heavy.

All of those lost people. All of that evil is right there burning and smoking in front of my eyes and I just want to scream until I die from it. My brain cannot form or find words that will ever describe this. I can smell the fuel—the oily residue of jet fuel hangs in the air with the burning of so many different materials in one place. Still.

It is just too big.

Way up on the pile of rubble are *tiny* men. I see a red bag with a circle of men around it way out there on the side. Just one more

lost soul coming home for the last time . . .

All of these people and all of that equipment, and I hear nothing. Strangely, this silence is becoming so soothing—I feel it wrapping around me. This place is so ugly, but at the same time, so holy. This is a land of extremes—opposites. I have a sensation of being wrapped in heavy cotton: fuzzy, muffled, colorless. The sacredness of this place is overwhelming, as overwhelming as the evil that created it. Out of habit, I keep trying to slow my breathing to keep my emotions steady, and my thoughts clear. It works a tiny bit. I close my eyes and try to breathe slow and deep, but my eyes immediately snap open, and I begin to pant when I realize that although I have closed my eyes, I can still see it—it has been burned into my brain, already.

In my head I think that the screaming of all of those souls must be the reason that there is no sound. Their pain has drowned out the world.

We have a Hindu family with us. A man in the family lost his wife. Her parents have come to visit from Pakistan. At home he has a five-year-old boy. They need a body to have closure on death in their faith. Tonight the parents will return to Pakistan with no body. We are trying to get an urn for them, early, from New York. They are praying at the railing. Behind us on the platform stands a New York State Trooper in full dress uniform, at attention, crying. Again I close my eyes and try to breathe. Bob's arm goes around my shoulders and he says softly, "It will never get any easier."

He tells me that I'm doing a good job. As the group is leaving, I linger. I realize that I have pulled my hands inside of my sleeves as if I were trying to get warm. I am not cold. I am now three years old and all alone with my fists balled up inside my sleeves, chewing on my thumb through the fabric. Never in my wildest dreams would I be able to relate to anyone being able to do something like this. How do you fly a plane full of people into a building on purpose? What kind of twisted . . .

At the Wall of Remembrance they cry. They clutch their teddy bears and cry. Some choose to keep the teddies. I put a kiss on the carnation in my hand, and put down the flower and a prayer of thanks for those in my circle who lived, and for those I now watch who are not as fortunate as I am. I know in my heart that I have changed somehow. The shift inside me was as strong as a shot. But I don't know how or where or what it means. I'm simply not me anymore. But what I have changed into I don't know.

The Wall of Remembrance is actually a line of bushes that wraps around the roadway next to the sidewalk. There is a little alcove where the bushes make a circle. Just at the outer edge of this alcove, a woman leaves her little brown teddy bear. She has tied her dust mask to its head like a little hat. Under the ribbon around its neck she has placed a folded dollar bill. She gives the teddy a pat on the belly, a kiss, and lays it gently in the bushes. My heart breaks for her and I want desperately to curl up under a blanket and cry. From next to me a voice says, "Yeah, that will last long." I don't respond, and don't even know who spoke. I make a mental note to bring a dollar each day— just in case . . . The woman cries, touches the little teddy's chest with tenderness, and walks away. The dollar flutters in the breeze.

Back on board the ferryboat, we collect hard hats, give water, juice, more flowers, soft words, tissues. Simply Band-Aids, tiny, ineffective Band-Aids. We remind the families to try to eat. Many have not eaten much lately. I see red eyes, puffy and hurting. But many seem almost relaxed now—like something shifted in them as well. . . .

Debriefing.

It means what? I feel lost. Hurt. Like somebody took out my insides and shook them like a mildewed blanket. There is a lump in my throat the size of a watermelon and I am so tired I could die. How do you debrief that? Does half an hour of talking fix me?

Following debriefing is my time to handle the logistical details for the next day: the buses, boats, head counts, snacks, special needs, security clearance, equipment cleaning, assembly and packing, faxes, phone calls, numbering stickers, locating tomorrow's rosters, firming up staffing, reviewing attendance of actual participants, and so on. . . . I watch the sun go down for a few minutes with some fellow sunset worshippers, and begin to make my arrangements for tomorrow.

Red Cross Mary is leaving, back to California. She brings me a Beanie Baby dog with floppy ears and says, "On the last boat over, leave this from both of us. Promise me you will remember." She will not get to go with us. I look at her sadly. One more is leaving . . .

"I promise."

Mary has been such a comfort, so funny, warm, and helpful. I tuck the little dog into my vest pocket and hug her good-bye. Everything here is about loss. We get to know each other just a little bit and then it's gone. Just a snapshot of a person . . .

I cry my way down the turnpike to exit 7A.

For me there will be a sunrise tomorrow.

October 7

Again no sleep. Another set of movies was running in my head. So I lay there all night and worked on relaxation breathing. And simply watching my brain. Good thing I have had about thirty years' worth of meditation training.

Rain. Hard rain. We gather together in a group huddle and say prayers for sun. It works. Yesterday worked like a well-oiled machine, and we patted ourselves and one another on the back a lot. How it worked so well I don't know, except that someone up there must have been pulling strings. It went off without a hitch.

I learn this morning that the family from yesterday returned to Pakistan with an urn. They have something to help them put some kind of closure—if there really is such a thing—on her death. I guess red tape can be cut.

How will I live through this?

It really hurts.

I have lunch with Bob and discover that we have almost identical training and work experience. We both worked many years in state psychiatric hospitals, both specialized in addictions treatment and both have experience with forensics. Weird . . .

Again we have staff orientation with nervous, anxious faces. Again the families are nervous and tearful—eyes wide and fear filled. Fear of the unknown.

I know.

I'm still afraid.

At the close of orientation, the Major gives us a blessing for our journey that he based on our conversations about collecting rocks for souvenirs. It was from the Bible—the story of Joshua:

> . . . the Lord said to Joshua, take up twelve stones and carry them over with you and put them down at the place where you will stay tonight. In the future when your children ask you "What do these stones mean?" tell them:
>
> "These stones are to be a memorial to the people . . . forever."
>
> So they took up twelve stones and they carried them over with them to their camp, where they put them down.
>
> We will be taking the victims' families across the river by boat each day to view the World Trade Center complex. And like Joshua and the tribesmen, each one of us who visits that place will bring back stones . . . stones in our hearts. Stones of fear and hate. Stones of revenge. Stones of loneliness and grief.
>
> When we cross back over that river we will have to find a way to put down those stones to build a memorial of hope that will rise like the phoenix from the ashes of that city.
>
> We will return as one people, one family.

Damn. It's only 9:30 a.m. and I'm crying already.

We offer soothing words and quiet talk for the families. We learned from yesterday to explain the maps to help families with their orientation to the building locations when they view the scene, and to add extra people for equipment. Make the smooth run even better.

Today America bombed Afghanistan. Before we began loading the buses the troopers found out that the bombing had started; their radios crackled to life all at once. Even CNN didn't know yet.

What do we do? We load up and go!

As we are boarding the families onto the buses, I see Bob walking up with Father Matthews. I open my arms wide to them at the same time as if to give them both a hug. As I stand between them, I tell them the news that the bombing has started. Father is ready in case we need prayer and counsel. I choose those among the crew today that I know I can trust to be quiet: those in charge of others, who I know are level headed—Sandy, Harry: the site supervisors for NOVA and the Red Cross. One by one I whisper into their ears, they tell only those who they know will remain calm and quiet, and we begin to circle the wagons. Enough of us are ready—just in case. . . . Please, God, let these families do what they need to do today!

Immediately before the families come out of the terminal building to board the buses, the sky is screaming blue, the sun is out and it's raining like hell. Huge drops *pouring* down like a movie on nuclear rain. As I walk through the downpour, I turn in circles to find the rainbow—but there isn't one. What is with this weather? Sunshine, no clouds, and it's *pouring*. For about ten minutes. This must truly be hell. I pass Blaze, one of our troopers, who looks up at the sky, back to me, and shrugs. "Creepy, huh?"

We board the boat. My circle of wagons looks as jumpy as I feel. On the outside deck of the boat the cell phones in pockets of those in charge begin to ring—orders have come for turning us around.

"What should I do?" says the trooper in charge.

"Throw that fucking phone in the river."

The order to turn back is refused: we have eighty-five people on board the boat that need to go to a funeral. Within seconds there is a Coast Guard gunner beside us on one side and the state police gunner on the other. My heart jumps, and I think they have come to force us back, but we go on. Fast. The ferry is suddenly going at full throttle. A man who is seated very close to where I'm standing mutters something about how they are "Really getting the royal treatment" to his family. His family nods, and he says to me, "You people really went all out for us. Thank you!" ... and I smile, thinking to myself—*if you only knew* ... I put a hand on his shoulder and say, "You are very welcome."

Armed national guards at the dock meet us. Humvees are parked nearby. They escort us in. New York is under full military alert and we're acting as if this is totally normal and routine. Another helicopter gunner has joined the single mosquito that has buzzed over Manhattan 24-7 since. The two buzz together up there now as a pair. We exchange nervous looks, and whisper about how to keep this quiet. We soon figure out that the families and most of the companions are clueless about the bombing, so we will have no distractions. We can let them do what they came for ... and they do: they cry, they hug.

Again we pass the fractured world of broken stone, glass, concrete, and burned and twisted metal. Again the workers stand at attention. Again they cry. Like some horror version of the movie *Groundhog Day,* my life has become this twisted repeat of itself. And I feel it as much, or more, than yesterday. I feel sooooo tired. Not sleepy. Worn down, beat up, flogged tired. As if I have done this for years.

Again, on the platform I see myself pulling my hands into my sleeves as if to make sock puppets. I'm feeling like a child again, and want to hide. I catch myself again nibbling on the edge of the sleeve that is wrapped around my hand. Again, as we begin to depart, I hang back. I hear Bob whisper in my ear: "I told you it doesn't get better. How are you holding up?" I'm not sure I even answered. I'm not sure I even am.

As we are leaving I see the same young New York State Trooper crying behind us—his position is to guard the platform. I'm not the only one stuck in a hell that repeats itself day after day. The repetition and sameness about this is downright unnerving. He is so young and strong and baby-faced. . . . I hand him a flower. He blinks at me and says, "Thanks so much," in a tone like I gave him a Porsche. The families are slowly filing out around me.

I go to the rail and lean on it. I realize Maria is leaning on me. We wrap our arms around each other, and hug as we stand looking out across the rubble, with tears running down our faces. "See that building? (she points at the Verizon building) Seven hundred fifty people got out alive. Remember that—seven hundred fifty people lived." Bless you, Maria, for trying, but my brain screams back at her—

But how many thousands died? IT DOESN'T HELP!

Right here, right now, I am incapable of seeing the good side of anything. I nod at her, wipe my eyes, hug her tighter and agree—it isn't her fault that the Band-Aid was way too small for the boo-boo. Two lost souls trying to make sense out of the loss of thousands of souls. . . . Please, God—take them home; don't let them stay here and be lost.

I leave the platform. In the street, the tiniest sobbing little old woman grabs me as I walk by. She has one hand over her mouth and the other one is digging into my skin with painful, amazing strength. She is clearly frantic and horrified and keeps saying "My son" over and over and over. She turns around and takes her hand from her mouth and points toward the pile of rubble, all the while digging deeper into me with the other hand as she says over and over and over, "My son, my son, my son, my son . . ." Her eyes focus on nothing, with pupils big and terrified. Tears run down her cheeks in a flood.

The strength of the despair in those tiny, digging fingers is amazing. I move around in front of her line of vision. She is so tiny she comes up to my armpit. I wrap myself around her and turn her away from the nightmare scenery and begin to walk. She lets go of my arm and grabs my coat, crying into me as we walk. I stroke her hair and tighten my arm around her frail, tiny shoulders as they shake with her tears, and say to her, "I am so sorry." *God.* What should I say? There is *nothing* I can say. Or do. She believed until today that he was alive. She knew now, after only one look, that he was not. I dab at her tears with Red Cross tissues and steer her to her assigned companion, who takes over.

I need to stop now.
I look down at my feet . . .

A scuffling noise comes from under the platform. As I look up and turn toward the sound, a firefighter comes ducking out from under our platform—taking a shortcut through. He jumps at the sight of me, looks down at his feet and says, "I'm so sorry. I thought everyone was gone."

"You look like a man who needs a hug."

He looks up, gives me a wide evil grin, and in the heaviest New York accent says "*Aww.* I'm all doity." That grin says, "Yes, please, I want a hug." (Actually—*I'm* really the one who needs a hug!)

"You look beautiful to me," and I grin back as I open my arms. He walks into them, picks me up, and about breaks my ribs before he sets me down again. I put a flower in his pocket and say, "Thank you so much." He gives me the smile of an angel and sniffs the flower, winks at me, and stomps off. I have to jog to catch up to the group at the Wall of Remembrance. On the way I pass a fireman in a golf cart. I stretch out my hand, which he grabs very tightly and holds onto. His face is pale and shell-shocked, but he brightens when he grabs my hand and he smiles. I smile back: "Thank you for doing this." He smiles wider and says—"Yeah—you too." I put a flower in the goggles that he wears strapped around his helmet. I get a nod in thanks.

I think I have found an addiction. That contact has made me feel almost human—setting a spark and a smile off somewhere in this crazy place has made me remember those words that my first supervisor in the world of human services, Joe, spoke to me in 1972: "If you can make one person smile today, you've done your job."

Since hearing that, I have tried to live my life that way. If you can ease the pain of someone for just a moment, than you have done that person a wonderful service. Maybe one smile a day—somewhere? I can't fix it. But . . . just one more smile . . .

I wonder for a moment what will happen to those flowers. . . . Will they ditch them immediately, or will they keep them as a connection with something besides death?

At the Wall of Remembrance, the families mourn, accept, deny, and say good-bye; they leave flowers and wipe tears. No one is coming behind us today—no appointments. We stay a long time. As I leave a flower at the wall today, I say a prayer for those lost men in there with their pale faces and dying eyes. Please, God, keep them safe and whole. . . .

Safely back at the boat, and halfway across the water, the family members are turning their cell phones back on, and they immediately begin to ring. "Oh God, we're bombing Afghanistan!" begins to waft through the boat. Thank you, God, for giving them time interrupted. . . . Many of the family members smile. A couple of the families actually clap and cheer.

I can really see the difference today in the families when we return to the terminal; worry lines relax, they become more animated, they smile, they eat like pigs. I find this to be so comforting, and take it as evidence that God is looking down on us. Something is working here. Not a fix, but just a teeny bit of relief. Just one more smile—please— just one more smile, just one more. It warms my heart.

The park is in lockdown. No one allowed in or out is the original order, which later changes to no one in. Bob decides to close tomorrow. It will be my first day off in over two weeks.

Debriefing. Tired, head aching, numb.

I cry again to exit 7A.

October 8

The FAC is closed today. I am suffering in imposed exile to a normal life that now feels boring, dull, *strange.* I'm not sure what I should do with myself, and I don't want to do anything. Is this how it was before? I don't remember what it was like before . . .

I sleep until after 9, and wake up feeling stupid.

My house suddenly feels like a luxury hotel. I linger over coffee. I watch TV. I do nothing at a slow pace.

I toy with the idea of driving to the FAC anyway, but I don't.

October 9

To try to lighten things a bit, we play the "How far have you come to be here?" game first thing in the morning, before we begin volunteer orientation. We clap and thank those who have come from far away. I consider anything outside of New Jersey to be far away. Camden is far away from this place. It might be south—central Jersey, but it's still a hell of a commute. Blows my mind that so many people have come from so far—Canada, California, and Texas—all over, just to help New Jersey people. And they seem amazed that anyone would thank them openly for doing it.

I back up without looking during my orientation speech today: *Ouch!* I look down at a potted plant that sits by the altar, behind me. Damn thing *bit* me! It has sharp nasty prehistoric spikes for leaves, and it *bit* me, through heavy jeans. It feels like someone just took a knife to the back of my calf. Something that ugly has got to be poisonous. After everyone files out of the chapel, I lift my pant leg and look at an actual cut on my leg from that evil plant. It drew blood. Don't want this happening again. . . . I bend down to lift it up and take it somewhere else, and it scratches me up both arms through my sweater and denim jacket. I let go of "Little Shop of Horrors" and decide that remembering it's there is probably better than fighting with it. I would obviously lose.

I do my customary peek out the door for the buses at 11 a.m. There are none. There is a huddle of blue uniforms near the sidewalk. I run over to our troopers and say, "Guys, have you seen the buses?"

Yup.

"Where are they now?"

Dunno.

"Did you do the bomb search and everything?"

Nope.

"When did the buses leave?"

Dunno.

Okay—not getting anywhere here.

I run inside to call the bus company. As I enter the terminal a NOVA worker runs up looking confused. She grabs my arm and gives me one of those scared whispers from horror movies: "There are no families here." I look around, and suddenly realize that by now this place should be *bustling* with people. She says to me nervously, "Where could all of the families be?" Someone passing by overhears her question and says, "The troopers put them on the buses and sent them away." *What????????*

"Where did they send them?" I ask, beginning to really get nervous now. Dunno.

A Red Cross person runs up, excited and breathless: "We were walking on the other side of the island, and we saw the buses and the families over there." She turns and points toward the Science Center. I turn and run full speed through the terminal, up the stairs to the state police office, where I find Sam on the phone. I interrupt, out of breath, to tell him the story of troopers putting families on the buses and sending them away.

"Sam, I want you to find the person who did this and shoot him for me."

"Don't worry!" as he grabs his hat and runs.

I begin dialing the bus company number as I follow after him, trying to keep up: "We can't find the buses. Do they check in with you?"

"They're with you."

"No, honest—they came and then they left. They have the families and we don't know where they are. Can you call them?" Dunno. Oh God, help me!

A tap on my shoulder from behind, and a shy Salvation Army person says quietly, "The flowers are gone." What? I just look at her with my mouth open. . . . She is obviously concerned by my lack of verbal response, so she makes another attempt to communicate. "They were here; now they're gone."

"Where could they have gone?" Dunno.

I feel like it's a bad movie with this dunno crap from everybody. I mean, like is this a *joke* or something? Did you all *plan this?*

"So do you know who may have taken the flowers?" Dunno. I can't *take* this . . .

"Do me a favor—ask the equipment people, the NOVA people at the desk, anybody—ask around a little and if you don't find them soon, tell Major Fred or Major Barb that we need more. They'll know what to do." She nods and skitters off. My head is starting to hurt.

Within a minute a NOVA worker comes up to me: "We found them."

"Oh, *great!* Where?"

"In the buckets." *What?*

"Someone put them in the buckets"—in an exaggerated patient, patronizing tone like I'm stupid or something.

"I'm sorry—what did you find?"

"The *flowers.*" Oh God, now my right eye is twitching.

"They're pulling them out of the buckets now—tacky, yeah, but at least you'll have flowers."

"Thank you so much!" I look over to see the Salvation Army staff trying unsuccessfully to look inconspicuous as they take flowers out of the buckets that decorate the walls, and gather them into a bundle for us.

In the history of disasters, no one has ever taken 200 people a day through four modes of public transportation into a war zone and had them all return without a hitch. No one, no place, ever. That is an incomprehensible, mind-boggling feat. Really—think about it: 200 grief-stricken people through buses, water, twisted metal, and devastation. But we did it. More than once. Without incident. Without problem. Without rules, regulations, or assistance. Now all of a sudden we lose the buses, the flowers, and *all* of the family members *at one time.* What is *up?* I just want to stand here in the middle of everything and scream at the top of my lungs.

"We found them." I turn around to find Sandy, the NOVA site supervisor. This time I ask, not assume—"The families?"

"*Yeah*—Corrections had a new guy out front. He was trying to be helpful, so he put them onto the buses and sent them to a parking lot over by the Science Center."

I look down at the clock on my cell phone—we are now forty minutes behind schedule. So much for our well-oiled machine. We have patted ourselves on the backs too much—God is taking us down a few pegs! *No one* is checked in. None have had lunch; it must be hot as hell on the buses . . . The state police come over, chests puffing up, jabbing fingers at both of us, and saying, "You have to check each and every one of these people before we leave. Is that clear? Every one of them."

"But the corrections guys checked their death certificates and paperwork on the bus. They haven't eaten; they've been on a bus for an hour. *Please* don't make us do that."

"*Every one.* Is that clear?" Yes. We nod. I look at Sandy; she has been a rock for me—a spirit to commune with. One of those people that I can communicate with almost nonverbally—she just *knows* what to do.

"What do we do—we'll never get through this many people!" I look down at the huge pile of green stickers in my hand.

"Half?"

"Oh yeah . . ." We split the batch and begin to put stickers on families as we try to soothe with soft words and apologies.

I do little more than apologize profusely to the families during orientation. We rush to get them loaded and off. Two blocks from the docks my phone rings. Jake's voice says, "Act natural, okay? The boat isn't there."

"What do you mean?"

"There's no boat."

I turn my head away from everyone near me and whisper into the phone: "What happened to the boat?" Dunno. I am truly in hell.

"What should I do?"

"Just be cool—it will come. I hope." Oh crap. Within a few minutes of our arrival the boat is coming through the harbor. I breathe deep. It turns out that one of the guys that works on the ferry had fallen off halfway across the river, and they had to pull him from the water, take him back, and send another boat. I can't believe it—what are the odds of a ferry worker falling off the boat. . . . Considering all of that—they made great time, and no one was hurt.

Once off the boat, as we approach Battery Park, a New Jersey State Trooper, along with a New York State Trooper, are pulling a kid from our group, snatching him up by the collar. They take him aside, behind the group, and are obviously reaming him out. He turns out to be one of the ferry staff who said that he saw the Towers being hit, and wanted to go in with us. He has three IDs that don't match. The New York State Trooper is hissing at him: "What's wrong with you that you would butt into a group of grieving families? I oughta put these size thirteens up your . . ." I touch the trooper's arm and say, "When you're done doing that, let's also make sure that whoever you hand him over to gets him into treatment. There's something wrong that he would risk this to go in. He needs someone to talk to." I am accused of being a tree-hugging liberal. . . . "Suppose you want to give him a flower too . . ."

On the platform, there is suddenly a worried voice in my ear: "Have you seen the EMTs? I have my eye on this older gent here; he's having a bit of trouble. I want them to eyeball him." I look around. I don't see them. "I'll get them." I walk around the platform—no EMTs. I ask a trooper if he has seen them. "No." I'm really worried now, and look down in the street—sometimes they hang out there. No EMTs. I go down to street level, and ask one of the Department of Corrections SOGs: "I can't find my EMTs. Have you seen them?"

"Anything wrong?" He frowns and looks like he is ready for attack mode.

"Really, no, but I can't find them."

"You did bring them, right?"

My mouth drops open. *Ohhhhh crap!* Now it's my turn: "Dunno."

I return to the platform with the news. "What do we do?"

"*Pray.*" We eyeball the gent together. He does fine—thank God!

I get a signal that it is time for our closing prayer. Our rabbi who is supposed to say the prayer is not there either. Sweet Jesus, *what else?* Major Fred pinch hits beautifully.

Once back at the terminal building I'm confronted by my missing EMTs, looking at their feet. "We missed the bus."

"Guys—big white things. Out front every day—Get *on them*. Don't make me babysit you." I don't know if I should hug them or smack them. They are looking so upset. . . . "No, I will not tell on you—but from now on . . ."

"*Okay Okay Okay Okay!*"

Everything has gone wrong. But everything has gone right. A family member gives me a hug after we return, and says, "I can't thank you enough. I can't tell you what this means to us."

You just did.

One of the troopers gives me a New Jersey State Police enamel pin. "You do a great job here." I tear up and hug him with thanks.

The more I come here the more I see God.

October 10

I bring someone to orient as my relief person, and she follows me, taking down phone numbers and organizing staff scheduling. I think my choice of backup is a good one. Bob is not happy at the prospect of a relief person. He frowns and warns me to keep the backup thing to a minimum. It also seems that he has clashed with her at some point in the recent past . . . I tell him I'm not getting in the middle: "You *know* she's capable of doing this, and she's bright, so . . ." He waves his hand at me to shut me up.

We are back to being that well-oiled machine, but now I dare not take it for granted. . . .

Outside, Jack jogs up to me carrying a green hard hat. We get donations of hard hats from various construction and building corporations. Our latest donation was from the Dick Corporation. He holds it up proudly—he has an organizational idea to make things run more smoothly: "We have just enough of these for 'administration.' Green hat people can be the ones that everyone goes to if they need anything—you know—we can run and get things, solve problems—whatever you need. Be really visible in the crowd. What do you think?"

"Sort of really antiadministrators." I laugh. Then I turn over the hat and see four giant letters across the front. "Wait. Jack, this is a joke, right?"

"No, baby. What do you mean?"

"Jack, look at it; it says DICK on it. I am *not* running around here with a hard hat that says DICK. Imagine the jokes: administration—all dick heads. See the DICK CORPORATION, our people in charge. Hey, everybody in charge here is a real *dick*. Jack, you can't be serious."
He was. But he laughs.

"We can put stickers on the DICK."

Okay . . .

Word of that conversation spreads rapidly. Jokes and giggles about the DICK helmets go on behind the scenes.

In the chapel this morning, before staff orientation, I get a complaint: independent consultants are supposed to be here each day to provide clinical supervision to the trailer staff. The consultants are really never here. When they are here, staff come to me later and ask why they don't help them when they ask for it. The staff beg me for clinical guidance and debriefing. I am feeling overwhelmed—I can't do the trailer *and* the boats. . . . I have tried to get the people in charge of hiring the consultants to understand that the needs of the trailer staff aren't being met. But they aren't on grounds here, either. I am told that I'm wrong, and it's working well. Management from long distance is easy—you don't have to see the staff's faces when they're confused and crying. Don't have to wrap your arms around them and bleed with them. So I fill in the gaps. . . .

Hurting staff are here asking for help and getting nothing. Jealous? Maybe a bit. Angry? Yeah—somebody should care for these people;

they give from their souls. Just as I begin fuming about the situation, Rich and George enter the chapel and look like salvation—as angelic as ever, smiling, always there, always ready to help. How can you not want to provide clinical support to people like this? They drive up from Camden County to be here for days on end. For free. Consultants are paid huge amounts and rarely show up. But they make the newspapers, discussing their opinions about our work here. Jack and the Major come in joking and bringing more smiles. . . . I ask the person bringing the complaint to me to contact those who are in charge of the consultants, to better describe what their situation has been. "Oh, but I don't want to make waves. I thought that maybe you could speak to them again. . . ." I agree. I know in my heart it will not help.

During morning meeting for staff I point toward the front of the terminal and in my professional orientation voice say, "The buses will be out front . . ." and after the fiasco yesterday, the room erupts in laughter, snickers, and a few snorts and "yeah, right"s. *Oh* man, give me some slack guys! I feel loved. They're actually picking on me!

I keep going with my speech, trying to stay professional in my delivery. When I get to "We have several different types of people traveling with us: state police, EMTs . . . ," again with the snorting and snickering! But I'm still determined to keep a straight face and straight delivery.

It totally falls apart when I hold up a helmet and start with "Everyone will be given a hard hat . . ." and hold up a DICK helmet. Most have heard about my conversation with Jack already. He has confiscated the red hard hat that I had grabbed for myself on the first trip over and substituted one of his green DICK helmets. They really crack up. I can no longer keep a straight face. By the looks on their faces, the new people in the group are wondering what land they have come to. I explain the story. They also join in the laughter. *God,* I love these people!

This land of extremes just bowls me over: people who give and laugh and cry and hug and just ooze compassion. People digging until their hands bleed and their bodies give out, and all the while they pray to find *just one more* . . . will they get their wish? And a huge reminder of hate and evil is all around us. The positives must be so strong to overshadow that mess that doesn't resemble what we used to call the World Trade Center complex. I wonder sometimes if we would not have just continued in a downward evil spiral if we had not found that counterbalance of strength and beauty. Humans are creatures to marvel at.

I wonder if I'm numbing out—I stand on the platform and see that scene, but the tears are not there. Until later. I look at it now and feel so small and empty. My mind wanders back to meditation lessons, where the teacher described the goal of meditation as being able to feel small and empty. But it should not be like this.

I feel the grief of all of those people on the platform with me— hanging everywhere. And it is overwhelmingly heavy. I feel the impact of the grief of *all* the families. I can't have tunnel vision and see one family like the companions can; I have them all. And the companions as well. I also wonder if it matters that I numb out. What happens over time? Can you get used to this? "Getting used to" is not the terminology. . . . For now I file it away for another time.

On the bus, before we leave the marina, I sit with a Red Cross woman from Florida. She asks me if I'm from around here.

"Yes, I'm from Trenton, New Jersey. About an hour southwest of here."

"I've never seen the Towers. I heard that they were amazing. Have you ever seen the Towers?"

My brain says *Oh my God.* Amazed, I look at her—"Not even in pictures?"

"Well, maybe, but definitely not enough to remember, or even picture what they looked like. So you have seen them?"

"God, yes. We come up here for plays and shopping and hanging out. I have friends here. You could also see them from the New Jersey Turnpike, so I saw them a lot."

"Were they beautiful?" I tell her about how as they were being built many people didn't like them, but they became a real symbol of New York—we got used to them.

"I wish I had some frame of reference . . ."

I am amazed at myself for not realizing that so many people have no picture of the Towers in their heads, no frame of reference. I stopped in the turnpike stores on the way home; they have postcards of the Towers. I had only a small amount of cash so only about a dozen postcards are tucked in a bag for tomorrow.

After we have been on the platform for a bit, Rich comes over to me and points out a New York policeman way in the back corner. The young cop is sitting on a chair with his hat off—held in hands that dangle between his knees. It is the same one who is here almost every day with us. He is slumped and looking heavyhearted and all alone. Rich tells me about how he tried, unsuccessfully, to talk to him, to see if he was all right. I watch his manner from the distance. The policeman looks up, shakes his head "no" to no one in particular. He apparently would not talk to Rich, or let loose the tears that filled his eyes.

"I'm worried about him. Go see if he'll talk to you. Maybe a woman would be less threatening."

I head toward the back. As I approach he makes eye contact with me and doesn't break it. His eyes are filled to the brim. He stiffens, and for a second I wonder if maybe I should just leave him alone, but something pushes me forward to check in with him. As I approach his side, I put my hand on his shoulder and say, "I see you here almost every day. Are you all right?" He literally melts: shoulders loosen, his whole posture relaxes, and he sits back into the chair, nodding. Tears spill out and run down his face.

"It's just too much. It hurts so bad. I don't want to see the families like this."

I rub his shoulder. "I see it hanging on you. And I know what you mean. Let it out. It will kill us if we try to hold it in." He nods and cries as he reaches up to give me a hug, which I return.

"It must be so hard for you to watch us every day." He nods.

"Kind of like that movie *Groundhog Day*?"

He nods again. *"Yeah!"*

"Me too. It hurts me too."

"What do you do with it?"

"I cry a lot." He sniffs and nods.

When I say "See you again tomorrow?" he smiles and nods. "Yeah."

I pop him one gently on the arm: "Good. If you need another talking to, you just let me know. I'll be right here with you, brother."

"You bet."

I turn to leave him, and Rich is watching. We pass each other. He thanks me. "No problem. Like putty in my hands. . . . " It is easy to commune with a heart and mind as overwhelmed as your own . . . day after day after day after day after day . . .

October 11

This morning the volunteers have a ceremony on the docks behind the terminal. I had to meet with Jake about logistics—we have some government people that will be coming in a couple of days and they want everything just so. Jake is one of our deputy attorney generals. He is here overseeing all of the activities of the FAC. Our Office of Emergency Management is in the attorney general's office. Jake is tall and thin, wears expensive clothes and shoes, and has a confidence that looks like arrogance. I hear people complain that he has all of the attributes that give attorneys a bad name. He does. I like him. He has a soft side. I like people who care about how their work is done.

With our government people coming, we have to be tighter with security and staffing. I am being read the riot act by a worried Jake who wants to make a good impression. Through the open window I hear voices singing "Michael, Row the Boat Ashore" and my ears turn off his words to listen. I grow impatient and want to go be with them on the docks. Screw logistics. I smile and nod and act like I take notes. I see balloons float by the window; they have released red, white, and blue balloons.

Today before beginning orientation we add the "Who has no idea what the Towers looked like?" game. A couple of hands go up. I tell them to see me at the end of the day, because I will have a present for them. . . .

On the way to the marina, a man on the bus suddenly turns to me and tells me his story:

> My family and I moved here from LA to be with my dear friend. Our plane landed at midnight on the tenth. By noon on the eleventh I know in my heart that he is dead. I never had a belief that he made it through that. I wonder: what have I come for? I know his spirit is not in that place.

"I am so sorry for your loss." What can I say that would be meaningful? Helpful? Nothing. Words are so inadequate . . .

He asks, "And you—you do this every day?"

"Yes."

"And what about the effect that this will have on you? What keeps you sane?"

"Right now, today, that isn't important. I consider it a great honor—a privilege to be able to do this for you and the other families. I wouldn't have it any other way, and would never consider not doing it." I want to cry just thinking about this sweet man who has come across the country to watch his dear friend die.

He touches my arm: "As long as you believe that way you will be all right. They picked the right person for this job."

"Thank you." What a gift . . .

The first month is over. Fitting that exactly one month later I should stand on the platform and see this close up. I watched it happen on TV. I watch it here every day. Today I will see it with eyes that feel as if they belong to somebody else, and feel as if they have aged 100 years.

When those planes hit I ached inside, and it has chewed on me since. I wanted to help but didn't run to New York that day for fear of being turned away. I would have liked to work with the firemen, but since looking into those dead eyes, I have come to know that the work with them will go on for years to come. Time for that in the future. My heart hurts whenever I see them—those sad sweet angels that dig in the pile until their hands bleed. They find tiny pieces—just fragments of humanity. They have eyes that are so hurt, so haunted. Every day I leave flowers and prayers of gratitude at the memorial. Today I will pray again for the diggers as well. God, why should your troops have to hurt so much? What lessons do they have to learn, these people that give until they don't exist anymore?

Part of me never thought I would be looking at this evil in person. Today fires are visible. That smell that belongs only to this place is so strong that it makes my eyes and nose burn. Plastic, electric, fuel, ozone, steel, death. I will never forget that smell.

The weather today is clear, bright, shining, and beautiful. I squint up at the sky so heartbreakingly blue, and think of 9/11. Just like today. Sky to die for. Warm. From the fractured catwalk that runs parallel to Liberty Street, birds suddenly take off and fly in a great circle before landing back again. They pass in a beautiful formation over that enormous red crane that is bigger than any machine has a right to be. My heart skips a beat, and tears instantly come into my eyes. I try without success to choke them back. How can they live here in this place? How can anything so beautiful and normal coexist with this horror? And how can I feel both horrified and awestruck with beauty all at once? So much at peace but so shattered inside? A land of extremes. . . I have a lump in my throat so big I can't swallow. I wonder about life coming back to this place, and decide that the birds are hope. Beautiful hope. They keep saying that we'll all remember where we were on 9/11. I'll remember 10/11 as well. The smell, the sight, the sounds. I stand in the center of many people, looking from the sky to the scene in front of me and feel so small. So completely alone. So lost. What could ever cause a human to do such a thing?

A family member comes up to me and thanks me for bringing them here. I give him a tearful hug.

On the platform the collective grief becomes very heavy. I feel it creeping inside me and I want to get away, so I escape to the street below. Two shell-shocked-looking firemen come clomping along dirty and heavy-footed in their boots. I hold out two flowers and suddenly their faces bloom with big grins. As they approach me the younger one wraps one arm around me, picks me up off the ground, and whispers in my ear: "Thank you so much for what you do." Can you imagine? *Him* thanking *me* for what I do! He puts the flower in the pocket of his overalls. Even though their mouths have smiles, their eyes look dead. Their smiles are sad. I keep thinking about how wounded these souls are from looking and touching this day after day. Searching for something they can never have, wishing for *just one more rescue, just one more body, just one more day to do it over.* And we wish it along with them from a distance. The older one has tears in his eyes and his smile is shaking from holding back the tears. I reach out and rub his arm and say, "Thank you for all you do. I see how much it hurts." He wipes his eyes and nods, looking down. They stomp off toward the river and the hazmat tents. Please God help them survive this life that they now have. . . .

As we walk out I am always the last to leave—to check the platform and the street to be sure that we leave no one and nothing behind. From the back of the group, I approach the hazmat crew standing in front of the tents, stiffly at attention with their helmets over their hearts. Every day they have taken this position as stiffly as if they were military. They stand so still they could be made of bronze. Yet they are simply two big men in dreadlocks with dusty American flag bandannas around their heads. And tears in their eyes.

I wonder, where do the workers, the families, and my boat crew get their strength? What superhuman thing allows them to be this way? American pride flashes through my head and my emotions as an answer to that question. I wrap my arms around the first hazmat guy and put a flower in his pocket. He doesn't move a bit. I think maybe I shouldn't have done that—maybe for him it was not the right thing to do. I thank him for saluting and honoring the families this way, and let him know that many of them remarked about the level of respect that the workers show toward them. The families are genuinely amazed at the honor that they are shown each day, and they talk about it after. He replies, "Oh God, thank you so much." You would think that I just gave him a million dollars. I guess in many ways I did. He sees crying families. We hear their thoughts, their impressions, and see some of them respond in a positive way to tiny scraps of beauty in this horrific experience. As I hug the second one he blurts out, "I see you every day. Please tell me that this helps them."

"Trust me, it does help."

"Thank you—I need to know that something good will come out of this." The tears run down his cheeks.

"I have to believe that too. Please be safe." He nods and takes a flower, which he puts behind his ear. "Thanks. You too."

Debriefing today was so hard, trying to put into perspective what I have brought back with me. I think back to the conversation with Major Fred about how natural it is to collect souvenirs, how I have rocks at home from a visit to Colorado.

I have one hell of a souvenir: I feel like there is a boulder in my chest. I have picked up a really big and heavy rock that is getting hard to carry. I try to explain to others about the faces that I bring back with me in my mind—the good that I saw. Tears come and the lump in my throat is keeping me from getting any more words out. My phone rings in my pocket—it's 4:30 (no escape). I answer to hear the voice of a co-worker, and quickly say, "I'm in debriefing—can't talk now." But the person on the other end says, "Oh, just one little thing—I won't keep you long." And because it's someone I just can't blow off, or simply hang up on, I get up to leave so I don't disrupt it for everyone any further. As I leave the room, I hear Rich call after me, "Hang up. Just hang up."

I walk from the room as I ask, "Can't I call you back in ten minutes? We just got back—I'm debriefing, and I *really need to be there.*"

"No—it's after 4:30, and I want to go home." Nice—wish I could—I have at least four more hours here. Self-centered *bitch.* My ear is being filled with talk, and I ignore it as I swallow the lump in my throat and wipe the tears and my nose on my sleeves, letting anger and disgust replace the heavy sadness.

I go back into debriefing and think about how hard it is to discuss this: the scene itself, but it is even harder to describe how I feel about it. Just no words to describe . . . language is not enough. Screaming might work—but who can scream long enough to convey something like this? Even here—where we have all faced the same demon to-day—even here the explanation is not easy. This is a club that no one should belong to. But then again . . . maybe *everyone* should. I don't want to numb out and shut down—I want to feel. I hope I really never can explain this—it would mean acceptance, that we actually had language for this. It is just too big.

At the close of the day, as I attempt to number stickers for tomorrow, I am having a hard time remembering the last number I wrote. Sequencing has become really hard. I write a sticker, turn it over, write what I think is the right number, check it and I mutter "shit" under my breath.

Try again, new method, leave them face up. It works for a couple of stickers, but then I start to go backward without realizing it. I decide to backtrack and check myself. "Shit." A pile of torn ones grows higher and higher next to me—about twenty of them. That means that I only have about 180 more of them to get through. "Shit." I hear a laugh next to me and look up. "Do you know you're having *symptoms?*"

"With a vengeance."

"How do you feel about that?"

"Like it's going to take me all night to number these things."

"No, I mean are you okay with it?"

"I know what you mean. I'm okay. I've noticed this for days."

"Does it worry you?"

"Nope. No point suffering over your own suffering, you know?"

"Good. You *will* be okay when this is over."

"Shit." Rip and toss. He cracks up. "You know we're going to have to tie a string around your wrist when you leave the trailer so you don't get lost."

October 13

I have the day off. A party that we had planned long ago is happening this weekend and I look forward to seeing people, but at the same time I wonder—what am I going to say to them? Every time someone hears that I have been working there they drop their jaw in shock. Sometimes they physically back up as if to get away. They ask what it's like. I can't answer. I can't find the words to tell them, so I simply tell them that. And then the question is the inevitable: "Are you okay?" And in answer my brain screams out *No, I'm not okay!* But I acknowledge their concern with the answer that I know they want to hear—"Yes, it is hard, but I'm fine."

Something doesn't feel right inside me, and I don't know what. I feel almost like I've been locked up somewhere and forgot how to act. Or maybe like suddenly waking up in Canada, or England: it's foreign, but everyone still speaks English, so it isn't too different . . . but it is . . .

My husband Fred and I drive through the countryside of Hopewell. Beautiful rolling fields and tree-lined farms. Surrounded by autumn colors and autumn sun, we are in search of pumpkins and flowers to decorate for the party. Warm day. Those heartbreakingly blue skies are *still* here, making everything all the more vivid and beautiful. "God, look at the colors . . ." comes out of my mouth as I gaze across the fields at the mix of gold, orange red, and dark pine greens. Geese are flying and it looks like a postcard. Immediately I get a flash of the World Trade Center complex—burning, crumbling. Tortured, twisted metal. An actual visual flash. It was the scene that I saw behind my eyes on that first family visit. I jump and my stomach turns. I squeeze my eyes shut and then look out of the car window on the other side. Beauty. But in a second another flash. And I can smell it. This is burned right into my soul, my heart, my brain. I have a Technicolor tattoo on my soul that brings smells and heavy feelings with it. I recognize the symptoms of becoming shell-shocked myself. It has not only started but blossomed. Trauma reaction. I feel suddenly very quiet, no longer belonging here in this world.

Now I know why they dig beyond their own limits, why they have those sad, dead eyes: their soul is etched even deeper than mine. Someone described to me once that his addiction was a sickness of always needing *just one more*. I am reminded of the slogan in twelve-step programs: "One is too many and a thousand never enough." It has become an addiction—I (we all) keep saying *just one more*—like some magic will work. If we can fix one more, find one more, have one more—over and over. *A million* would never be enough. Never enough of anything—never good enough, frantic and desperate. Make it better or die trying.

The behaviors that we think are our salvation, our protection—the things that we think keep us going are the ultimate behaviors that will eventually kill us. The people digging go beyond their limits because they just can't do it any other way—the element of choice is gone and the compulsion for *just one more of something* has taken over. And like an addiction, they would rather die than stop. . . . Me too.

I have also discovered what that vague sensation of something not being right was: it was me. I am no longer right. Maybe I'm no longer even me. Life is going on all around me and I'm no longer part of it. Is it right that I am frozen in time and space in Manhattan? What happens when I finally rejoin my life? Will I be replaced by some ghost? I don't even know what my life is anymore. I'm not sure who I am anymore. I can't even handle a day off.

I distract myself with cooking and decorating and party preparations and practicing an "it's all right" attitude. Friends arrive for the party wearing smiles and bringing with them good food and great hugs and questions and all that looks so blessedly normal. For them. Life is indeed going on—and I am not in it. I hear events and catching-up talk. They seem to be missing me, but I can't shake the sensation of being at my own funeral or something. They are talking about me as if I were not in the room. They have all shared a span of time that I have missed. I'm a ghost. A hologram in front of them that they aren't really sure if they even see. And they feel *sorry* for me. *What the hell for?* Christ, how do you explain . . . They worry out loud on my behalf. Do they see something? Would any one of them trade places with me for even a moment?

I really am a ghost. Every hug and conversation and bite of food reminds me that I am a ghost here. I no longer belong. My life is gone.

A hockey game with the home team later in the evening brings fun. I guess I need violence to feel comfortable. I can sit in a stadium full of people and not have to talk, or explain, or feel like I don't belong: I can live in suspended animation and just deal with *now*. I can sit in my assigned seat just as if nothing ever happened—just like the old days. I think of Bob in north Jersey, my fellow hockey nut, and want to bring him a gift. Four of us at the FAC are season ticket holders for the Trenton Titans—our home team. I settle on an enamel pin for Bob with "Trenton Titans" on it, and a team flag to hang up in the trailer. Bringing a little piece of home to the war zone.

October 15

I am tired and dragging. Feels exactly like the tail end of a bad speed run. I walk into the trailer and begin to put my stuff on my desk. Bob looks up and says, "What's wrong with you? You're not your usual bouncy self." I simply turn around, walk out, come in again and jump up and down, cheerily saying, "Good morning, everyone." It was painful. It really physically hurt. They crack up. Bob says, "That's better; now sit down." Now I feel like I belong. I wish life could be this way—people who could relate this way all the time—no games.

I unload my stuff and give Bob the Titans pin. He grins like a kid. "Any good fights? Who won? What did I miss?" I give him a blow-by-blow description of the game and the fights as I hang the team flag in the back of the trailer. "Yeah?—Cam and Forbes—who'd they hit? Great! Any blood on the ice?"

We have a new team of NOVA workers who came in from Florida about four days ago. I sit next to one on the bus, a young blonde girl. I am on the side of the bus that faces the terminal and the Statue. She looks toward me and says: "I can't wait to get on the boat so I can see the Statue of Liberty. Can we see it from the boat?"

It backs me up for a second . . .

I look over my shoulder; out of the bus window and directly in her line of vision is the Lady Herself. Big as life, green as ever, taking up the whole window. She has to be able to see it—you can't miss it; it takes up the whole backyard of the terminal.

"Yeah, you can see it from the boat."

"Ohhh, I'm so excited!"

I don't know how to politely tell her that the big green thing in the backyard is the statue and she would have a much better view if she simply looked over my shoulder and out the widow. I guess she'll figure it out after seeing it in the harbor. I wonder if she has even gone outside during the time she has been here . . .

Family orientation is filled with quiet and tearful people.

No staff are in the trailer today.

No firemen are in hugging distance. I feel cheated.

I have opportunity to reflect on the well-oiled machine at its finest again today. I have such gratitude for the people who come here to work. Our resident polished attorney, Jake, takes a ribbing from a family—one of the fathers turns to me, jerks his head and thumb at Jake in his customary stance in the front of the bus, and says, "Who's the suit?"

I can't answer with a straight face. "He works for our attorney general's office."

The guy snorts and replies, "Knew he wasn't FBI—his shoes are too expensive." One of the other family members laughs and says, "Pretty boy." I can't help but laugh. Later, I had to tell him what they said. He cracks up. Genuinely.

Bob is grumping around and dealing with the press, who have turned up at the front gate, apparently invited by one of our families. He stomps and swears. I run off to schedule, confirm, manipulate, and wrap up loose ends.

During morning staff orientation I am still asking for a show of hands of people who don't know what the Towers looked like. On my way home I stop at the turnpike rest areas and buy postcards of the Towers. I ask the people who have never seen the Towers to find me when we return from New York. Tonight, three staff approach me when we return, and I give them each a postcard. One woman looks at the gleaming photo in her hand and drops into a chair with her mouth open, "Oh God, I had no idea." They all agree that the Towers are beautiful. They are amazed, as we all are, that from something so huge nothing is left. We talk for a bit about the void, the new perspective they now have—a debriefing before we actually debrief. One of them brings his postcard to the all-staff debriefing and shares his feelings about now seeing the picture at least. They all want to see, to refresh their minds. As the photos are handed around we all take a look and remember with tears . . .

Because there is no one else, I have taken on the task of staff debriefings most days. NOVA or the Red Cross have occasionally been doing it also—to help fill in and give me a break. They are tied up tonight. I keep thinking about the stones that the Major told me about in the Bible story of Joshua, and how I collect stones from vacations, so I ran with it:

> It is natural for us to collect souveniors of places we visit. Shells, stones, and other objects bring us back to places we have been; they remind us of the experience. Sometimes when I go places I like to pick up stones. Some are brown with dirt; they aren't always pretty at first. What did you bring back with you today from New York? What does your souvenir look like? What does it feel like?"

We discussed the impact of the visit on the senses; many experienced it as "deathly quiet." Silence. That place is actually unearthly in its loudness. The visual and the smell and the emotional impact are so great initially that our ears shut down—it's a protective thing our brain does to prevent overload. It is similar to what happens when we seriously injure ourselves: there is a time when the body provides numbness—time to get somewhere safe and have things attended to. A protective device to guard against the overwhelming onslaught of pain.

Some people described the experience of loss of the visual—"I can't remember what it *looked* like." "I don't think I could *see* anything while I was there." We discussed our sensory input: size, smell, taste, thoughts. And some put into description the heaviness of their hearts: the sense that we all shared of now carrying something very heavy—in our hearts, on our shoulders. Heavy like boulders. Like Atlas with the weight of the world resting on our backs.

We discussed the impact of the trauma that will occur later. The sudden crying jag for no reason: tomorrow in the grocery store, on the way home. The inability to discuss it. The sense that spouses, family, friends who have not been to this place, and cannot understand; there are simply no words to describe this thing. We discussed how now the abnormal is normal; we now belonged to a very small club of people that cried at the drop of a hat without provocation. But considering . . . that is normal. Cautions were given about the importance of trying to talk to others about the experience, about the importance of giving ourselves a break, and the importance of self-care.

As an ending I wanted them to have a sense of the positive, the beauty:

> Sometimes when I go away and collect those stones as souvenirs they may be heavy, brown, and ugly at first. But you know how sometimes when you brush the dirt off, those stones can suddenly sparkle like diamonds? Instead of something heavy, brown, and ugly, I now have a true gift: a real treasure to remind me of the experience. Tell me about the diamonds you picked up today, the surprise gifts you received.

And we marveled at the strength of spirit, the courage, the compassion and the angels that we encountered along the way. . . . And of how they had just done angels' work, and the importance of remembering what a wonderful thing it is to offer compassion to someone in need. It was one of the lightest feelings I've seen yet in debriefing. I actually felt better afterward.

When I arrived home, I listened to several answering machine messages left from yesterday's partygoers:—had fun—thanks—great to be together—missed you. Makes this tired headache a bit easier. Do ghosts even get headaches? They must—when I was human in my former life I *never* got headaches. . . .

I discuss with my husband, Fred, about how I want him to go with me to the FAC, so that he understands what this is about. He keeps looking at me as if I'm some kind of creepy thing—which by now, I probably am. I can't explain it to him, and he really doesn't want to hear it. He has anxiety about it—the great unknown—but he agrees to go. He has no idea what he is in for, and I could never explain or convey the magnitude.

October 16

Bringing Fred is scary. I don't want to ask permission because I'm afraid they will say no, even though many people have brought their spouses in to volunteer. He needs a dose of understanding, gratitude, and compassion and I'm hoping that this will provide it. And he needs to understand what I'm going through. I *know* that will happen . . .

I try to let him know what to expect, show him around. He wants to play hugs and kisses in the trailer and gets pissed when I back off. All that I said to him was "Please—not here," but it sets him off and he decides to have a tantrum. He has never taken my work seriously, and has no concept of my desire to maintain a professional image. He considers me a piece of fluff. I want to say, "Go ahead—get me yelled at—act like you're at the mall and not work. No biggie. *For you!*" But I don't have to say anything. He stomps out before I have a chance, and I simply let him—not in the mood to play the fight game. I turn to confirmations and faxes and doing the job.

When I catch up to him later in the terminal, I find him upset at reading the notes that family members left on the memorial walls. I had explained to him about the walls being there for families to write on. Curious to me that he understood them—what they were—intellectually. He didn't get it emotionally until he read them. Tears. I put an arm around him for comfort and let him talk. Yes, love—this is the heaviest thing you will ever know. . . . I take him to Jack and he seems to settle into the equipment routine. I keep an eye on him as we walk that eternal eighth of a mile through Battery Park. His teeth are clamped together. Afterward in debriefing anger comes.

As soon as I got on the platform today I felt *heavy*. Dripping with HEAVY. I really needed to escape it for a bit, so I went back down to the street to find police or workers to talk to for a minute.

I found hazmat guys to hug today. "Where you from, girl?"

"Jersey."

"What exit, Joisey girl?" They laugh loud New Yorker laughs.

"7A."

"Yo—Trenton girl. Thanks for being here, sweetie." They don't look tired and dead. Fresh arrivals, I think. I say a little prayer for them to keep those smiling eyes and laughter. Now that I can breathe again, I go back up to the platform. Standing next to me I see a volunteer looking like a deer in the headlights. "First time here?"

"How did you know?"

"You have that look that we all get the first time." I put an arm around her shoulders and hold her close as she cries and wipes her red nose. I wonder: shouldn't I be crying too?

I move to the other side of the platform and end up standing next to a family member. There is a "clunk" and a sensation of impact at our feet. We both look down. A bolt about one inch thick and a couple of inches long has landed at the woman's feet, missing her toes by less than an inch. That would have *hurt*.

"Oh my God, are you all right?"

"It didn't hit me."

We look down at it again, then at each other. "Can I keep it?"

"Looks to me like you were *supposed* to have it."

She scoops it up and shoves it in her pocket.

On the way home Fred and I talk. *"I'm all right."* Yeah, maybe now. Wait . . . it comes when you least expect it. He doesn't want to hear it.

October 17

This morning Ant'ny is busting on me as I pull up to the checkpoint. In his heavy North Jersey accent he says, "Hey, you got yer ID?"

In my imitation North Jersey accent I respond: "Yeah, Ant'ny, I got my ID," and I hand him a picture of himself that I took a few days ago.

"Hey—where'd you git dat?" He laughs and blushes as he waves me through.

"Keep it, handsome."

My cell phone rings as I'm in the trailer organizing my day. Fred calls me—tearful. "Someone asked me about yesterday and I just cried. I couldn't answer." Oh yeah—I know the feeling, welcome to the club, love. He seemed to know the normalcy of that response. I am glad that he heard me yesterday, even if he wanted to not deal with it then. Normal is really so relative these days. But I think he knows that the reaction is okay. We talk. He calms, for now. The trauma reaction will come back.

It's odd—I've heard from several people that they have those "normal" unexpected crying jags in places like the grocery store. It's happened to me as well. Grocery stores are apparently the place where things fall apart. I think it's because the grocery store is so *normal* that our brain suddenly feels compelled to vomit out the abnormal. The contrast between the devastation we have seen, and the everyday blandness of the grocery store is simply too great. Don't know—I'll have to ask some of the veteran disaster workers about this . . .

The mental health trailer isn't staffed again today. There has apparently been a problem with getting enough mental health agency volunteers to work in the trailer. Over 200 family members and survivors come to the FAC each day. Of that 200, we generally have about 85 to 100 family members going with us to Ground Zero. The rest of the families are there for services such as referrals, help with access to services in the community, counseling, completion of paperwork.

Today I have enough staffing to spare. I also have six volunteers on my list who are all from one place. I know all of them, and think that they will be the best choices for staying to staff the trailer: they haven't driven as far as some to get here. They are arriving together and they know one another—they can stay with one another. I let the trailer know that I'll ask them to stay behind to staff the FAC. One of them arrives early, on his own, and I approach him to explain the situation. He gives me a good-natured smile, and a "No problem—anything you need." I tell him to pick any day to return—I'll see to it he gets on the boat, and thank him profusely.

Morning meeting begins. Stickers are handed out, and the staff poke fun at me because some have the same numbers. Oooops! I really can't sequence too well anymore. . . . I take out my marker and write A, B, C, etc., on the duplicates. They ask, "Is this legal?" Yeah—no problem!

At the end of orientation, I ask the five others from the group to gather for a minute: "Guys, we have an emergency situation here; we have no staff for the trailer . . ." I am interrupted in midsentence by "You aren't telling us we can't go, are you?"

"I'm not staffing that trailer—I'm not here for that!"

And the best complaint of all: "You can't make me."

I tune them out to take a deep breath, and I see a room full of volunteers from the Red Cross, mental health, NOVA, and the Salvation Army watching this conversation. Bob is talking to someone over by the door and doesn't notice. Good thing for them. They wind down, so I try again: "You have to understand that 100 people a day come here while we're gone . . ."

"No, I didn't come here for that." And they start up again.

Now I'm pissed. I'm losing it. I hold up both of my hands: "You know what? You all have one minute to decide. You can either go home or staff the trailer."

"I'm not staying here."

"I came to work on the boat."

"I'm not here for that."

"Fine. You have one minute. Or I pick up the phone and you can tell the person I call what your decision is—okay? One minute." I'm getting a headache.

I walk away from them to let them decide what to do, and to take a deep breath. I go back to the middle of the group. "Your minute is up. What will it be?"

"You can't make me."

Blessedly two of them respond with "Whatever you need us to do." I thank them and ask them to go to the trailer.

"I'm leaving then. I didn't come here for this."

"Okay. You can do what you want, but you're not going with me." I turn and walk away. The good, the bad, and the ugly—extremes of people as well in this place.

They apparently all decide to go to the trailer instead of going home. At lunch the person supervising the trailer brings two of them to me, *begging* me to take them. She tells me that they have continued to complain loudly, and are being disruptive and embarrassing. I give them passes to accompany us, working equipment. I should have sent them home to get in trouble with their employer. I should have had them escorted out by the state police. What misguided idiot lives inside of me that I would show compassion to people who behave like this?

In New York the scene has changed: before there were office chairs in the street—piles of stuff that had been cleared from the buildings. Today the chairs were gone. The hazmat tents were moved. The cross that was found in the center of the customs building last week has been moved into the street beside the Verizon building, in the middle of West Street. We can see it from the platform, and many people ask about it, wanting to see this strange thing. Looking at it sends chills through my whole body—up my back and standing my hairs on end. It has a strange orange glow about it. To think that this object was formed so perfectly. Discovered in the center of nothing.

Extremes. There they are again—extremes.

Today we have a nine-month pregnant woman. I can't imagine how I would go on if I were in her place. Today is also very cold.

A married couple gives up as we arrive at the gate. They can't bring themselves to go in. They look at me panicked and are clutching each other shaking their heads. No words. I rub their arms, reassure them, and ask them to stay where they are for just a second until I can get someone to walk them back to the boat. They readily agree. One of our SOGs, Chuck, who has a red face from the cold and is visibly shivering behind his sunglasses, volunteers to take them back to the boat with a grin. Poor boy, his teeth are chattering. He wants to get warm, and is not even remotely trying to hide his motives. He looks *so* cold. I smile at him and tell him to go ahead. He dashes to them and takes them toward the dock. He's sweet, gentle, and has an engaging personality and grin—they are in very good hands.

As we enter, the mother lode of firemen pull up in their truck, and park it on Liberty Street. Major Barb hands me a bunch of flowers: "Well, what are you waiting for?" I go up to them and hand them each a flower. They laugh and begin to decorate their truck—flowers are put under the wipers, on the dash, on the hose clamps. They look like they're getting a kick out of it. I know I am. I make sure that there are a couple of flowers in pockets before I go up to the platform.

Jake takes his lapel pin off and hands it to me on the boat. I have been teasing him about wanting his pin because we are collecting them from one another. This isn't just a dollar's worth of enamel—it's a formal little gold one that government people wear. I protest only a bit when he gives it to me. He insists that he has a bunch more at home, so I keep it. I really couldn't keep it if that weren't true—I'm going to make sure that he shows up with another, or he gets this one back. I put it next to the New Jersey State Police pin and a couple of others that are collecting on my jacket.

When I am fresh off the bus and wandering through the terminal from the back, raking my fingers through my hair and wanting to drop dead, the director of my agency comes walking in from the front door. I had no idea he was coming, and it's a nice surprise. He looks directly at me, walks up to me holding out his hand and says, "Are you okay?" Takes me back a step. I want to be bratty and complain, but I'm too tired.

"You want the real answer or the polite one?"

"The real one." I laugh and give him the polite one—"I'm okay. Tired." He points out the fact that I'm a liar. I give him a tour.

When I get back to the administrative trailer someone tells me about another news article in which one of the outside consultants takes credit for the boat trips. This is becoming a habit—people talking about the work they do here when they came here once, and strangely enough it's my job that they are taking credit for. I am beyond angry. I would really like to smash the person's face. Bob reassures me with "Well, at least she's never here—you don't have to look at her or listen to that drivel in person." Somehow it doesn't soothe my wounded ego. I sit and look at him and beat myself up for this petty wish that someone would let me have the credit for my job. I wish I had the nerve to call the newspapers and tell them about what I do here. Especially since I really *am doing it*. I wish I could just be happy for her and not be resentful. I try to practice acceptance and inner peace. It isn't working.

I talk to Bob about feeling slighted. He lets me know what a good job I do and how I *should* feel slighted. He has a way of being so supportive and telling me what I need to know, even if I don't like it. He jokes and tells me he's going to buy me a T-shirt that says, YOU SPELL

IT B-E-D-A-R-D. I laugh. I remain stuck somewhere between resentment and anger and rational thinking. Whenever I read about Bob being interviewed, hear praise for him—I can smile at that. I am happy for that. Not doing this for a pat on the head is one thing. Being walked on is another. Life's a bitch. . . .

I have been able to grab some snatches of time with Rich—to talk about everything and nothing. He is capable and caring, the kind of person who is always willing to help, to do anything that is needed. I would bet that if I asked him to clean the portable toilets, he would. I'm sure he'd look at me funny for a split second, but he'd do it without question. When I started to work on arranging the visits to Ground Zero, I stopped working in the mental health trailer. Rich had come to me then, troubled about the need for clinical supervision for the staff, because I was pulling back. The staff needed guidance and were asking for help. I was preoccupied and overwhelmed with the responsibilities I had. I told him I could no longer do both. Rich took it upon himself to take over clinical supervision of the trailer staff. He spends time working with the trailer staff first thing in the morning, and stays late evenings to be sure things run smoothly. *And* he goes with us on the ferry. On days that he feels the strain of it all, he works equipment rather than dealing directly with the families.

Rich has an uncanny ability to always be in the right place at the right time. We have shared thoughts and feelings about how hard it is to hold together a normal life and be here. I ran into Rich at the end of the day. He has recently returned from a little break at home. He talks to me about how strange it felt to be home again with his family. He uses the word *ghost* to describe it.

"Holy shit! I feel the same way."

"Do you really?"

We take inventory from some of the others; Bob feels that way also.

I feel more comfortable here than anywhere. Like an addiction, it invades your body, mind, and spirit and eventually takes over every part of your self. Life is going on out there and I don't really have any desire to join it anymore. Scary stuff. Yes—I know why they dig over there until their hands bleed and they drop. I would join them if I could.

If we could get just one more survivor . . . we would all feel better. By now there are no more. . . .

So cold today—so windy: a premonition of things to come?

October 18

This morning the main breaker failed. We have no power. It doesn't change the disposition of those cheery Red Cross morning people who hand me my breakfast each day as I pass them on the way through the terminal: a bottle of water, a Rice Krispies Treat, and a smile. I yawn out a sleepy "good morning," and raise my water bottle in salute as I continue on through to the back door.

I go into the administrative trailer to find that Bob was given a reclining chair today from the Salvation Army. In the middle of the trailer sits a blue, reasonably worn BarcaLounger. Ya gotta love these people. We have no heat, no lights, but we got a comfy chair! And Slim Jims—Bob's favorite food. Bob is not around, so I sit Red Cross Jack in his comfy chair and take his picture holding Slim Jims. Bob is an Archie Bunker about this chair and we don't *dare* sit in it.

I wander back over to the terminal—the bathroom is *so dark*. I have never seen such heavy darkness. Not one shred of light. I really need to pee, and have waited long enough for the power to be restored—soooo—people who are blind can do it, right? I grope along the wall to a stall—*How in the name of God do blind people do it????* Jesus, it is so black, it's disorienting. I swear it's blacker than closing your eyes. The outside door to the bathroom is always open anyway, but this doesn't even break the darkness (guess *not—no lights out there either*).

A woman calls from the door, "Hello?" in a little voice.

"Hi."

"Can you see in there?"

"Nope."

"How are you managing?"

"Well, I know where everything is, and I figured people who are blind can work it out, so I can too."

"I'm scared."

"I won't bite you."

"No—that I'll fall or something. You really can't see? Your eyes don't get accustomed to it?"

"Nope. Want some help?"

"I'm leaving—I'll hold it."

I grope to the sink to wash up. I dry my hands on my pants—at least I don't have to feel around for *them*.

The lights come back on and we cheer. It's those little things in life . . .

The heat comes on with a vengeance. We feel like we're being poached during the morning meeting in the chapel.

I trade Red Cross Vera my New Jersey pin and ribbon for a Washington State pin. We are beginning to decorate one another. A NOVA worker tells me that I started a fad. People are beginning to come up with pins and treats for one another from all over. Major Fred gives me a Salvation Army shirt. Later I get into Bob's stash of NEW JERSEY AND YOU: PERFECT TOGETHER T- shirts and give one to Vera. She *loves* it. We really are easy to please around here . . .

We have a loud, boisterous group of companions today. Strange. Major Fred at my request gives us a blessing with Father Mychal Judge's prayer [Father Judge was the first responder to lose his life at the World Trade Center. Along with being a Franciscan priest, he had also been a chaplain for the New York City Fire Department. He said this prayer every time he went out to minister to someone]:

> Lord, take me where you want me to go
> Let me meet who you want me to meet
> Tell me what you want me to say
> And keep me out of your way.

I don't think Father Judge was thinking of companions when he wrote that prayer, but it is so fitting. I ask the Major to use it as our morning blessing each day.

With devilish grins, our EMTs continue to announce themselves everywhere they go so we won't leave them again. "The EMTs are entering the chapel." "The EMTs are boarding the bus."

The mood in the air is odd today. The families arrive tearful and shaky. Nervous. As I go through orientation they cry openly—more so than in days before. I don't know—does that mean I should do it differently, or that I'm doing it right? Seeing all of those crying faces makes me feel so helpless. I want to make it go away for them, turn back time—just one more month—and let us all do this over again without airplane crashes.

We walk through Battery Park and enter the gates. A big blond fireman is stomping from inside toward the gate. He stops in his tracks, and looks at us as we enter and begin to file up onto the platform. Tears immediately begin rolling down his cheeks, leaving clean streaks. He sits down in the middle of what used to be Liberty Street and puts his face in his helmet and just cries—sobbing *hard*. As companions begin to take the families onto the platform I go to him and touch his shoulder—"Hey, what is it?" He has a totally wet face, crying so hard and without even caring.

"I feel for them so much that they have to see this. It must kill them to come here and see this." He reaches for my hand, which he holds very tightly, crying his eyes out. He puts his head down on his knees.

I squat down and put my other hand on his shoulder. "You have to understand something; they wanted to sign up to come. For some, when we go back they eat for the first time in days. They relax, they smile. For some it helps to be here. To see this." Poor guy is sobbing so hard.

"*Aw fuck. Please* tell me you mean it. Please don't lie to me."

"No, baby, I swear to you. I have seen some of the families begin to relax and smile on the way back on the boat. I wouldn't lie about that. Not here. Not now."

He looks up at me and actually breaks into a huge smile. Yes, this is a place of extremes. . . .

I hold my hand out and he stands up with me, sniffing and wiping his nose and face with his dirty hands, making mud out of tears. I offer him tissues and he shakes his head no. "We worry about them, you know." He looks over my head at the platform.

"We do too. And we worry about you guys working here like this. You okay now?" He smiles and nods. Suddenly tears fill his eyes again and begin running down his face. "You promise?" He grips my hand tighter, but is still watching the families.

"I promise. For many of them, it helps."

"I'm going to tell the guys. You come here every day. We see you. You're doing good work. We worry about you too."

I want to cry. "Thank you so much." I put a flower in his overalls pocket and tell him to be careful. He wraps his arms around me and says, "I will. Promise." He stomps off toward the water.

A young man on the boat tells me he is in trouble with his employer for coming today, and he asks if I can intervene. His work doesn't believe that he was coming here with his family to mourn. I write a note to his job, call them, fax in the note and let him know that we will do anything to help him. How can you get in trouble for wanting to mourn? Is the world without soul? Maybe that is simply why I would rather be here: too many ugly rat bastards out there—nothing but angels here.

Our Rabbi Ron is feeling chatty. I think he gets nervous here—it hurts his sensitive soul. He tells me that I'm soothing. I don't feel soothing. Far from it. I feel frazzled, crazed, and dead on my feet. I'm glad that I soothe someone!

October 19

Days run into one another in a blur. No sooner do I get home—I leave again.

Fred is at a hockey game today. Without me.

We have "The Mrs. Rabbi Ron" as our clergy from the community today. She has the face of a saint, gorgeous. She says a tearful prayer at the railing. So quiet you had to strain to hear her.

Again the birds take off from their perch on the catwalk and circle. My heart stops, sinks, and soars all at once. It finishes with sad and heavy. This place is so surreal—birds flying as if nothing is wrong, with that twisted steel as a backdrop. I wish I could take a picture of it—but here and now the camera is not appropriate. . . . No matter; I think the picture now lives in my heart anyway. This place has a way of embedding its image into the soul. A photo forever burned, whether you want it or not.

A tall priest is with us—he has to be about seven feet tall. He towers above me as we stand next to each other. He looks very disturbed. Frowning and wincing as if he is in pain—he probably is. "Welcome to hell, Father." He looks down at me. "It truly is." He looks back.

I meet a fireman stomping out again—they look like they move in slow motion in those heavy boots. He actually appears to be aiming toward me. He is crying and watching the families on the platform—in exactly the same way as the one I spoke to yesterday. He walks up to me, grabs my arm, and says, "I hear this helps them. Is it true? You told somebody that yesterday, right? That was you?" I am shocked, finding it unbelievable that the conversation I had yesterday has come back—complete strangers forming a circle.

"Yes. It helps many of them." It amazes me how these guys can feel so comfortable crying in front of a woman they don't know. Not the typical American guy I'm used to meeting. . . . He wipes his eyes and says, "It's so sad." I stand with him, rubbing his arm, trying to soothe.

As we stand talking, four more firemen come stomping by. They make fast glances between their feet, and the families, and me. It is really hard to just let them pass. I want to do something for them. . . .

I give a blue flower to the fireman I'm talking to and he smiles. "Thanks. Smells like life." Sure does, buddy! He walks off to join the others. Bob pokes me in the arm from behind "Do we have to find you a twelve-step program for firemen?" Yes, I'm afraid so. . . . I give him a grin.

As I look up, the first fireman has joined the four that passed, and they have gathered on the corner of West and Liberty—across the street from us by the Salvation Army tent. They're looking at me. They motion for me to come over. I cross over Liberty Street to join them. I see the blue flower poking out of my guy's pocket. Sweet. I wondered if they threw them away. . . . One of the other guys scoops me up without any warning and gives me a big hug. I laugh. "What's that for?"

"No reason. Just because we see you here every day. Thanks. You're pretty special." He sets me back down and I give the others flowers. I get a bear hug from each. Imagine—them thanking me. I will never get over *that*. . . . I run like hell to catch up to the group at the Wall of Remembrance. The SOGs are waving at me impatiently. They can't serve and protect stragglers. . . .

We talk in debriefing again today about heavy rocks that we picked up and carry in our hearts. They describe the pain they acquired very visually. Good group. I ask them to discuss the gems, the gifts, and one woman smiles and thanks me. "I would never have seen that if you hadn't made me think that way. This really is a gift." Bless your heart, you don't know the half of it yet. Stick with me—I'll show you true beauty beyond belief. . . .

October 20

The bills are coming in, so Joan, Bob, and Vic are all running around trying to gather the data that will justify and prove. . . . All of their reports will cover my area so I am blessedly immune from this activity. I can fax and number stickers to my heart's content. Bob had a weekend off scheduled, but it is not to be.

Joan is a tiny, sweet lady from the Port Authority who worked in the Towers. She is our connection to much of what we need from New York and is also our person who handles much of what is requested from our governor's office—hence the running around gathering information. . . .

Today it seems as if every physically sick person in the state has arrived to go with us:

- An older man who has had four heart attacks and a recent brain tumor: he suffers from lack of balance and is always breathless.
- An eight-and-one-half-month pregnant woman who calmly says that she "Delivered the other four all early in the eighth month." (*That* does not inspire confidence.) Rough water on the river today; she's upset . . . it is past "early in the eighth month. . ."
- A family that is very overweight, one of whom said that she was't sure if she could even get through the door of the bus. All of them claimed that they could not make the walk and had to ride in the golf cart. There are five of them and the cart holds four regular-sized people.
- Three older folks who describe themselves as "feeble."

- A person with uncontrolled asthma who tells me that she needs her inhaler about every half hour and was hospitalized this week. Today there is a *lot* of smoke over there. They have opened a fire pit. . . .

Altogether about twenty family members are in need of watching and attention for medical issues—serious ones. This far exceeds the capacity for the golf cart to drive them through Battery Park. I consult with the EMTs and we decide that all of them should go on one bus with the EMTs. They will triage who walks and who rides. I ask each family with special needs to get on the first bus, and explain that we have concerns for them. They are so good—so understanding. They readily agree and recognize that we want only to keep them safe.

One of our "feeble" people loses it about halfway through Battery Park—her knees begin to buckle. Because we had so many in need, through triage, she was walking. We hold her up and dry her tears. We manage to pile her into the cart in place of another and we continue on.

At the Wall of Remembrance, the families begin their task of arranging things—their expression to their lost ones. One family has a large roll of wide cellophane packing tape and photos that they wish to hang on a tree. The mother begins taping and taping and taping and taping and taping and taping . . . and *oh God,* all that can be heard is the sound of the packing tape being wound around a tree to hold photos and messages there forever. It seems like an eternity. She is sobbing loudly as she winds that tape. Her companions are nearby and the winding of tape continues. Someone next to me—and I don't even look up as she speaks, because I have become frozen and stuck by the sound of that tape—says, "I want to scream." Me too. I can only look at my feet.

Finally they begin to pull her gently from the tree and the taping. She does not leave willingly or easily, and turns to go back. Wanting to tape more, she asks, "Do you think it will last?" To leave this symbol behind for her is so important, so vital. So much so that she crosses the line to that other place of existence where there is no rational power of reason. And she has taken many of us with her, as we hear the desperation, pain, and torture in the sound of unwinding packing tape. Like the smell of this place, I believe the sound of unwinding tape will be in my soul forever. . . .

This group is in so much pain, and we seem to have made a transition to really *arranging* things. In days before, we had families that wanted to keep the teddies and flowers or simply lay them down. Today, arrangements have become important. Placement, choosing the right spot, trying to make it just so . . . We are building headstones, but unlike granite, these headstones will not be there for eternity. They are susceptible to wind and weather, fragile. Just like us . . . no matter how thick the tape . . .

Our pregnant lady puts both hands on her lower back and announces that she NEEDS to walk. She is holding her back and refusing to sit. I glance up at one of our EMTs, who raises eyebrows and whispers, "oh oh . . ."

"Don't they do that right before they deliver?" She nods. "Hey, now, don't even *ask* me if you can use my helmet to catch, okay?"

"Well, don't think I'm using my *own.* . . ."

I continue my own ritual of leaving a flower each day with a little prayer of thanks and gratitude. I set my flower today by the dollar teddy—who still proudly wears his dollar bill, in the middle of New York City. When he was left on our first visit, someone whispered that the dollar would never last out here. He remains safe and intact, dollar tucked under his little ribbon, fluttering in the breeze.

October 21

The scramble for information for the governor's office continues. Bob is very involved in gathering paperwork and data, meetings, phones, scrambling. He wears a frown that really makes him look like a beast. I am not used to him not being on the boat and I want him to be there to get him away from the drudgery of bureaucratic justifications. I feel bad for him. The stress of bureaucratic compliance is showing on all of them today. I try to talk him into going with us during a conversation in the trailer. Vic overhears the conversation and asks me if I want him to go in Bob's place for support. I tell him he's welcome, but I'm good with it.

Bob later decides to come with us but he gets on the boat having forgotten to eat because he got so wrapped up in what he was doing. He is sweaty, dazed, and shaky—his blood sugar must be *way* off. I can tell when I talk to him that he isn't really with it. I feed him crackers and ask the EMTs to keep watch on him. They talk to him and report back to me their worries. I watch him closely. This guy would probably kill himself for this place and these families.

A NOVA worker tells me a story about the family he is with. The father has not been able to come on the ferry visit. He desperately wanted to, and they have already changed their appointment with us a couple of times at the last minute. Every time it drew close, the father became physically ill. This morning, after a sleepless night, he was so ill he just couldn't come, and asked his wife to go without him. Even though he wanted to go, he just couldn't bear the thought of seeing the place where he lost his child. The wife wants a rock—to take to him. The NOVA worker says, "I know that you are able to go down there and get closer than we can. Can't you get her something? She said it would mean so much to him."

Yes—I have been inside, out of sight of the platform but had never picked up anything. . . . We have been told that nothing can be taken out. . . . "I'll try, but I can't promise you anything. I'll try." He nods and thanks me, and runs off to be with the family.

I go up to the Major and tell him the story, and ask him if he will help me to get her a stone or something. "Is it really that wrong to take a rock?" He pats my shoulder. Once inside the fence, the Major takes me over to the Salvation Army tent, just across the street a bit from our platform, but out of sight of the platform. He simply bends down in front of everyone there and picks up a stone, which he pockets, giving me a wink and a devilish grin. No one reacts. He introduces me around inside the tent where firemen and construction workers are resting and getting a bite to eat. As he talks to the Salvation Army staff working the tent, I read notes from schoolchildren that are hung on the tent walls with duct tape. We head back to the others. I catch up to the companion at the Wall of Remembrance, and tell him that I have a stone for the woman. He grins and says that he knew I would come through. I tell him that I'll give it to her at the terminal building so that no one sees. I don't want to have others feel slighted. . . .

As we leave the bus, I find the companion and tell him to ask the woman to put down her belongings and come over to shake my hand. I see a small woman speaking to him, after which she puts down her coat and purse on one of the outside benches. I hold the stone in my right hand and begin to walk toward her, as she does toward me. Like a drug dealer, I hold out my right hand to shake hers and my left arm to hug her. As our palms touch, the transfer of the stone is done. She makes contact with the stone and her eyes register something that looks like a cross between shock and pure delight. "Oh my God, oh *my God*. You have *no* idea what this means to me. What it will mean to my husband," she says as she wraps her other arm around me. I feel like I have been suspended in time and space—somewhere magical. She holds me tightly for a very long time, with both of our hands together around that stone. She thanks me over and over with tears rolling down her face and a smile all at once.

I really hope that people who hijack and kill feel the torment of these people for an eternity. I pray that this stone gives these parents some kind of comfort or relief. I don't know how a chunk of cement could in any small way relieve the loss of a child, but for her it seems to be important to bring to her husband. She believes it will help him. Her smile warms my heart. Please, God, let her be right. . . .

The story of Joshua comes back to my mind and I think of my former conversation with the Major about collecting things from places we have visited. Wish they would just *give* them stones . . . not like they don't have a lot . . .

As we are leaving the platform today, a young guy tells me he escaped Tower Two. His wife did not. Through tears he tells me, "I got out. I am so grateful that I lived. I feel so sad for the firemen. I want to thank them." When we are leaving is *not* the time to ask for favors—*Damn*. I look frantically around and see a group of EMTs within a somewhat reasonable distance leaning on their trucks. I had visited them when we arrived. "There are some EMTs there." (I point.) "I don't see any firemen nearby and I can't take you in any further. Are the EMTs okay?" He nods and says, "Anyone. I just want to thank someone." I grab his arm.

"Walk very fast and don't listen to anything you hear. Just go." From behind I hear *"Hey*—where are you going? *Hey, get back here!"* The young guy pauses.

"No, keep going. Don't listen."

"Are you going to get in trouble?" He hesitates.

I give him a smile. "No, I'll plead insanity. Don't worry, but we probably have to be quick." He nods.

I stop a bit short to give him some privacy. "Go ahead; it's okay." He hugs an EMT, crying. The EMT cries also. They talk. I don't hear their words. The young guy turns back to me. I put an arm across his back and we hurry toward the group. "Thank you. I really needed to do that." A couple of the troopers are waiting for us, watching. I brace for a talking to, but get none. They understand. After all, anything for the families. . . He joins his family at the Wall.

A young fireman behind us stomps toward the water, not yet looking shell-shocked, but bright-eyed and smiling. He walks directly to me and asks me what we are doing and where we come from. He gives me a hug and tells me that he is on a break and is headed to the water. "We like to sit by the water to rest."

"Sounds like a good place to be."

"Smells better there."

I hand him a flower. "Smell this."

He laughs. "Yeah, right," and waves as he walks on.

Another comes along behind him. God, I *know* that face from somewhere. . . . He walks right up to me and holds out his hand, introducing himself. He has lively eyes and a great smile and the face of an angel, and *God,* where do I *know* him from? He has a really peaceful and serene face and energy. An angel, no doubt. He tells me he has been there from the first day, and says, "You've been here a long time too. Thanks so much for bringing them here. It must be hard but it's worth it, right?"

Oh yeah!

I tell him I know his face. He grins. "CNN." He was interviewed a lot for being involved in pulling out the first survivors. He smiles on his way.

Again the families are involved in arranging things. Obsessing. Getting everything just so. . . . We are running very late, and one of the New York State Troopers is coming up to begin to shoo us along our way. As he approaches me I see that he has tears in his eyes. I give him a hug and beat him to the lecture I know is coming: "I know we're late. We'll go as soon as we can. This is very important to them." He nods and whispers, "I know." We stay.

Tonight I cry my way to exit 7A.

October 22

Our Commissioner of Human Services calls and requests to meet us at the dock to take the ferry with the families. I go up to get clearance from the state police. The sergeant in charge asks,
"What's his name?"
"Joe Jones." I get a look.
"No, really. What's his name?"
"Joe Jones."
"Not funny—*what's his name?*"
"Joe Jones."
"Stop playing and tell me his name if you want him cleared."
"His name is Joe Jones. I swear."
"What kind of name is that for a commissioner? Sounds like an alias."

I shake hands with Joe at the dock. I know him to be a quiet, soft-spoken, caring person. As we board the boat he looks quiet and frowns, going straight up to the upper deck of the boat. On the platform he appears to be shaken. I touch his arm and ask if he would like to go down to the street. Relief goes through his face and he nods. I walk him over to the state police standing in the roadway. I check on the time—the fifteen minutes we have either goes by like lightning or lasts a lifetime. . . . On the way across the street, four firemen are approaching. I excuse myself to indulge in my addiction. There's that slogan again: "one is too many and a thousand never enough. . ."

I return to the platform to help huddle the families together for the closing prayer that serves to help them to get going, as well as (hopefully) feed their spirits:

> In the rising of the sun and in its going down
> We remember them.
> In the blowing of the wind and the chill of winter
> We remember them.
> In the opening of buds and the warmth of summer
> We remember them.
> When we are weary and in need of strength
> We remember them.
> When we are lost and sick at heart
> We remember them.
> When we have joys we yearn to share
> We remember them.
> So long as we live, they too shall live, for they are now a
> Part of us
> As we remember them.

I am struck with the way that the words can mean either the people or the Towers themselves. I wonder, since it is called the "Prayer for Ground Zero" if it was chosen for that reason. . . .

A companion asks me if I realized that I crossed myself after the prayer. "I'm Catholic."

"Yes, but that was a *rabbi* who gave the prayer. And you're not the only one who did that. I've never seen anyone cross themselves for a *rabbi* before." I never thought about it, but she is right—here there is one religion, one family, all the same. No rules, no boundaries. When there is so much pain there is no room for prejudice. I smiled.

The commissioner leaves a flower at the Wall of Remembrance. Back at the dock, before he leaves, he makes it a point to thank me for doing a good job. Sweet guy.

In the administrative trailer, as I begin my organizing activities, the phone on the Red Cross desk rings. I pick up and hear a very shaky voice say: "I think something is wrong with me." My heart jumps about four beats. It's the kind of voice that says "something really bad is going to happen. . ."

"What's wrong? Can you tell me?"

"I was in the Towers when they were hit, and I'm afraid to go outside. I'm scared all the time. I don't know what to do. . . ." She begins to cry. I wait for more. . . .

"And my husband thinks I should just get over it, but I can't . . . I think I'm going crazy."

"Do you have a pencil and some paper?"

She sniffs. I can tell she is interested; she didn't expect that. "Yes, somewhere . . ."

"Can you go and get me a pencil and a few really big pieces of paper?"

"Big pieces? How big?"

"Big as you have. I'll be right here waiting."

She puts down the phone and comes back: "Okay. I have it."

"Good, now take one sheet and write this down. Ready? 'It's okay to be scared when really horrible things happen to me.'"

"You want me to write that down?" She is no longer crying.

"Big letters. Use the whole page."

"Okay. I'm done."

"Good. Now another sheet. Write down 'Having a building fall on my head is a really horrible thing.'"

"Okay. You *really* want me to write that down?" She actually laughs.

"Yes. Trust me."

"Okay."

"Now write 'There are lots of people who are scared just like me.'"

"Oh my god, there *are?"*

"Yes."

"You mean other people feel this way too?"

"Yes. If I were there when it happened I think I would feel just like you do. It was a horrible, scary thing that no one should ever have to go through. You're afraid. It's normal to be afraid when a building falls down around you, don't you think?"

"Yes."

"Now, one more paper, okay?"

"Yes."

"Write 'I can get better, but it is going to take a lot of courage and some hard work to get over my fear.'"

"It will stop?"

"Yes, but you have to work on things slowly and give yourself a break. Now I want you to hang those papers up or put them where you can get them if you think you're going crazy again. Understand?"

"Yes."

"Now, we can come there to see you. Would you like me to send someone to talk to you? You don't have to go outside yet."

"Oh yes, *please*."

"I'm going to talk to a really sweet lady named Barbara. Barbara works for the Salvation Army. She will call you back and let you know when we can come out to your house. Is that good for you?"

"I'm really not crazy?"

"No. You are not crazy. You can get through this."

She sounds almost human by the time we hang up. I scurry off to talk to Major Barb, who readily accepts the mission.

I had taken the photo of Red Cross Jack in Bob's chair and propped it up on Bob's computer keyboard. We await his reaction when he enters the trailer. He sees the picture, studies it a second, and gives us a loud "HEY . . . !" With a huge grin. "You were in my Slim Jims *too?!*"

October 23

During morning staff orientation my three EMTs are in the back, standing, leaning with their arms on the pews. They have heard this speech so many times. Paul is back there mouthing the words as I talk, and he is mimicking my movements, Steve Martin style. I can't hold back from laughing. I'm the only one in the room who can see this and knows what's going on.

"Paul, come on up here and do this for me."

"*No.*"

"Come on—you've heard it so many times you probably know it better than I do. I'm tired; you do orientation." I sit down.

He does. A perfect imitation. He holds up the hard hat, the whole bit. They laugh.

A NOVA worker comes up to me, laughing. She tells me that yesterday, next to the platform there was a fireman taking his clothes off—right down in front, stripping down to his underwear, no shoes, no shirt. "I thought it would be inappropriate to yell over to you 'Hey, Kat—naked one here—come see!' You know we *really* need a signal— he was cute!" We shared a wicked chuckle. It would be so great if we could just be this way in real life—honest, raw, friendly as hell to people we don't know, trusting . . .

Today we have a small group of policemen going over with us— early responders who have lost their brothers. They have come for closure, to try to understand, heal, come to terms. We are all concerned for them—these big tough guys rarely give themselves permission to feel, and even more rarely allow themselves time to talk about it. We offer support and we receive "I'm okay," generally said with eyes down and shaking voice, so we know it's a lie. Sad that their superiors and their work doesn't allow them to be human, feel human—just cut loose and cry.

I reflect for a moment on the crying habits of the men I have met here. It seems to me that firemen cry openly, with no hesitation. Given a chance, they grab on to you like a bear in a trap, and tell you how they feel. Demonstrative, open. I see policemen cry here, but differently—their tears slide down their faces almost as if they don't have permission. Policemen stand more quietly, reserved. And I wonder: Those two groups preserve life so differently. Sometimes to save a life you may have to take another. I think that policemen, like surgeons, need to detach enough to actually harm another human. To be able to shoot someone requires detachment, coolness, objectivity. Firemen wrap their arms around others as they carry them from burning buildings. They attach; they can be passionate. Does it affect the way they cry?

Our family group today is angry, testy, snapping at the companions—expressing their grief outwardly. In the stages of the grief process, a period of anger comes as we try to resist accepting the loss. Everyone does it. It seems that enough time has passed that the families are entering the anger phase of grieving. A man gets into an argument with his companion because he wants to take pictures. "There are pictures in all the magazines." *Yup.* But New York says we can't, and they confiscate cameras from those who don't listen—and the cameras are apparently not being returned. . . The companion asks me to intervene. He yells at me also when I very quietly try to explain to him that these are the restrictions that we have—that we agree with him, that we would like to let them take pictures, but we can't. I simply reply, "I'm sorry" very softly when he finishes yelling in my face. He shrugs and shoves the camera in his pocket, then asks, "Do they really take the cameras?"

"Yes."

"They really watch?"

"Yes. Not only that, but the families who don't have cameras are likely to rat you out because they want pictures too."

He nods and says, "Okay. I don't like it, but what can you do?"

My favorite therapy dog, Mabel, has developed a habit: each day after family orientation, as she sees me wander through the dayroom looking for stragglers who need to board the bus, she begins to turn in doggie circles, and lays down at Beth's feet. Beth tells me that she lays there quietly until we return from New York, then she gets up to work again as we come in. I smile as I walk into the room and Mabel spies me and begins turning to settle in. For some reason Mabel doesn't like me today—she turns away when I try to pet her. Beth is puzzled, and it troubles her. I put it off as her picking up my frazzled energy. "But she's supposed to be used to that. . . ."

October 24

The wife of a Port Authority chief who was lost in the attack arrives at 10:30 with friends, looking for State Trooper Sam. She has apparently been told that the ferry leaves at 11 (which is the wrong time), and no one she has encountered yet has been able to locate Sam for her. She is bordering on hysteria. Her friends are holding her up on each side, and one of them tells me that she has barely eaten since 9/11 and has been throwing up what little she does eat—living on coffee, cigarettes, and tears ever since. I assure her that I will take her to Sam, who I assume is upstairs, and assure her that she will in no way miss the ferry, because I was going to be on it—so as long as she saw me, she would make it on. She is fixated on finding Sam. I take them up-stairs and we are told that Sam is not there—he isn't even at the FAC. She wails. Her knees give out. She is so fragile. We tell the state police in charge the story of how she is supposed to see Sam and be on a boat by 11. I take the sergeant aside and whisper, "You guys aren't taking her separately, right?"

"*No.*"

She becomes more upset by the moment. I try to soothe her, and promise we will straighten it out and get her there. She insists she *must* see Sam. I talk quietly to the sergeant: "You guys have to talk to me, if I knew she was coming and he wouldn't be here we wouldn't have to upset her even more—I could run interference." He nods. I tell her that I personally guarantee she will get on that boat. The sarge agrees. She seems to feel better that at least the sergeant in charge has joined in and agreed that she will go. I take her downstairs and try to coax her to eat. She accepts soup. They want to hang out in the front of the terminal. I provide times for orientation and departure, point out where the buses will park and reinforce to her that even if she simply sat right where she was, she would see me come out to leave and would make the bus. Poor lady is so tearful. A bit later they want to write on the memory walls; I take them to one of the newer ones with lots of blank space. They seem pleased. She tells me a story of seeing a shining star that she believed was him, coming to tell her he was okay. She has a strong spiritual orientation, and despite her grief can talk fondly and with conviction about her love for him.

Rabbi Ron calls me a mensch and tells me that my orientation is helpful to families. We chat about it a bit. I wonder sometimes . . . am I doing it right? It is good for me to hear from the companions and other staff what they think helps and doesn't help. Rabbi Ron is such a sweet and decent guy. Funny and quick to give.

Major Fred takes me for a walk way inside the damage area today. I have been wanting to get a picture of the cross and see it close up. He takes my camera and as we walk up he snaps some pictures. I fret about going so far, because my Mother Hen sense of responsibility takes over—I worry about something happening in the ten minutes we are not there. He laughs at me. A policeman comes up to me, and my heart jumps because I'm afraid that they are going to yell at us for wandering around loose. He takes my arm and yells over the noise into my ear, telling me to keep my eyes wide open because the noise level is so high that you can't hear the trucks running behind you. "Don't get run over on my watch—I'll be really pissed!" He turns me around and sure enough, within inches of us is a dump truck rolling past us. Didn't see it, hear it, or feel it. I tell him not to worry—I'll be very careful. As we walk toward the Verizon building, a fireman is passing and holds his arms out. He picks me up off my feet and swings me across a puddle—setting me down on the other side of the muck. What a love. Major Fred stops to greet workers in the shacks. Inside one of the shacks are teddy bears, cards and notes from kids, home-made necklaces and charms. Sweet. They cover the walls.

I am *extremely* tired today. Soul tired. But the families are so appreciative. When we get back to the terminal one family comes up to me and gives me the ultimate compliment: "This was so well put together, so helpful, so sensitive. You just don't know what this means to us." I could have died on the spot and been happy. That makes anything that I go through before, now, and in the future worthwhile. I can't relate to how it would help to go there. These people are so strong, so amazing. I don't think I could go. If I had lost my husband there it would be the *last* place I would want to see, but fortunately for me . . . In my head I understand the need to be where the loved one was lost, but my heart says *no way* could I ever do that. Seems too horrific, and I'm just not that strong.

We have a young girl of about sixteen who has been so tearful. After we return to the terminal, she continues to be red-faced and crying. Jack goes to the back and gets her a teddy bear, which she buries her face in and then smiles. He laughs and tells her, "I knew you needed that." She returns his laugh and brightens.

My favorite therapy dog, Mabel, wants no part of me again today. She turns her head away and snubs my attempts to pet her. Beth, her owner, is beside herself with apologies: "She isn't supposed to act this way. I don't understand it." I noticed that each time I wore the perfume I have with pheromones in it she has acted this way. Damn, to be snubbed by a therapy dog. . . . How low can life go? Beth asks me to try different perfume to test the theory.

More new memory boards are being brought in—the others are becoming full from messages and photos. I wander over and start to read the newer messages.

I feel like someone just ripped my guts out.

For some reason I decide to continue reading for a while and choke back the tears. I go back to the trailer to do the next day's confirmations and write out my faxes to New York and the bus company. I go about my work with tears running down my face—they just will not stop. Another staff person asks if I'm okay. "Yeah—this is probably the only place where you can work at your desk crying and not really look out of place." I find I need some air, so I go the front of the terminal and look out over the water for a long time. Rich comes up to stand with me to check up on me. He shows me pictures of his kids and makes small talk to bring me back to earth. We stand together and watch a duck as it dives, eventually so deep that it disappears completely and we never see it come up.

Sometimes lately I wish I could dive so deep that I don't come up . . .

As I become more human, I turn to find George and Joe on a bench behind us, talking. We join them. George is smiling and animated—a nice surprise, as I have never seen him looking that happy. He has a wonderful smile. We chat for a while, share Oreos, and then depart for the parking lot.

The trip home feels tired, but I feel soothed. Guess I needed to lose it for a while . . . needed to put down some of those big stones I've been carrying around.

October 25

Bob did get some time off and is back. There is to be a ceremony this weekend, so another flurry of frantic activity has started. Plans for an unknown amount of people to go to New York, to sit who knows where, with thousands of others. A long day for the families.

We typically have about five new volunteers out of the thirty-plus who go on the ferry each day. Today we have twelve newcomers, so they are very curious, full of questions, and a little lively. We hold a group massage before orientation to help dispel some of that energy. We have a big group of families who are also very active.

After family orientation, a father approaches—in response to me telling them that if they have any special requests or needs, to please make them known to us as soon as they can. He is sobbing and holding a picture of a beautiful young woman with long curly red hair. It is obvious that he *loves* her—his pride and joy—Daddy's little girl.

All of my hair stands up when he says, "They found what was left of her on her wedding anniversary—October 11. Her husband had brought her new rings for their first anniversary. The rings are how they identified her. This picture was taken at her wedding rehearsal." He had made a card on his computer with her photo and a thank-you note and the date she was found. She is extraordinarily beautiful.

"I want to give this to a fireman. A fireman found her. Will there be firemen over there that we can talk to?"

Boy did you come to the right person. "There may be firemen, but sometimes they are not nearby. But EMTs and construction workers may be. Would that be okay if there are no firemen available?"

"Anyone will do."

"Then I will get you someone to talk to, and I will try my best to make it a fireman."

I approach our trooper in charge, Sergeant Tom, who is usually so quiet and serious-looking. I'm worried that he will refuse me when I ask to go in alone and hunt for a fireman. He simply nods and says, "Anything for the families." I assure him that I will be smart and not get into trouble.

"I know." He smiles.

Once we are inside the fence, I see that a group of about six firemen are standing not too far away. They are all huge—the biggest humans I have ever seen. One in particular has an enormous walrus mustache and must be over seven feet tall. Sergeant Tom nods in their direction and smiles at me. I approach them and tell the story. They all readily agree to meet with the father. One asks me for a hug. Another looks at the bunch of flowers in my hands and says, "Jersey girl, are they for me?" I give them all flowers and hugs and thanks and go up to the platform where the father stands crying with his family. I ask him if he would like to go now or to wait until their time on the platform is over. He nods. "I'd like to go right away." He sobs harder as we walk. I take his arm not only to guide him, but because I'm afraid he will simply drop. Poor man. I step back a couple of paces to give him space with them. He wraps his arms around the fireman with the big mustache and hugs him so tightly for a long time, just crying. The looks on their faces show obvious pain. One takes the father's paper and tells him that they will take it back to the station house to hang up for everyone to share. The father is very pleased. He shakes all of their hands and sobs "thank you" to each of them. I hug the big-mustached guy again and tell him thanks, that I know this was hard for them too. I take the father's arm and guide him back to the platform to join his family.

Our companions are behaving in a clinging way. They hover too close. I hear several family members ask companions to go away. One companion asks a man if he is okay. "I'd be better if you'd just leave me alone!" he snaps as he turns and walks away. She follows him. This must stop. I consult with my peers in NOVA and the Red Cross. They see it too: Is it simply a function of having so many new people?

Those who work in disasters have told me about what they call "disaster whackos." Apparently some volunteers have a need to soothe their own issues through this type of work. Maybe they had trauma or grief in their lives that they can't deal with, so they come to places like this to be close to others. The outcome is that sometimes they get so caught up in the impact of it all that they smother the victims in their attempt to make it better. Because they are so wounded themselves, they can't give the space to others; they cling. Sad. Clinging, along with the natural anger of the families produces a situation we need to nip in the bud.

As we are returning on the ferry two companions are leaning over a family seated around one of the tables. This leaves the companions with their butts in the aisle. I ask them twice nicely to sit—we are all tripping over them on the way by to hand out juice and take care of needs. They shouldn't be hovering over people anyway. They don't sit. The third time I pass them I tell them to sit *now*. They both squeeze in with the family. A couple of the family members did not hide their reaction to the intrusion. I try to hide my disgust at their invasion of these people and hope I was successful. In front of the families is not the time to bristle. . . . Yes, we need to fix this clinging, smothering behavior.

I consult with the other team leaders and they tell me that during straff meetings they give clear instructions to companions about keeping distance from the families, but for some reason this group doesn't seem to understand boundaries and privacy. . . . My peers ask me to be very firm and "mean" in the next orientation. I don't want to be mean.

"But apparently they don't listen to *us*."

Okay. Different orientation tomorrow. . . .

Later, back at the terminal the father comes up to me with another copy of the card that he made. He asks if I will take it into Ground Zero and hang it up in one of the shelters around the perimeter—somewhere where the firemen will see it when they take breaks. I promise. He turns toward a memory wall and begins to hang her photo. I lend a hand to steady the picture as he staples. Tears are still running down his face. She was so well loved. The father is rummaging through his things for something as I hold up the photo. He has brought a staple gun, which he uses to put heavy-duty staples all around the edge of the picture.

Even later that evening, I see the father again—this time with a contagious grin on his face. What a great sight!! Smiling as if he had just become a grandpa. He has more paper that he has shuffled through. Smiling, he holds out a photo of an airman in full battle gear writing his daughter's name on a *bomb*. "Look, they dropped it the same day they found her—October 11." He is simply bubbling over with happiness at this. I touch his arm and reply:

"I don't believe I'm saying this, but, congratulations."

"Thanks—isn't it great?"

He hangs this photo as well.

I am so grateful that I was able to give this man a chance to express his appreciation to a worker over there. It may not have been to the same men who found his daughter, but it seemed to help him feel more at peace. He gives me his e-mail address and I promise to check in with him when I get back. I also promise to send him a photo of his daughter's picture hanging in a shack inside Ground Zero . . . your daddy misses you so much.

Mabel loves me again! She runs into my arms and gives me lots of kisses. She almost knocks me over with love. Different perfume. I think the effect that the dogs have on the families is great—they smile, they reach out. The looks on their faces show the amount of soothing that animals can give—that nonthreatening way we can reach out to them and feel like we have received affection in return. As I pet Mabel I think about the George Carlin thing—would we still pet them if they didn't have fur? I think at least here it would be guaranteed—bald dogs would get love too.

I'm feeling tearful, sad, and vulnerable. I want people to stop asking me what this is doing to me. I'm not totally sure what it is doing to me. I am sure that I don't want to worry about it—it won't help or change things. Maybe what it is doing to me is good. I do know that leaving it behind will be hard. People ask if I'm worried about the damage it will do to me. I believe that whatever happens, if I develop something I can undevelop it, so what's the big deal? I don't worry about damage—don't believe it will happen. I do worry about how I will figure out what normal is. . . .

A couple of days ago someone gave me a very emotional compliment; she told me that I am the heart and soul of the boat operation. I was flattered and embarrassed all at once. For someone to give me such a compliment was a great feeling. Today I find out that she wrote a note about what she did here on the two days she went with us as a companion, and she took credit for everything. Even to the point that she listed the content of my orientation speeches and briefings as hers—verbatim—like she had tape-recorded it. She gave me a copy of the note. I read it and wondered why she would want me to see it. Does she think I will be happy that she takes credit for my words and my work, or did she do it to put a knife in my ribs? Or am I totally seeing it wrong? I wish that when I hear about these types of things I could simply let it ride and not resent it. I feel cheap and petty that I should want to grab a spotlight for this work. And I feel cheap and petty because I resent people for not even mentioning my name. I show Bob the note and ask him, "Is it me? Am I wrong to be upset at this?" He teases me by saying he'll put up a billboard that says, SPELL IT B-E-D-A-R-D. Fame is just not in the cards for me. . . . Why do some people have to step all over others? Do they feel that bad about themselves that they can't allow someone around them to do something good? Do they believe when they take credit for something they did not do that it really means anything? I guess for a moment it feels really good to get the praise. To come here to work for even a day is a wonderful, amazing thing. Why isn't that enough?

I watch the sun go down and talk with my fellow sunset worshippers about the amazing reds tonight. And about how the sunsets have been unnaturally beautiful since 9/11. I understand that dust in the atmosphere is what makes the sunset vivid. Is this a gift that the Towers left us with—glorious sunsets? I really believe that God has sent us these sunsets to ease the pain. Not us here at the FAC, but us in general. Perfect weather, beautiful-hand painted skies at dawn and dusk. Warms the soul to see the world in all its glory. We are developing a ritual of pausing to watch the sun. NOVA George is a frequent watcher with me. Sometimes we cry, sometimes we laugh, get philosophical, or just watch quietly before going back inside to finish the day's work.

"Hey Major Fred, I'll race you to 7A!"

October 26

Major Barb gives me good news: "Hey, guess who was here at the FAC yesterday?" I don't have a clue. "Your girl from the phone the other day. Came in all by herself. She wanted to meet you and thank you, but you guys were out on the boat." I sit back and smile and soak it in. *Thank you, God, for telling me what to say to her.* "She looked good. She's on her way. She'll be fine." I just grin.

Today I have a mission to deliver a young woman's picture to an FDNY shelter deep inside Ground Zero somewhere. I shove my camera—that I am never without anyway—into my pocket. I search for tape. As I leave the boat, I arm myself with a fistful of flowers. The Major says he'll go with me to protect me from trouble. He takes my camera from me. We walk as quickly as we can toward the cross. Up close the cross is even more eerie. . . the rust from the beam somehow catches the light in strange ways. I want to climb up the concrete base it sits on and touch it.

They are digging in an ash pit. The air is thick with ash and heavy, nasty. The burning smell is so thick it goes right through my brain. Ash is up my nose, in my mouth, stuck in my throat, immediately stuck to my skin. The wind today whips so hard I can hardly walk. Hard hats don't stay on without a lot of holding.

About another half a block over from the cross is an FDNY shelter. I decide this one is a good place to hang the picture. As we enter and explain our mission, the guys inside choose a prominent spot near the door. Unlike the shelters closer to the edges, this one is not as decorated inside, so a lot of wall space remains. I tape up the picture and thank-you note, and add a red flower over top for decoration. These flowers dry well, so it will not look too funky. I take a few photos to be sure of a good one. The Major is busy chatting as I work on my project. The firemen wander over to stand and watch my work. As they consider the picture one says, "She was really beautiful. How is the family?" I tell them of the tearful father and of the bomb story. They smile and nod—not happy smiles—vicious, wicked smiles. One says, "Good! Hope it found its mark."

We walk on a bit farther to another shelter. Outside the shelter is a hand-built plywood altar with a cross on it made of welded chain. A vase of dead flowers is next to the cross. Across the front of the altar is painted a legend about a little girl who brought the flowers in to thank the firemen. From inside of the shack comes a fireman. As I look at him I get chills—his eyes are dead, as if he has no soul left. Dead, blank eyes that are so full of pain. All I can think of is *he's dead already—walking dead.* I feel so bad for him—God, what must those eyes have seen to die so fast? He stops in front of us and just looks at me—or through me. I ask him if he's all right. He wraps his arms around me, buries his face in my neck, and cries on my shoulder. I return the hug, and just hold him. When he turns me loose, I ask him what I can do. "You did it." I put a flower through the strap for his goggles on his helmet. He takes a flower from me and puts it on the altar, telling me the story about that little girl who left the vase of flowers and a note asking her daddy to come home. Sadness just hangs on this guy. What can you ever say or do to help suffering this deep?

We walk on a bit more and a deputy chief calls us over. "Hey, take our picture!" he says to the Major, laughing. He motions me over and puts an arm around me. Here in this shack brightly colored pictures from kids are hanging in obsessively neat and tidy rows. Cheerful greetings, pictures of rainbows, sun-filled pictures, animals and trees, notes, thank-yous, people holding hands. What a strange contrast. And each one with a complete frame of duct tape, hung with absolute reverence. I wonder what will become of these pictures—will they take them home or leave them with the rubble for burial? Scraps of sweetness in hell—there are those extremes again.

The pile is still belching black ash everywhere. Fire hoses are dumping water on the scoop from four different locations to keep the flames and the soot down. I wonder what will come out when I finally do get to blow my nose. . . .

What horror it must have been to see that cloud of dust rolling through the streets and be trapped inside that smoke, dust, and ash. It looked like an avalanche. I can't imagine living through that, choking and running in terror. It is no wonder they ran to the docks and just kept screaming and running to the water. As the Major stops to talk to someone I look around at where the buildings were. I look up. I am now standing not too far from where the south edge of Tower One would have been. I turn in a circle just gazing up into an empty hole of sky where there used to be so many windows. So many.

How could something so big be turned so completely to dust?

The Major finishes his conversation and we turn into the wind to head back, bending to walk, holding helmets on. Debris is falling from the buildings. Grit is in my eyes and crunching in my teeth. My nose is so clogged with ash that I resort to mouth breathing. It tastes so indescribably nasty—worse than it smells. I think about the photos and hope they come out. I really want to be able to let the father see that his daughter is with the firemen inside as well. I hope it gives him some comfort.

We go to the Wall of Remembrance. The little teddy from our first visit still sports his dollar bill tucked neatly under his ribbon collar. I fear for him being in the open once Monday comes: New York is opening the Battery Park area to the public once again. With the public roaming free, I think that the premonition that someone whispered to me on that first day will come true: that dollar bill may not last long. I still carry a dollar each day just in case. I also found out that I'm not the only one with a protective eye on that teddy. Bob and the Major also have dollars waiting.

A mother walks up to me and hugs me, thanking me for bringing her to say good-bye.

Despite my being "mean" in orientation, this group of companions is still clinging to families and being possessive. What is this behavior? A desperate need to fix? NOVA Ed, Sandy, Red Cross Jack, and I meet and discuss keeping orientation very simple. Perhaps we give them so much information that they become overwhelmed and overcompensate. We decide to tell them that their *only* job is to preserve safety— keep the families from tripping hazards, keep distance, flank them as we walk, file up to the platform after the families, and stay in the back.

As we follow the families into the terminal, there are two *huge* state troopers immediately in front of me. A bit in front of them are two very tiny state troopers—smaller than I am, I think. The contrast strikes me as funny. I nudge one of the big ones. "Hey, what are they? Sprouts?" He laughs.

A group of troopers is inside the food tent, and some others are reading the walls. I go up to the second group and ask them if they saw the note that was left for them. They look confused. I motion for them to follow me, and take them to a wall where very high up is a message that reads NJ STATE TROOPERS ARE THE BEST. They seem surprised. I tell them that I watched one of the family members write it.

"They love you. They are forever telling us how much they appreciate you guys. They are so pleased with how respectful you are, and they talk about how safe they feel, and how nice it is to talk with you. Most of us regular people don't get to really *talk* to state police. I think it's great too. All of you have been so friendly and easy to talk to."

They get bashful—as they always do when you give them a compliment: big guys with fat necks who blush and do the *awwww shucks* at a little praise. I know from talking to them that they are not used to compliments, and being and interacting with people this way. It's always a perk to be appreciated, no matter how hard it is to get used to compliments. One trooper asks, "How'd that message get way up there at the top?" The message is on the very top of a memory board that is about eight feet tall.

"They get on chairs or boxes so that they can reach."

He grins but then suddenly turns away, looking down. He turns back and says, "So sad."

"Yeah." And I leave them to their reading and to get more teary-eyed.

Tonight I walk through the kitchen door at home to a very enthusiastic dog greeting, which is typical. But they begin to eat my clothes. Not nibbling like grooming. Not licking or sniffing.

Eating my clothes.

Gnawing on my pant legs, my shirt, my jacket. Chewing. It's ungodly strange and disturbing, and I have never seen them act that way. I am so stunned that I can't think of what to do about it, so for a few seconds I stand and watch them gnawing at me. I feel like a rawhide chew toy. And with two rotties and a pit bull, it's becoming hard to remain standing. I'm looking down at them, doing the *whatthehell?* Fred is sitting at the breakfast counter, watching, with a puzzled grin on his face. He laughs and says, "What did you do, roll in raw hamburger on the way home?" They are still chewing on my clothes, and now are also pulling as if to get the clothes off me.

Then it hit me. That heavy dark ash. That ash was everywhere today and I was in the middle of it—covered in it. All of my hairs stand on end and I can't get out of my clothes fast enough, right there in the kitchen. Oh God.

There are people in that ash.

October 27

Still the scurrying behavior for the ceremony in New York on Sunday. We are planning for 2,000 people for dinner . . .

Our urns arrive from New York by police and firefighter honor guard today.

We have planned to change our walking pattern through Battery Park to send the message to our symbiotic companions that they should be there *for* the families, not *on* the families. I'll be happy when this group cycles out. I consult with one of the troopers on the fine points of crowd control. Companions used to walk next to the family group. Now they will walk around the outside perimeter.

The Major has pulled a Salvation Army trailer into the terminal building, pushing it into the opening of the breezeway. It will serve as the depository for the urns. They begin to decorate the trailer with draped American flags. A Red Cross worker grabs my elbow and takes me to the trailer and says, "It's awful. It looks like a coffin. Talk to them and get that thing out of here."
"Can't do that. They need it for the urns."
"But it looks like a coffin."
"It is a coffin."
He shrugs and walks away.

Salvation Army cadets arrive about 9 a.m., by the dozens, all dressed in navy blue sweaters and slacks. The Major lines them up in two long parallel lines stretching through the terminal. I run into him out back, and he asks if I have seen his cadets. I shake my head no. "Come with me; let's go and look for the caravan out front and I'll show you." He offers his elbow as a royal escort. He's in his Salvation Army majors' dress uniform, looking more imposing and splendid than ever. . . . We walk arm in arm through the back door of the terminal, where two lines of cadets stand at attention. The lines stretch through the terminal almost to the front door. "There—aren't they beautiful?"
"They are. Very. What are they doing?"
"Waiting."
I look confused at him. He laughs. "They sing very nicely too."
As we stroll arm in arm through the flanks I say: "I feel like I'm at a wedding."
"Would you like to hear them sing?'
"Yes, please."
"What would you like to hear?"
"'Amazing Grace'?"
He stops and turns back toward them, gesturing with his arms like an orchestra conductor: "Sing 'Amazing Grace.'"

They do, beautifully, like a choir. I laugh and am totally a five-year-old in a joyful mood. "They are really *good.* Nobody has ever sung just for me. This is so great!" He laughs and takes my arm again as we continue to the front door. As is everyone else, we are anxious and waiting for the caravan to bring the urns. We spend a couple of minutes chatting with others who are out front waiting and setting things up. We discuss some planning for later. As we go back through the terminal I realize the cadets are still singing. I stop and ask the Major: "How long will they do that?"

"Until I tell them to stop."

"No, really?"

"Yup." He laughs. I am astounded.

We continue on—searching for troopers. About ten minutes later we return again to the terminal. The cadets are still singing. "See? I told you. They'll do that until I tell them to stop."

"Now that's getting creepy. Tell them to stop. I really like their singing, but they must have rotated though those verses sixty times already."

He laughs and waves his conductor arm again, and in a loud preacher voice says, "Sing something else." Their highest-ranking cadet announces "America the Beautiful," and they launch into that, followed by an assortment of other hymns and songs. Each time I pass through the area, I giggle that I actually had an army of cadets sing just for me. And I let myself soak in the beautiful sound. Feels like lying on the beach in the sun—warm and relaxing and soft. They sing all morning.

Lights are flashing in the distance on the drive; the fire engines carrying the urns are entering the park. They are escorted by the state police. Firemen and New York State Troopers in dress blues emerge from the caravan. Bagpipers group together and begin to tune up. It is *freezing* and the wind whips their kilts. They are visibly shivering. The drummer goes off to the side and appears to be praying. From the two fire trucks they begin unloading onto hand trucks large boxes containing the urns filled with the ashes from the World Trade Center. The boxes appear to be extraordinarily heavy, but the men, even though they are straining to lift them, handle the boxes so gently, as if they contain eggs. Each box is placed on the carts, four deep, and once they are finished they stretch out

American flags and drape them over the boxes. Two hundred urns have arrived to serve as containers for bodies for our families.

First in the formation are the pipers, and then the New York State Police in full dress blues followed by the firemen escorting the flag-draped urns. Our New Jersey State Troopers, also in full dress, join with them as receiving escorts. The pipers play a marching tune and they march through the terminal toward the breezeway, where the Salvation Army wagon waits to be filled. The cadets, still in two single rows, hold up one finger pointing to God: the Salvation Army salute. Not crying is not an option. They load the heavy boxes into the Salvation Army wagon, and one by one fold the American flags into triangles and hand them up the ranks. The pipers play "Amazing Grace," and we sing. At least those of us who can both sing and cry at the same time.

The formation leaves as it came—but in silence—except for a drumbeat marking left foot. The Salvation Army cadets sing "America," and those of us who can choke it out sing along. I choose to cry.

It suddenly becomes time to do orientation for staff. It is a hard transition from the urn ceremony to this. I feel bitchy and would rather stand there and scream. I bite my mood and speak softly to overcompensate for how I feel. Today will be the day that the public is allowed into the fringes of Battery Park and the Mercantile. I ask companions to flank the families tightly so that if we meet up with the public they meet us first. We need to be a cocoon to insulate and protect even more.

People are standing and staring at us from in front of the Mercantile. I am glad that I warned the families that the area would be opened to pedestrian traffic. Now that the Mercantile is open for business, the workers are out in the sun on their lunch break, smoking and talking. Pedestrians are hanging out at the dock area. As we walk toward the platform, people in the street are snapping photos. I herd the companions to the back to shield the group from the camera lenses, and we herd the families forward and inside.

We have three British firefighters with us today. They lost many people who were here in New York for a meeting. One is a quiet, white-haired guy with impossible spiked hair. He is so sad, so sweet in mannerisms. I provide him with extra flowers at the Wall of Remembrance. He didn't think about leaving anything at the wall, so he begs a pen and hastily scribbles a note on a scrap of paper. He wipes tears and hugs his buddies who openly cry for their lost comrades.

We have four young brothers in their teens. We had their mom last week. They lost many from their family: cousins, father, nephew, and an uncle. They are young, fresh, and have that adolescent sassiness, but they are polite, tearful, and supporting one another. They stand together at Ground Zero huddled as a group hug, letting tears flow without talk. The oldest, who looks about seventeen, cries on the boat on the way back. I bring him a teddy and say in a squeaky voice, "Will you take me home and hug me?" He smiles, wipes his nose, snatches the teddy, and folds his arms around it on his chest, hugging for dear life. He rubs his cheek on the fuzzy teddy, still smiling.

The weather and time is taking its toll on the Wall of Remembrance; flowers have fallen. I pick them up and poke them back into the bushes and lean them back against the photos and messages. As if tidying up can make it better—*if I can keep it clean for just one more day* . . . I don't even know why.

Ash is blowing around even at the Wall of Remembrance. I look at Judy and she has a bit of ash in her hair. Judy is an intense person with big, soft, soulful blue eyes and a contagious laugh. I reach out and gently take the ash and try to set it on the wind, but it dissolves—melting onto my finger. I had wanted to set it free, let it drift, but it simply melts on my fingertip, and for some reason that really hurts. It must register on my face. I look back into her eyes. "I know," she responds. She does. I feel it in my bones.

Judy is a Red Cross mental health clinician, a veteran disaster worker—and probably able to handle anything. I am not sure when I actually met her (at least in this life!); it seems she has always been here. She quickly became another one of my rocks: steady, even, someone I don't have to talk with to communicate. Several of us here are like that—I believe we communicate at a spirit level, that we knew each other before and will again. And I believe we were sent here to work together, to keep each other strong.

That tiny fragment of ash takes my mind back once more to that cloud billowing out over the river and through the streets. Please

God, take care of that new army of angels, and send them to Afghanistan to watch over those who fight . . .

Today is my day for compliments. One from our group of adolescent boys comes up to me as we leave the buses and thanks me. He also thanks me for taking care of their mom last week. "She said you were good people." I ruffle his hair and say, "Thanks. You're pretty special yourself." Those guys were great together. Holding one another, talking to one another, being so adult and so strong. As we walk into the terminal, I bring up my usual spot at the rear, a family member comes up to me and says, "I just want to tell you how important this was for me. Thank you for making it possible for me to say goodbye."

I ask if I can give her a hug. She opens her arms and welcomes me.

"It was a privilege to be able to do this for you."

Back in the trailer I chatter with Vic, who gets me in a silly laughing mood. He tells me he thinks I'm doing a great job and thanks me. I start out the day bitchy and tearful, and end with sweetness all around me. God really provides, because if this didn't happen to balance me I think I'd lose it. Soon.

I sit for a bit in the trailer and think about what is going to happen to me. I think that soon a new chapter of my life will open with the subtlety of elephants. . . .

Tomorrow will be a day off for me—there will be the ceremony in New York, dinner for 2,000, and the beginning of handing out the urns for those who want them. In the terminal several men are erecting tents to provide shelter from the wind that has been blowing through the breezeway and the platform. Tomorrow will be a chaotic and cold day, and for many a turning point toward closure, if there is such a thing. I ask God to send some angels down to help the dinner for 2,000 run smoothly.

One of the troopers motions for me to come to him: "Remember the other day, you asked me if those little guys were sprouts?"

I nod. He has a nasty twinkle in his eye, and is obviously about to be a very bad boy. He nudges the trooper next to him. "Tell her."

The second guy leans down to me and says: "We keep them in our backpack, or three or four in our pockets—just in case we need a spare."

Oh yes, there is beauty here!

As I wrap up the day in the dark trailer, CNN describes a quake at Ground Zero last night, 2.3 on the Richter Scale. When the Towers fell it registered 3.6. One of the NOVA workers at the desk looks up and says, "*Shoot!* I'm from California. We sneeze harder than that!" The reports on the air quality have been full of toxic warnings. Hey, Rudy, maybe you should think twice about that ceremony?

October 28

I have the day off, and find myself with a husband who thinks he is the only person in the world who is ever affected by events. He acts like a spoiled five-year-old at every opportunity, and I have to swallow it and smile as usual. My hope that he would learn not to sweat the small things from working with me in that great smoking hole is apparently just a pipe dream. . . . I don't understand why caring about someone else is so hard for him to do. I end up in a really foul mood and seriously consider driving up to the FAC just to be with nice people. I guess someday I will just pack it in and give up trying. . . .

I begin bringing my houseplants in from the cold—bit late for that—and feel cold, tired, angry, and impatient.

October 29

Okay, so I recognize the sickness in feeling like being at a disaster area is better than being at home.

The family visits are winding down in enrollment. This coming Wednesday and Thursday are supposed to be the last. Even though I knew this would happen, I am feeling the loss. I dread the end—when I have to go back to whatever life I will have now. Do I just go away and pretend nothing happened? *What?*

Another bright beautiful day. Fred comes with me today, and trots off to join Jack and their equipment routine. The security in New York is now noticeably low. Our trooper in charge today has very long legs. As he walks, we have to run to keep up. The front of the group is entering the gate at Ground Zero as the back of the group is leaving the dock. The Major gives me a wink and says: "I'll walk with him on the way back and slow him down." People—the general public—watch, snap photos, try to walk in our group. They don't seem to be able to understand how rude it comes across for grieving families to have their pictures taken. I can understand wanting a part of history, but how would they feel if they were on public display without a choice? I can even understand wanting to take pictures to share the experience, be a part of it, identify with it. It is so invasive, and we are so protective of the families.

As we approach the gates there is a small group of three people on the platform. Fred goes up to the platform and tries to be nice by giving them a "heads up" that we are bringing a large group of families up in a few minutes. A man in the small group looks at him and says, "Fucking families. I don't care about your fucking families." Fred comes down and tells me what had happened. I pass the comment on to a couple of our troopers, who silently go ballistic—puffing up their chests and getting a look like "show me where it is so I can kill it." We discover that the man is part of a government group from the Ukraine and was sent up ahead of their president's arrival—like a scout to scope out the area and situation before the dignitaries came through. A couple of minutes pass, and they leave the platform and the area.

We have three elderly women, one in a wheelchair. Jack and Fred carry the one who is using the wheelchair onto the platform. We also have several Port Authority workers (survivors) with us, and we put them in the back of the group so that the families can be at the platform railing. We hoist those in the back onto chairs and support them so that they can see without falling.

We are only on the platform for about five minutes, and have just settled into place when Blaze approaches me in his best state trooper tone and says that they have asked us to leave. He is being very professional and coplike, probably because he wants unquestioned obedience. I look at him over the top of my mirror shades and quietly and simply say, "No." He looks amazed—he didn't expect that. He actually twitched. He patiently explains that dignitaries from the Ukraine are here with their president and they want to come up.

"No. We just got here; we're staying."

He is looking very troubled now . . . civilians are not supposed to be this disobedient. He shuffles a bit, looking very disturbed. He seems to be searching for a peaceful way to settle this—or he thinks I've totally lost my mind and isn't sure *what* I'll do if provoked further . . . I'm having trouble not laughing at his distress, but I'm still peeved at the man being so obnoxious for no reason.

"What do you want me to tell them?"

I calmly say: "Tell the president of the Ukraine that he can kiss my American ass. Our families have fifteen more minutes." Blaze is now looking at me like he doesn't know whether to laugh or yell at me. He definitely is confused by my behavior. I tell him the story about the guy with the trash mouth.

"He said *what?*" comes out in a really vicious whisper. *"No, he didn't!"* I look over my sunglasses at him and just nod. Blaze turns and walks down to the street. I think his hair might have been smoking. We stay.

A few moments later he returns, "What did the scumbag look like?" I describe him. Blaze leaves again. The Major takes me by the elbow, pulling. He tells me that the entourage is arriving at the gate. I go around the corner and see the limos stopping and guys in religious-type headgear and long robes get out.

"Bishops, holy men," the Major says. "My kind of people. I'll talk to them."

He goes to the cars, greets the men, and explains that we have families on the platform. They appear to be having a friendly conversation. Their president says he will not interrupt the families. At least *he* has class.

The FBI comes up to me and asks about the trash mouth. I repeat the story. "We can't find the guy. If you see him, yell." I nod. As we are leaving, trash mouth is standing in the street smoking a cigarette, talking to a woman. I tell Blaze, who sets off running. A secret service guy—I knew he was secret service because his jacket had "secret service" stitched on the front of it in at least four-inch-high yellow letters—comes up to me and says, "Point the fucker out for me." I do. They go toward him. Lots of them. HA!—he doesn't stand a chance. . . . I continue to walk with the families toward the Wall of Remembrance. Blaze catches up, walking next to me with a grin on his face, looking very smug and satisfied.

I grin at him. "Did you shoot him?"

"Nah . . ."

"Beat him half to death, then?"

"Wanted to."

"Why didn't you?"

"Nah . . ." He laughs. "I didn't know *what* to do when you said that to me. I *never* expected anything like that to come out of your mouth. You're always so easygoing."

"I know. Sorry."

"I don't think I'll ever be able to look at you without laughing again."

"Good!"

He cracks up and returns to crowd control—serving and protecting.

People have begun to arrive for urns and triangular-folded American flags. One family wants two, one for the wife and one for the parents. The only way it can happen is if they are estranged and the daughter-in-law will not allow the parents to visit the urn. Like there is a shortage of ash over there. I can't understand a world where parents and wives should have to split an urn, but the position from New York is that if it were a body there would be only one. Logical, but under the circumstances, cold. They ask people to split it by opening the urn and pouring some of it into a baggie. Really nice—let's put a baggie of dirt on the TV and call it our son. I plead their case with the legal staff and the family gets their wish.

I have discovered that the turnpike rest stops now have Twin Towers enamel pins, so I stop in all of them on the way home and clean out the supply to decorate my peers. I really find it amazing that the New Jersey Department of Tourism has no New Jersey pins for sale. They come to the FAC from all over, bringing pins that represent their states. We have none. The New Jersey Turnpike Authority sells New York pins. Go figure. I also replenish my stock of postcards for the out of towners.

On the way home, my husband tells me about a woman he met today—a beautiful, young blonde woman who arrived with her sister-in-law and a friend. All of them were well-dressed and well-groomed. Being a hairdresser, he notices those things. The woman had lost her husband. As we walked past the Wall of Remembrance on the way into Ground Zero, she saw her husband's picture hanging on the wall—left by someone else. She screamed and her knees buckled. I was in the back of the group and remembered hearing that scream. Fred was the one who caught her, and he held her up as she walked on.

Later, as we were leaving for the boat, she was put in the golf cart to ride because she was still feeling shaky. Fred walked beside her. She thanked him for being there for her and for volunteering to be with the families. Fred said, "Then she asked 'What do you do for a living?' I was afraid to tell her I was a hairdresser. She kept asking me over and over what I did for a living that I could come here and work. I told her I would rather not say."

"Why? What are you, a *spy* or something?" was her response. He hesitated, then finally told her: "I own a hair salon. I do hair." Her hands went up to the top of her head and she said, "Oh God, don't look at my roots!"

He shakes his head in wonder and laughs. "Women. At a time like that, as soon as you see a hairdresser, all you can do is worry about being scolded for your roots."

I can see that this experience has shown him so much. Since the first day he volunteered, he has returned three days a week to work equipment with Jack. I remembered the first day, when in a sudden panic he said to me, "What can I possibly offer these people? I'm not a therapist."

"Yes, but you're a hairdresser; you know how to talk to people. Therapy is not really what they need right now. Now they need someone to stand next to them and give them a hug if they need it. Believe me—they will let you know what they need. You know how to hug. Just be human, be nice. There are plenty of therapists all around them, watching. They'll handle it if it gets scary. Besides, you'll be doing equipment with Jack. He'll take good care of you. I'll watch out for you too."

I have seen him step outside of his normal role and give to strangers. Service really is good for the spirit. It's so great that he has this chance to do something—to contribute something. It's nice to share this as a couple, to have someone at home who simply understands. I don't have to look for the words to explain why I go there without a break, for such long hours: it's in his soul now as well. He feels that place tugging at his heart too.

October 30

Another beautiful bright day. The weather has been incredible this year. I would like to continue to think that God is doing this for us, so that the families can have the blessings of not being cold and wet over there. And especially for the diggers, so that they can do their work.

Today we have survivors from the Port Authority offices in the World Trade Center. The booking sheets say 125 people. New York has a fit that we are bringing that many, plus the usual thirty-five or so companions. At the last minute chaos erupts because Port Authority wants to add people. We are stretching the bus and equipment capacity to the limits, as well as the boat capacity. The state police also add people at the last minute. Jake also adds attorney people. By the way, have I mentioned to you that we *have only 140 seats????* They don't care. Bob tells me to start pulling companions to make room for the add-ons.

In the middle of the chaos I have State Trooper Sam come up to me and grab my arm: "Gimme another sticker," with a seriously bossy tone. I have *no room* for anyone else, am overbooked, and New York is threatening to not let us in unless we have no more than 100 people total. I hit personal overload with his remark, and his attitude of ordering me around.

"No."

"I said gimme a sticker. I want to put somebody on the boat." Again with the tone. Rich and Judy are standing there and they roll their eyes behind him.

"No. I have no more room and I'm throwing off companions to make room. I don't know how we're going to do this now."

"The guy is on the list. Give me a sticker."

"If he is on the list then NOVA has his sticker. I gave them the stickers for all of the registered people this morning, including the blue ones. You can get it from them."

"Gimme the sticker." He is *really* getting rude now. . . .

"Sam, NOVA has them."

"Why are you doing this? Just give it to me."

Three times already. What is with this guy? "Sam I told you, NOVA has the stickers." And because I know this is going nowhere, I turn and walk away before I say what I really want to—*Can't you hear—I told you I don't have them!!!!!!!!!!*

The Port Authority people don't want to move to board the buses and are so slow to respond. Guess I can't blame them—if I were in those buildings I wouldn't want to go back there either. Because they are moving so slowly, we are running very late. They are cranky and rude to companions, who are feeling stretched to begin with—we have less than ten out of the original thirty-five companions going.

The Port Authority staff don't want to leave the platform, and become rude to Bob, who takes it in stride, but gives me an eye roll behind them. Yeah, me too, buddy. I guess we all express fear and grief in a different way. . . .

Sam has been bad-mouthing me all over to anyone who will listen, because I dared to tell him "no" when he jumped on me this morning. And of course, they have all come to me and ratted him out. Five state police brass have arranged a meeting with Bob and me—to squash me. During our meeting, Sam tells a story about coming up to me sweetly and saying please and getting a rude response. "She just walked away." When it was my turn, I said, "Sam, you demanded a sticker. I explained to you that I was bouncing companions so that we had room. When you finally told me he was previously registered, I explained to you that NOVA had his sticker. Then you demanded the sticker three more times. Each time I told you his sticker was with NOVA. I didn't even have any stickers with me."

"Oh, Sam wouldn't do that," the in-charge cop says.

"He did. And he knows it. He also did it in front of several other people who can verify what I'm telling you. I'll give you their names. Ask them yourself."

"Sam was brought here because he is so polite and so good with people. He would never do that." *Okay. . .*

They look at Bob. "So. Who is in charge when it comes to the boat issues?"

He looks at me. "She is."

They look surprised, and I try not to let out the grin that I feel, and the urge to say "Nah nah, I win!" Bastards.

"*She* has the final authority?"

"Yes. And I support her one hundred percent." I could jump across the table and hug this man!!!

I admit to them that under the stress of having to change so many things at once that I probably had a tone of voice that was not as pleasant as always, and apologize for appearing gruff. I ask them to let me know if they have a guest in advance so that I *have* their stickers and we don't misunderstand each other. Especially since it has happened before; people arrived and said they are to see Sam, and he is not there. I can't run interference or provide support if I don't know what's happening.

Sam again swears that he was nothing but sweet to me—he can't let it go. He has to be in control, in charge, and *right*.

Bob discusses with them the fact that he has had trouble with Sam's attitude before . . . and I have seen him save Sam's ass several times. Bob repeats that I'm in charge of the boat. The brass tell Sam and I to work it out between us. I respond that it should have happened that way to begin with. Bastard runs whining behind my back because he isn't man enough to talk about it. He's so into control and looking good that he ends up being the one person in the crowd who gets everyone else to fight with one another so it's a big mess. He also ends up being the one that everyone asks—behind his back—"What's up with him?"

After the meeting, I let Bob know how much I appreciate his support, and how I think that it was probably the first time in my career that I didn't have to go to bat strictly for myself. I really don't remember a time when someone stood up for me like that.

"You deserve it. He's a bastard and they know it. They just protect their own no matter how off base they are. You are in charge, and you do it well."

God, thank you for this man! Stress is taking its toll on all of us . . .

A Red Cross guy comes up to me at about 9 p.m., and says, "Hey, did you know that there has been a running bet on when you're going to drop?"

I laugh. "No way."

He nods. "I hear you've been here from the start, and have been on the ferry every day. They won't allow us to do that. Even more than a two-week rotation at a disaster site is a no-no. They have bets on you."

"How much you got riding on me?"

"Five dollars that you won't last until my tour is over next Friday."

"Sorry, love. I'll be standing a *lot* longer than that. I have plenty more energy and much more work to do."

He laughs. "You're a tough cookie." Yup.

"Hey, if I never drop, do *I* get all the money?"

"You *should*." Yup.

October 31

No boat running today. Not enough people signing up, so we consolidated them to other days. Shades of things to come. . . . So I drive up just to lend a hand.

I had another totally sleepless night where those damn movies were playing in my head. I woke up feeling angry and depressed about that meeting yesterday. Letting Sam get to me like that just lets him win. I know that. I can't help it. We were both wrong in the long run, and I feel used, abused, and like I've been treated like a piece of fluff. No respect. I could still hug Bob for standing up for me like that! Wish I could just let it go. . . Gotta expect that we'll get on each other's nerves: too much for too long . . .

November 1

As I go up to the state police office first thing this morning, I meet Sergeant Tom who says. "Hey did you see your *boy* on TV last night?"

What do you mean?"

"The riot between the police and the firemen. You heard about it, right?"

"Yeah. So sad that those guys had to go against each other."

"But did you see who threw the first punch?"

"No."

"It was your boy. The big guy with the mustache." He's talking about the fireman with the big mustache who spoke to the dad with the picture. He had been so nice, so considerate, very soft-spoken and gentle with the father . . .

"No *way!* Seriously?"

"Yeah, seriously. He was a big guy too. Suckered that cop right in the face." His tone is very angry now. My "boy" has obviously committed an act that the sarg is not happy about. I hear strong emotion in his voice. He isn't usually like that—always professional, quiet, polite, detached a bit, but quick to smile. I didn't think he *got* angry.

"I really feel for them all. They shouldn't have been put against one another that way. Didn't they think that would happen? Emotions are so raw there. They are all so tired, so passionate about what they do, so stressed and burned out. That really makes people unpredictable and prone to something like that."

"Cops never expect to get punched in—the—*face*. Especially by someone who should be like a brother. That was uncalled for."

Now I get where his anger comes from. It was too real. Being punched in the stomach is not as personal, not as mean-spirited. "Yeah, you're right." I hear a few comments about "my boy" from other troopers throughout the day.

They have been finding bodies lately. A shame that we get caught between the desire to hang on and have a recovery with honors, and the business of running a city and having to cut back workers. They have such strong passion and desire to bring home their lost brothers and our lost family members. They are cutting a couple of hundred firemen down to thirty-five. Maybe if they had not been finding bodies I could agree. . . .

A woman arrives who is not on the list for the front or back check-ins. NOVA points her out to me and explains that she was very insistent that she was invited here by the attorney general's office and was insisting that she was going to stay. She is having lunch. I let them know I'll handle it for them and go upstairs to ask the AG's office if they have invited anyone. So much for meetings where we agree that we will work *with* one another and give a heads up. . . . I find Sam, who doesn't know and pretty much dismisses it. Jake from the AG's office knows nothing about anyone being invited. I explain to him that she insists that the invitation is from his office. "Maybe one of the local offices"—and he explains a bit of their organization so I have some reference. "Check her out some more, and if she doesn't sound right, have her thrown out if you want."

I return downstairs to see if her story jibes with the possibilities that Jake gives me. She tells me: "Three people from the administration called me to tell me it was okay to come." She can't explain who, but her story about where she works matches Jake's description of their system. She explains that she is coming separately from her office; they are going over with the police to increase their understanding of how to work with families. She appears to have no strange motives, so I apologize to her if it seemed as if any of us were giving her a hard time—security, you know—and give her a blue "official" sticker and information about orientation times. She calms greatly and asks if she can sit on one of the buses to read a book until orientation time. "Don't see why not, as long as the bus driver is okay with it. Do you have a watch or should we come and get you?" She had a watch and turned up for orientation on time.

I have three staff no-shows, so we scramble for more volunteers. Then for extras, because we have many people signed up today. High numbers of families with not too many people in the family causes a need for more volunteers: we need to take two companions for each family in case someone wants to turn around.

My mystery lady from this morning comes up to me, upset. Sam approached her as she sat on the bus reading and she claims he said, "This is not the bus to Newark." Yeah, he is really polite and knows how to talk to people. She is a very well-dressed, well-groomed, intelligent and obviously well-mannered black woman. I am confident that he was trying to be lighthearted with her to find out why she was there. But . . . she is very offended, and is asking where she can lodge a complaint. I tell her that his supervisors are upstairs, as well as a rep from the AG's office. I offer to take her up.

She says, "You know, these guys generally stick up for one another. I think I'll wait and file an official complaint when I get back to work."

There are no state police in New York anymore and we feel vulnerable with the public staring and snapping photos and crowding toward us on the sidewalks. Some volunteers bring it up in orientation for discussion. I joked that I'm going to count to three; and on three we should all hold up a middle finger to spoil their pictures. Our troopers are busy running down people with cameras and taking the film. Some respond with understanding when we ask them not to take pictures of the families. Some could care less. Some get downright obnoxious. Everyone reacts to horrific events differently—to some people it seems to end up being like a movie—unreal. I think they mean no harm when they crowd in with cameras. I think they have just lost track of it being *real*. Personal. Someone's *family*.

The Major brings his family with him today. Happy, smiling, and proud Grandpa—his son's little newborn baby sits bouncing on the Mrs. Major's lap. A good-looking and sweet family. They look happy and peaceful together in the lunch tent.

The Major and I go way inside of Ground Zero. A fire pit is belching smoke—orange and nasty. Someone tells me that the orange color in the smoke indicates that it is steel burning, which means an excess of 2,000 degrees. They spray water through fire hoses and dig at the same time, and because the wind blows the other way it is bearable. Little golf carts full of various sports figures are running around. Guided tours. Their names are pointed out to me, but because I don't recognize their names, I haven't got a clue. A cart stops near us, and in it there are three very black-haired guys—Goth-looking—big guys like wrestlers, dressed in black leather. The Major looks at me with "WWF in town?" Police are running everywhere.

Once we return again to the terminal building, my mystery lady again approaches me. Her hands are shaking and she has tears in her eyes. Oh Lord, what now? She tells me that one of my mental health companions has mouthed off at her in front of a family and she is horribly embarrassed. I apologize for everything that we have done to make her day so hard and ask her to please tell me the details and point out the person so I can be sure it never happens again. I ask if she wants an apology and she responds that she just wants the person to be dealt with. No problem.

Apparently the lady had taken out her book on the way back from the marina and was reading on the bus. She did so because she wanted to cry and didn't want to cry in public, but wanted to wait until she got home. She was reading as a distraction. I can relate. . . . We had her going as an "official," as we do with all "organizational" types of people who are there to observe and not to mourn, so she didn't have a companion. No one to talk to about how she felt, so she did what she could to care for herself. I assure her that I will deal with our companion, and let her know that she can feel free to also lodge a complaint in our mental health trailer because she seemed to need to ventilate some more. She decided that was a good idea and headed off.

I catch up to the companion in the parking lot, getting into her car, and ask if she can wait and speak to me. She tells me her version of what happened: an absolutely more horrific story about what she said to the woman. I explain to her that confrontation of someone's behavior here is not appropriate, that the woman was a guest and was offended by being confronted out loud in public that way, in front of a whole bus full of families. She didn't care, and was firm that reading books on the bus should not be allowed. Scary. She doesn't get the fact that anyone who travels with us should have the freedom to pretty much act out in any way they want. Besides, I can't think of a time when *public* confrontation of someone is therapeutic. This companion thinks reading was an inappropriate activity. If it were porno, maybe, *but*. . . in the scheme of things, coping by reading is not the worst infraction I can think of. It didn't warrant public attack. I explain to her that we will not be able to have her back as a volunteer if she can't practice acceptance.

"If you are going to condone inappropriate and outrageous behavior like that then I think I *shouldn't come back.*"

Yup. I agreed with her. I head for the mental health trailer to talk to the person in charge there about the incident—"She did *what?*" Our girl is now banned from volunteer service in the trailer as well.

NOVA Ed is fretting about the control issues and some renewed clinging behavior in his newly arrived replacement team. Here we go again . . . full moon? I need to race home for a hockey game. I promised my husband I would make it. We do make it to the game—late, but there.

God, I'm tired.

November 2

I can't wait to get with Bob because first, we won the hockey game last night, and he loves to talk hockey the day after. Second, I want to tell him about yesterday before someone else does. At least he will hear about it from me. After all the trust he has placed in me, I would hate for him to hear from the state police or elsewhere that someone was reported or got in trouble. He doesn't seem concerned after we talk, and is happy that the companion incident was resolved; at least he is satisfied that my part was handled.

During orientation we again have to stress staying away from families and not smothering or getting too close. I can't relate to why companions would treat these poor people that way. Would they want a stranger hovering at them if they were in this situation? Crazy to have to tell grown people this.

After family orientation a young widow comes up to me with a special request:

"I have something to leave that is really inappropriate, but it is really important to me." She stands with their husband's sister who has a shit-eating grin on her face. *Oh God,* what could this one be????? I'm afraid to ask. . . . I wait. She is visibly pregnant.

"Maybe if I just tell you the story you'll understand. Every night when he came home he would say, 'Hey, babe, get me a beer' so I brought his favorite kind." She pulls a can of beer from her pocket and holds it up. The sister-in-law pulls a can of beer from her pocket and grins even wider.

"The baby is always giving him half-eaten cookies (she pulls a chewed Oreo out of the same pocket), and I have a juice pack from our son, and a dog biscuit from Jake (the dog). *Please* can I just leave it? I know it's inappropriate. You can take it away. Just let me put it down over there, and turn around—then you can take it and throw it in the trash. It's just important for me to *leave* this for him."

I want to cry. "You can do anything you want. I don't think it's inappropriate at all." Jesus, it's the sweetest thing I ever heard. How can that much love ever be inappropriate? "Honey, you do what you need to do. And I'll make sure no one bothers you."

"He was a real character," she says. His sister is laughing, nodding in agreement.

"I'll bet he was."

She has a devilish smile—quite a character herself, I'll bet. I couldn't do it—be strong and smiling and have a sense of humor if I were facing what she was. I admire this lady—so full of courage and love.

In New York, the state police are back because Battery Park access is even greater. Our pathway has been shrunk even more. Cameras are everywhere aimed at our tearful families.

One companion, Lauren, tells me she has a request—she wants to hug a fireman. She isn't assigned to a family today and is one of our free floaters. She asks me as a favor—"I know that you can go in there and I know that you get to talk to them and give them hugs. Can I hug just one?" There's something about her I have always liked, and agree to go and find her a fireman, but I spy one coming, and motion to her. She runs over and waits as he approaches. I step back and watch: vicarious hugs are good too. She stands and chats with him for a long time. Along come four more big dirty ones clomping right by her. She never looks up, she is so intent on their conversation. I'll have to talk to my girl about quantity! I try to signal her but she is lost in conversation with the first one. She returns, is thrilled, and hugs me with thanks. I tell her it was my pleasure to share my addiction with her. When I ask if she saw the others stomping by she looks amazed. "No. You mean I could have had four more?" Gotta keep your eyes open!!

We have a Hispanic family that sings beautifully in Spanish and prays by the wall. What an amazing sound in such a crazy place. I leave one flower at the feet of the dollar teddy, who still wears his dollar in spite of the area having free public access; and place one through the fence for Rich at the Penn State hat, hanging still. I had promised

Rich that I would leave flowers for his "favorite" family by the Penn State hat when he can't be here: a blue and white one—the Penn State colors. They lost a young man who was a Penn Stater, as was Rich. Through apparently not so random or coincidental selection, Rich ended up being their companion. They hit it off immediately and he had much to share with them about Penn State, which comforted them so greatly. I miss his smiling face being here, so I leave a flower for him as well. Maybe at home in his office he senses it?

A sadness grows in me as I realize that the visits are coming to a close soon. But I know that even if it went on forever, it would do so without me. I can't go on much longer anyway. Here I feel useful, purposeful, competent, appreciated.

But it's killing me.

I enter the administrative trailer to stash my hard hat and check on incoming fax confirmations. I find our consultant curled up in Bob's comfy chair. She is reading a magazine and munching on his Slim Jims. Must be suicidal as well as not too bright. I grin at her: "You're brave, sitting in Bob's chair."

"What do you mean?"

"He doesn't let just anybody sit there." She laughs. But I know that *she* knows that I'm giving her a warning, not kidding. "You're eating his Slim Jims too. Got a death wish?"

"He won't care." Ha—if it were me, no. Her? He will care all right.

The trailer door opens and she makes a mad dash out of the chair trying to hide a half-eaten Slim Jim, dropping her magazine, looking really conspicuous and guilty. It wasn't Bob. I can't hide my laughter—I bust up. It's only Jack, who looks at me and whispers, "What's up with her?"

"Too much caffeine."

November 3

Fred and I come as a family unit again today.

EMT Sharon has brought cards from her little grandson's school. The school has kindergarten through sixth grade. He told all of the other kids in his class what she does at the FAC, and they have decided that we need cheering up. This class of first graders has also decided to raise money for the World Trade Center victims. They raised $4,000. Amazing. First graders! The cards are also amazing. There are also cards from other grades, but it's the little ones that rip your heart out. Everyone who picks a card from the pile cries. Everyone. I'm passing them out, staff are holding me and crying—they show me their cards and I cry with them. This is nuts—everyone crying all over the place all morning as we share cards with one another. Feels damn good, though!

One Red Cross worker named Jenny picks a card from the pile and it is from a girl named Jenny. She absolutely melts. Gives me chills.

One of the Red Cross nurses chooses one made by a first grader. He has made a huge yellow blob that is the sun, with a tiny cross on the bottom corner. Inside it reads "Don't worry the sun will be bright tomorrow." She has to sit down after reading it. I meet a group of troopers and let them pick from the pile. They all start to tear up at once. As I hand one to Blaze he simply turns around and looks down at his feet. "You okay?" A very shaky "yeah" comes back and he wipes his eyes. Big softies, all of them.

Sergeant Barry is particularly touched by the cards and asks if he can type the thank-you note to the school. I tell him "Sure. Let me take you back to the trailer and set you up on a computer." About thirty minutes later, I go back to the trailer to collect things for orientation. He is still at it and has only typed about a half a paragraph. He is typing with one finger, *very* slowly. Chewing on an unlit cigar.

"Barry, can you type?"

"Not at all."

"Oh man, when you asked if you could do this, I thought you could type. Do you want me to get someone to give you a little help?"

"No. I'll figure it out." This is really important to him. He is now chewing his lip as he pecks slowly at the keys.

"Better take your hat off, love. I think your brain might be smoking from all that work!" He laughs and takes his hat off. I let him know where I'll be if he needs help with the printer.

About a half hour later, the Major comes up to me and says, "I read that letter that Barry's working on. Do you think he'll be offended if I send one of my girls over to help him? He needs help; he isn't doing well."

"No, I don't think he'll be offended. I fear he'll be there all night if we don't help him. Just tell her to be gentle. This is really important to him."

A few minutes later Sergeant Barry comes up to me, all smiles, with his finished letter—a touching, sweet response to the little boy's class from the perspective of someone who goes with the families each day. He tells them a story about being on the ferry, in gentle, plain language. The Major has his staff run around with the letter to collect signatures from the boat people in attendance that day. We write another thank-you letter for the whole school as well and circulate it for signatures from the other FAC staff. EMT Sharon takes the letters in an envelope to deliver to her grandson's school.

Tiny people have moved so many of us with such simple words, such simple drawings. Why is it so hard to hear sweet, simple words from babes in this place? Is it the ugliness and evil that burns across the river, or is it the wounded baby inside of all of us that now cries? The biggest, baddest, and bravest are reduced to blubbering mush by a first grader with a crayon—what a weapon! We stand among grieving families, looking at burned and broken buildings and we can keep our composure, yet we cry and hold each other over the simple words of a child. What a world . . .

Our families today are amazingly healthy—no one having any health issues at all. This has never happened.

The mix of people in our group is odd: some are angry and snapping, and behaving very contrarily—not keeping their hats on, trying to walk away from the group. I don't for a minute begrudge them the right to be as nasty and angry as they want. I would be as proud to be their whipping post as I am to be a shoulder to cry on, or a warm body to insulate. When they stray from the group it becomes hard to shield them from pictures. Even though they're grown adults, I can't help but fret over my flock being wide apart. Once in Battery Park we become spread apart more than I would like to see, because pedestrians are now walking into our group.

Still the fires are burning with that sickly orange smoke. Orange and yellow. Unearthly color. This time the fires are at Tower Two, which is almost gone. Bob tells me that the toxins in the air are reported to be heavy now. I have noticed that the day after there is particularly heavy smoke my nose bleeds in the morning.

I stand next to NOVA Ed on the platform. We are leaning on each other. So many times I have come to the realization that I am next to someone and we are leaning on each other. Without thinking of it— unconscious snuggling against the pain. And not once have any of us been startled out of leaning, or surprised. It appears to be a perfectly normal behavior that is simply accepted. Try that in an elevator— even with someone whom you know. . . .

Many stories up, a paper flutters on the wind. Someone's life is floating on the breeze. A memo, a letter, a payment receipt—what? The breeze carries the paper up and over toward the huge crane—up higher. And the birds fly in their great circle. So many people. . . . So many. My heart hurts. The tears in my eyes are scalding me and I can't swallow. Still higher the paper flutters, suspended in this surreal place that I keep wishing was a bad dream. Ed says in my ear, in his slow Midwestern drawl, "Is that a phone booth?"

He has yanked me out of my paper-watching trance. "What?"

"Look there, see the sun shining on it? Is that a phone booth?"

They have uncovered a phone booth. Seemingly intact. The great golden ball is very visible now. Fractured on one side. I have heard that an airline seat is imbedded in it. It looks like a cracked egg, and for a crazy moment the Humpty Dumpty rhyme flashes through my brain. "I think you're right. I think it's a phone booth."

He answers with "It doesn't get any easier, but it isn't harder." I just look at him, and we continue to lean on each other. No, my friend, never easier, just different. I look back skyward and have lost the trail of my paper. Perhaps it has found a place to land. Rest in peace. . . .

I know that the shock and sensory overload causes this place to seem very quiet when first visited. So much hits the eyes and the emotions that the ears shut down so the brain can process; it's a protective mechanism. After a couple of times the brain allows the ears to also take in the noise, which is deafeningly loud. The heavy equipment, the motors . . . I have almost turned around and walked into tractor trailers moving inside the damage zone, because I didn't hear or feel them moving right next to me, within inches. And I think about how strange it is; the sounds of this place are so overwhelmingly loud that you must scream in the ear of the person next to you. Yet if a family member sniffles or whimpers fifty feet away, you would have no trouble hearing it.

Today there is a hush—a quiet so deep I wonder if my ears are working. Like deep snow and no traffic. Like September 12. Ungodly quiet. I wonder what has caused my ears to shut down—what is overloading me today? It's never easier, just different. . . .

Some of the families are very tearful, crying hard and openly—like in the beginning when we were all very raw and hurting. Some are laughing and interactive, wanting to talk and joke. So many different stages of grieving now. . . . And at the Wall of Remembrance there continues to be arranging of teddies and notes: headstones being painstakingly constructed and made just so. The arranging has taken on a frantic quality. They are asking for assistance to complete their elaborate offerings. I have been climbing into flower beds five feet off the ground, helping to tape or tie teddies to the fence with rubber bands, place little flags where directed, and position and reposition for them, until everything is just right. I have been sucked right into the obsessions . . . and I am feeling frantic myself. I watch as Jack has also become more and more involved with helping to arrange as the families realize that their time here is short (perhaps in more than one way!) and they have a strong desire to be sure that a mark is left for their lost loved one. What must it be like to never have a body? To try to bury someone who isn't there? It's no wonder the families are becoming so frantic in their arrangements: it has been so long without having their person found.

Today I am in a flower bed almost upside down, positioning rocks that a family had brought from home to help spell out an "I Love You" headstone. It makes me sad to think that their mark here will be simply lifted up and thrown away someday soon, as life returns full force to Battery Park. . . . The families linger; they walk away and return. Frantic. Fussy. Troubled and frantic.

Again I leave a flower for Rich's Penn State family, a flower for those working, a flower for those lost, and a flower for our dollar teddy. Still sporting his dollar proudly in the wind, in the front for all to see and take. And he has been in public for a long time now. They have not robbed him. I pray that he goes to his dumpster with his dollar intact. He has renewed my faith in humans. The cans of beer still sit as well, along with the dog biscuit from Jake. Unopened. Untouched.

Today, as we are leaving the platform, I see a fireman across the street, alone and sad-looking, dirty in his helmet and heavy coat. His face shield is down over his face. He stands with his hands folded in front of him, and simply watches us with his head very slightly bowed. He looks almost like he is praying. But he is obviously watching. We are behind the barricade along the sidewalk in a long line, and we can't get into the street from that spot. They have stopped us from leaving for a moment to let vehicles through. Because we bring up the rear, Bob, Major Barb, Jack, and I have been stopped halfway to the gate. Out of the corner of my eye, I see an armload of white flowers move in my direction. Major Barb is in front of me, and is obviously reading my mind. I pluck one, and motion to him.

"Come here, love—have a flower." He smiles the biggest smile and begins to take a couple of steps toward us, but he is moving very slowly, as if he is hesitating.

From behind me I hear a voice: "He was waiting here for you."

"Were you waiting for me?"

He smiles wider and shrugs. "Maybe."

"Well then, come *over* here and let me give you a big hug!"

He laughs out loud, opens his arms as he walks, and wraps them around me, rocking me back and forth. "Thanks so much!" These guys give the best hugs.

Karl, our Methodist minister, is at the end of his two-week rotation. As is our custom, we have the clergy who are leaving give the prayer on the platform. He writes a beautiful one for us:

> To this sacred place I come, drawn by the eternal ties that
> bind my soul to yours.
> Death has separated us.
> You are no longer by my side to share the beauty of the
> passing moment.
> I cannot look to you to lighten my burdens.

And yet, what you mean to me neither withers or fades.
For a time we touched hearts and hands;
Still your voice abides within me.
You are part of me forever.
Something of you has become a deathless song upon my
    lips.
I hold you still in mind, and give thanks for love and life.
You continue to bless my days.
I will always give thanks for you.

Thank you, Karl. We talk together about how leading the prayer today at Ground Zero brought him some closure and gave him the beginnings of termination. I am really glad. I hope I can figure out a way to wrap this up—find a termination ritual. Changed forever and don't even know how. How do I decide to just walk back into life?

Fred and I take NOVA Ed to Newark airport for his flight home. Ed is a quiet, sweet, gentle guy with a deep, soft voice and a great laugh. You can tell as soon as you meet him that he's the kind of guy who would give the shirt off his back. He gives me a long hug goodbye. I don't want to let him go. It feels sad. "I'm changed forever," he says.
    "We all are."
    We all are. But changed into what? Going home one at a time. Wounded warriors or simply compassionate spirits who have fulfilled our missions?

After dropping Ed off and returning to the FAC, Fred and I chat with troopers for a few precious minutes outside. We discover Blaze is from our old neighborhood, same high school even. Sergeant Barry also has some people in common with me. Tom was related to childhood friends. What or who put together this circle that brings us all here? What events in our birth, our childhood, marked us for members in this circle? Suddenly the coincidences are too close. We've all been on the fringes of one another for years. I've heard of six degrees of separation, but this is too much!
    "Hey, you went to the same high school?" Tom asks Blaze and me. "What year did you graduate?" he asks me.

"Seventy-three."

He looks at Blaze and asks him the same question.

I hold my ears. "Oh God, don't answer that!" I realize that this large guy with the big neck and the gun could be my child . . . and I don't want to have that confirmed out loud. I could be his mom all right, with room to go! *Ouch.*

No one is around, it's late, so the troopers gather to watch the football game on the big screen TV in the dayroom. Blaze talks about how he generally likes to yell at the TV when his teams are playing. "But today I'm being solemn." Everyone cracks up. He's being serious. Sergeant Barry gives me his hat. I kiss the top of his head. It is now my most prized possession. Barry is definitely one of my favorite Staties. He is tall, wiry, and has deep blue eyes that crinkle in a great way when he smiles. He is funny, and is always quick to tease and joke. He is also deeply moved by so much here, and I catch him sometimes with tears filling his eyes. He speaks so lovingly of his kids and family. Barry is one of those people who is simply hilarious and really doesn't know it.

November 6

A day for arranging and unarranging. President Bush is going to visit the World Trade Center complex, so all day we have conflicting orders: cancel the weekend, never mind—we're on again. No, cancel. . . . I plod along arranging, canceling, arranging, canceling . . .

Bob loads me into a golf cart that typically lives in the breezeway of the terminal, and takes me for a ride to take some pictures of the Statue of Liberty's butt, which is really the only angle that New Jerseyians can see. I remember the NOVA woman from Florida who asked me about the Lady when we were on the bus. Never did ask her if she found the statue. . . .

Bob takes me on a tour of the island gift shops, introduces me to the director of the Science Center. A fun diversion. Chilly, but relaxing and nice after all of that scheduling/rescheduling stuff.

After returning from our field trip, I find a stuffed puppy on my desk wearing a nautical dress and a captain's hat. Bob says, "It's Captain Kathi." So sweet. I hug her close and thank him. He tells me about getting it from the Baptist child care people, Bill and Betty.

They hid it for him so I wouldn't see it. Another treasure. . . . I take her home immediately. I'm afraid she might wander away.

November 7

Trooper Sam has apparently told NOVA how many people we should have on the boat. They complain to me because they are short staffed and can't do what he says and they are upset that he is "barking orders" at them (their words). I take him aside and confront him. Why do we have to act out our personal burnout by manipulating one another? He acts as if the issue is not his fault and everything is resolved—no problem. He tells me sweet-faced that he never said *anything* to anyone about scheduling—they are making up stories. Behind my back he bad-mouths me all over again. We have been here too long. . . .

Major Barb brings in poems—one about where God was on 9/11. I read them, then sit and cry as morning meeting begins. Must be a record; usually I don't cry until the first orientation. Our Methodist minister says Mychal's Prayer and a blessing for our journey in Major Fred's absence.

Today we have about 115 Port Authority survivors and only nine family members. I meet with the small group of families alone for orientation. We discuss the fact that they will be with a group that has very different needs from the needs of family members. We talk about their fears of being a small amount of families in a sea of others. I assure them that we will move them first and be sure that they get what they need. They seem okay with that. They do well.

Blaze is our interference runner today—blasting ahead in his patrol car to stop traffic at the intersections. He's doing his best movie stunt driving—the guy is good! Sam and Jake are talking on the bus about how good he is to work with, how talented he is. I tell him later about how they remarked about his great driving and his good work. "Your momma didn't call you Blaze for nothing, did she?" He gives me a wicked grin and a chuckle.

Lately the burning smell has been strong. My nose still bleeds on the mornings after the stronger-smelling days. I've also noticed that one of our EMTs, who has asthma, uses her inhaler almost every day as we are leaving. The air really makes it hard for her to breathe. Makes me wonder . . . Today it is worse than it has been in a long time. That yellow/orange smoke of burning metal rises from another new spot. A crane drops its scoop and as it rises, flames shoot up. Some of the people on the platform gasp.

After so long, it still burns.

While the group is slowly going up to the platform, I see two firemen by their truck. I wander over and say hello. They give me a hug and I put flowers in their pockets, asking them about how long they have been there. I hear a voice from inside the truck say, "Hey, I know you." I look inside the truck, where I see their fire chief. I don't know him and tell him that. He looks at me with a smile and says, "I know *you*."

"I don't think so . . ."

"Yes, I do. Your flowers have been decorating my men all over this pile since the beginning. I recognize those flowers. We *all* know you."

I don't know what to say, so I stand and look stupid with my mouth open. He comes out of the truck and shakes my hand. "Thank you for doing that. You brought smiles to a lot of faces. The guys like that. Thank you."

I cry. I put a flower in his pocket. He hugs me. I now have the answer to my wondering about whatever became of the flowers I stuffed in those dirty pockets.

I have continued to use the cards from children for "payment" for the ferry volunteers. We get so many cards from children all over the country, all over the world. Each time I open a new box of them, I write a thank-you note to the school. Staff choose a card from the stack before orientation each morning as their reward for going. "Pick a card, any card—try your luck!" Today I bring a bag full of cards to New York for our corrections guys: the SOGs. They smile and get all choked up and tuck their cards in their pockets.

One of our EMTs brings me a defibrillator hat. Another prized possession. *So* many treasures . . .

I linger behind the group all along the way—to take photos of the ferry visits for posterity. I have promised Bob the double prints set. I snap a few of the arrangements at the Wall of Remembrance as well—

the ones that I know have been left by our families. The volume of teddies, flowers, and mementos is astounding. There are bushes under it all, but the green is no longer visible. The families have begun to use the granite wall that runs toward Liberty Street, and it is also rapidly filling. So many people . . .

During debriefing I try to focus staff on the good things that they have seen and experienced. We share the horrors that bind us together like some strange family. It is easy to find the horror. But the beauty binds us as well, as intimate as if we have known one another forever, but we are strangers. And will remain that way.

Before leaving, Blaze checks in with me—"Be here on Friday?"

"Always." He grins and walks off. Rabbi Ron gives me my weekly hug, overcome with the blessings of it all.

We truly are all becoming compassion vampires.

Together we huddle for a late discussion as we watch the sun set, and their talk turns to the "puffing up" habits of troopers. I am quiet, but listening to a group of mostly new people who are trying to process this place and the people in it. They have fresh eyes.

"How can they start out at five feet four and grow to seven feet tall just to intimidate someone?"

"How about the way they grow to 400 pounds and look down on those people saying 'S'cuse me, but you're going to have to leave this group, sir'!"

"How do they *do* that?"

"They must have puffing up lessons in trooper school."

"They all do it. They actually grow before your very eyes."

"And they get this voice that is almost like a horror movie."

My brain wanders during their chatter and I marvel at the way these new people are seeing with their new eyes. I can't help but smile at them—they remind me of how I felt way back. . . . My eyes are old. My eyes have adjusted to the ever-changing appearance of that place, but the history of the first sight remains with me so strongly. A tattoo on my brain.

So many changes . . .

Piles of debris were ten stories high, and then five, and now streets are emerging from underneath.

Sad shell-shocked workers everywhere. Now few are visible—only the construction workers way inside.

Heavy smoke was rising everywhere, now fires are visible but in spots.

A phone booth appears and is removed.

The gold sphere was uncovered, removed, and the area cleared.

Tower Two ribbing has given way to digging in the subfloors—a hole.

Fencing that was once empty is filled with the remembrances left by our families. So many. Oh God, so many.

The National Guard at full salute gave way to the general public taking pictures.

Birds are moving back into the area. People are walking through.

So much has changed . . .

I wish the new ones could see for just a minute with my old eyes. Will it be burned forever in my mind or will it be lost in this ever-changing scenery?

During one of our talks, Rabbi Ron said that each time visited it becomes a deeper wound. I want it to be the opposite—that with each visit the light grows brighter, the evil smaller. My heart bleeds over this. My soul bleeds. How can it go any deeper? I pray that he is wrong.

November 8

I wear Sergeant Barry's hat. Immediately State Trooper Sam jumps on it, attitude overflowing all over.

"Where'd you get the hat?"

"I'll never tell."

"Really, where'd you get the hat?"

"I never kiss and tell."

"Come on, tell me where you got it!" He obviously wants to make a case of it.

"From the backseat of your car." He makes a face. Right. Like I'm going to tell him so he can yell at the guy and cause a fuss.

A few minutes later, Bob comes up to me laughing. Sam had just grilled him about the hat. "Where'd she get the hat?"

"Ask her."

"I did; she won't tell me."

"Then I guess she doesn't want you to know."

I'm enjoying the torture. Evil and sadistic. He's dying to know so he can run and make trouble, and I'm not going to give him the chance.

At lunch I get motioned over by one of the sergeants: "Who gave you that hat? It's regulation issue. Must have been an officer."

"It was."

"Did he tell you that it was part of our official uniform?" I nod.

"Did he tell you that we would get in big trouble if our superiors came in here and saw you wearing that hat?"

I shake my head no.

"You really didn't know that part?"

"No. I'll take it off."

"Hey, you can wear it anywhere else, but not here where we could get busted for it." I take it off and put it in my car.

Bob says, "Where's your hat?"

I tell him the story about getting them in trouble. "Bullshit. They just get off on yanking your chain. Sam didn't want you to have it, so they teamed up on you. Go ahead and wear it." No. Better to keep the peace. Game over. Point to the blue team.

Bob and I get into the electric golf cart and head toward Ellis Island. Our typical front gate guy, Anthony, is at the back today, holding down the checkpoint at the walkway to Ellis Island, keeping foot traffic away from us. The wind is so cold it cuts through to my bones.

EMT Sharon took our letters to her grandson's school. They read them in front of all the children at an assembly. So nice. I hope that hearing from us was as important to them as those little cards were for us.

November 9

Today we have another Port Authority survivor's group: this one large and mouthy and nasty. They are in so much pain. We also have eight families, who will be lost in the crowd. Again I hold a tiny briefing for families to explain how we operate, and that we will surround them and insulate them from the large group so that they have a quality experience. We discuss the way in which the process of grieving for someone who was in one of the Towers and survives is different from grieving for families, and that being co-workers, they will behave just like any large group of co-workers who are out somewhere together. The families—as always—are understanding and great about it—expressing appreciation for the insight.

When we arrive at the platform, several of the Port Authority guys *run* to the railing and push an Asian family—who was there already—away in the process. The family becomes separated from one another. I separate the Port Authority people to get the family back together, and back in front. They aren't even one of our families, but to be treated with no manners . . . I apologize to them profusely, especially to the grandpa who was rudely shoved. He nods and does not speak. As we move our families to the front, one of our clingy-type companions pushes through to hover and stick to her family. *Again* the poor grandpa is shoved away from his family, this time by a companion. I grab her arm and pull her gently back from the railing, motioning for her to come with me. I talk to her about staying in the back so that the families and the victims can be in the front to see.

"But this is *my* family."

I say in her ear; "No—everyone here is your family. And they need private time. You almost knocked that poor guy over. Please stay to the back so that the families can be in the front to see."

We form a human chain to separate the Port Authority from the families to give them air. The Port Authority staff have all worked together for years, they know one another, they grab at one another, move forward and lean on one another, pushing to see better. Normal behavior for co-workers, not normal behavior for families. A Port Authority guy who is next to me is being very loud, talking and yelling to a couple of people over his shoulder about the fires and smells of burning people in the stairway. A family member hears and looks at him, startled, and chokes sobs. I quietly remind him that he is next to families. A second later he yells over his shoulder again, "Hey, remember all of the bodies we had to walk over? Bodies everywhere . . ." The rest of the family next to him now loses it as well, looking at him and sobbing. I touch his arm and say, "Please be a bit more quiet. The families are upset hearing that."

"I don't give a shit. You have a hell of a lot of nerve. Don't tell me what to do. You think they are the only ones hurting here? Fuck you and them too. I'll grieve any way I want. I have a right to say what I want and you can't stop me. Where do you get off telling *me* how to grieve? I'll express my grief any fucking way I want to."

I just look at him and let him go on. He finishes his speech, looks at me for a second with sad and angry eyes, but quiets down. I can see that other companions who are trying to maintain air space for the families all across the platform are being yelled at as well. Sad that administrators can't realize the differing needs of people, and allow the survivors to be only with survivors. They insist that we take families with them. If those in charge would listen, this man would have the right to grieve as loudly as he wanted. I try to explain clinical issues to these people. They don't get it. It is becoming a pissing contest—power knows best and will manipulate for their needs and wants. To hell with the reason we are there—the families. I try to look at it as God's way of making me leave without regrets.

A Red Cross volunteer talks to me on the ferry back about how she was amazed that I was able to explain everything to her in orientation—that she had no doubt about what she was supposed to do. Funny, because I say nothing but

> Stay away from them.
> Keep them from falling down.
> Don't hover.
> Treat them as you would want to be treated.

I really never tell anyone what to do. We just seem to be able to do it. I think God tells us what to do. I'm feeling like a brat, so I ask her: "What was the most helpful thing that I said to you?" She thinks for a second, and then frowns. She can't come up with anything, because I didn't tell her anything. She looks confused: "I'm not sure."

I laugh. "You know, I really didn't tell you anything, did I?"

"No. But how . . ."

I point up. "Not me."

"You think?"

"I *know*. I've been doing this for a while. Somebody a lot smarter than me is running this show."

She nods. "Thank you for being there, anyway."

"Welcome."

Upon returning, I am intercepted by several messages from people who have tried all day to help a family get onto the boat. For some reason the system is not working today. I take it up to NOVA. They promise to straighten it out. I check back periodically for two hours. They can't seem to pick up the phone and call these people. I call and book them myself, telling NOVA they will have to call them and let them know what to bring because I don't have the scripted information that they give to each family.

Holiday traffic tonight on the turnpike was crazy. I sat and sat. I rolled down my windows and talked to the guy in the next lane. He told me several great jokes that I have forgotten already. I stopped in every rest stop just for entertainment. They are out of World Trade Center postcards. The company has pulled them from the shelves. I find a few pins and key chains from New Jersey, which I purchase. At the New Brunswick rest stop, a lady from Florida is asking what's up with this traffic? They are telling her calmly that it's always this way on a holiday weekend. It takes me three hours to get home.

We are canceled for the boat going on the eleventh. President Bush is coming and they are redoing the platform—making it fancy for the president and the cable TV broadcast. I'm sure if he knew he was displacing families by this visit he would change his plans. . . .

November 12

At 9:15 this morning a plane crashes in Far Rockaway. Looking out the back door of the trailer we see the smoke billowing up in huge black plumes. CNN is reporting—showing footage. We leave the back door of the trailer open and watch the progress as the fires are put out. They are unsure about terrorism, and send our troopers all out to guard the bridges. We are briefly in lockdown. Since we have no troopers, we are forced to call the families, some en route, and cancel them. We reach them all in time.

After hanging around a bit and completing bookings for tomorrow we head out to the area of the island called Meditation Point to take photos of the Statue, visit the gift shops, nibble cheese crackers, and head home.

Fred has come with me again today. I am standing in the food tent, and Bill, the child care guy from Ohio comes up to me smiling and holding out his closed fist, offering something. I open my hand and he drops this thing in my hand that looks like a chestnut, but it's much, much smaller. "Know what that is?"

"No. Looks like a chestnut."

"Nope it's a buckeye. It's just a worthless nut—they're not good for anything." Just then, my husband Fred walks up. I put my arm around him and say to Bill, "No thanks, already got one." Bill cracks up. Fred looks confused because he didn't hear what we had been saying. Bill gives him one too, and explains the worthless nut thing again. "HEY—!"

November 13

Today the boat runs—back on schedule. By the description and photos on the news last night, it is quite a nice platform they have built for the president's ceremony. The Secretary General of the UN was in attendance and they dedicated a memorial wall on the platform.

We have a small group today, so we fill up with FAC staff who have not yet had a chance to go. We have many new faces in orientation. At the last minute, we realize that NOVA has forgotten to staff the center, so we have to pull some people back to cover for those who will arrive for other types of services while we are gone. The plane crash and seeing the black heavy smoke is still very much on people's minds and they are chattering about it. The world has changed so much. This is getting really hard to watch.

Today the group is lagging. *So* slow to move—apparently all in a stage of holding back. Getting them out of the building and into the buses is like pulling teeth. They go back; they walk in reverse. They go to their cars—anything but making the commitment to get on the bus. This would definitely be my behavior if it were me going to those buses. I think actually I would have to be dragged. They are very quiet as we walk. A solemn procession. The Major brings me stones for some reason, putting them into my pocket at the Wall of Remembrance. Again I am reminded of a drug deal, sneaking stones. And I think back again to my conversations with the Major about Joshua 4, bringing back stones for a memorial. I wonder if we can get enough for everybody on the last day. . . . Especially for my frequent flyers—my crew members who come a lot. Would they like a rock as a termination symbol? I have been thinking also about the rest of the story of Joshua; we also have all tribes represented: Red Cross, NOVA, Salvation Army. But we have eight of each . . .

We have received boxes of *really* nice teddies from a school. All of them have little construction paper hearts tied to their neck ribbons. On the hearts are written personalized notes, with the names and ages of the child who sent them. They are so sweet, and very cute teddies—all different. We snitch a couple and put them aside. I tell a couple of my frequent flyers crew to snitch themselves one for a souvenir. Some do. Martha has especially fallen in love with one stuffy—which is actually a lion. We didn't have many, but they were cute! I tell her we will check when we get back for a stray lion left in the back room. There are a couple, but as soon as I walk out of the door with one, someone says "What a cute lion—can I have it?" After about four tries, I go back for another, and have to hold it for dear life before passing it to Fred to deliver to her—everyone wants it!

"Quick—find Martha and give this to her, and don't let *anyone* else have him—he's the last one!"

My friend Jeanne has come with us today as a guest. She works with the mother of a victim in a state administrative office. Her co-worker is distraught over the loss of her daughter but is not seeking help. They are all concerned for her and would like to talk her into coming to the FAC. Jeanne is checking us out to report back to her workplace—to encourage the woman to come. She holds it together well, teary but strong. She tells me she is impressed with the sensitivity, the compassion, and the way that we work together so smoothly. I wonder sometimes: is it still as meaningful, as compassionate, as wonderful as it was at first? So much has changed; so much will continue to change. I hope that it remains fresh and giving for these families. Funny, has it become "common" to me? Have I been here so long that I am taking it for granted? I think that I am taking it for granted a bit. I think I have jaded, tired eyes. I give Jeanne the rocks that the Major had just slipped into my pocket, and she tears up.

The compassion vampire inside me wants this to go on forever. The person in me wants it to be over. Mostly, the vampire remains in charge.

I have been digging through the incoming boxes to keep my boat people in cards for payment. Sometimes they get drawings or flags made by children. I find an absolutely *beautiful* book made by a Cape May school. I take it around and show it off. At Bob's encouragement, I take it upstairs to the park service to ask them to keep it for archives. It deserves to be preserved. It should be seen and inspire awe in many people. I have been doing a stream of thank-you notes to the children's groups that send cards, pictures, and stuff. Some have been from Canada, Scotland, and all over the United States. Sweet babes.

Jake has been sick—he has a cold he can't shake and is grumpy and quiet lately. It is time for him to go home. He makes statements about cramming as many families on each boat as possible. Cram 'em on. I understand that we can't do this indefinitely, but we should at least do it well, with consideration for the humanness. You would think the AG's office is paying for the boats. The Salvation Army is paying the $2,000 per day fee, not them. Joan is designated as the person to be in the middle of the current squabbles to fix it. She is not a happy camper. They fight and argue and she gets ordered around. The more frazzled Joan gets, the more Bob laughs. She gives him the finger. He laughs harder.

On the way home we find the mother lode of World Trade Center pins at a rest stop. We buy them all.

November 14

Today is another Port Authority day. We also have all new teams from both Red Cross and NOVA in orientation, not a veteran among them. We have precious few family members again. With all new staff, it is difficult for them to conceive that the Port Authority does not want us to companion their staff—they simply want a ride over. It is a sad thing actually that they don't want them to have the benefit of human support in such a scary time . . . but . . .

Our families arrive. They are a tearful group. We encircle them, insulating them from the onslaught of the public in Battery Park and from the pushing and crowding of the Port Authority staff. Sergeant Tom is with us today, so it is easy to cooperate with one another for movement and seeing that the families are taken care of: moved first, getting the best spots, having space and air and support. The sarge keeps us wrapped tightly together, a perfect cocoon. Everything runs well when he is with us and it seems much more relaxed.

As we reach the platform we link arms and wrap around the families at the railing, forming a human chain to give them space. We generally try to give the families about three feet of open space around them. I turn my back toward the rail, and see one of the Port Authority survivors standing behind me, a man with long dreadlocks. He stands teary-eyed, quietly respectful, hurting so much inside because of what he had seen, and currently unable to see anything because we block his view. I reach for his arm and pull him to stand in front of me toward the railing, to a spot where there is a view. He no longer has to wait for a glimpse that he would not get. "Better?" He nods. I hold his arm as we stand close, and make him a part of our human chain. He wonders aloud to nobody about the fires that are still burning. He realizes that he spoke, and looks at me and asks so quietly: "It is really still burning? How hot is the fire, do you know?"

"Up to 2,000 degrees, they say. They tell us that the orange smoke is steel melting."

He is disoriented. Many of them who knew this area every day for *years* are disoriented and unable to figure out where they are, where their buildings were. He asks, like so many do: "Where was the Burger King?" I point to buildings and name them for him. Very slowly his face shows me that the pieces of what *should* be are forming in his mind. He nods, thanks me; tears run down his cheeks. "Look there; there is where my office was." He points skyward to show me where he worked in the Tower that no longer exists, then looks around.

"Oh God, look in that building. The computers are *still on*"—which is really half a question, the old—am I losing my mind or what? "Yes. Are you all right?" He wipes his eyes and nods. I rub his back.

I remember a man on the platform who told me that he worked in the World Trade Center complex for twenty years but once he was there with us could not remember which building was which.

I turn to monitor the crew. As I turn, a group of loud Port Authority people butt into our human chain, pulling in members of their little group and shoving a father backward into me and displacing him from his family about four deep. He looks pained, and then looks down. I offer to move them and get him back to his family. He sadly shakes his head and says, "No, let them look. It's okay."

"Are you sure?"

"Yeah." He lies, but is obviously a giving and considerate man. He continues to look longingly at his wife who is a few yards away. I want to make him a path and bring them together, but I allow him to have his compassion for the Port Authority staff. It's obvious that it isn't all right, but I let it be.

At the back of the group three Port Authority women are crying *hard*. Leaning on each other, crying, shaking, and hiding their faces. In much too much distress to be left alone with it. It is such a shame that their workplace can't see the pain they have, can't allow us to give them companions. Debriefing afterward back in the workplace is just not enough. Being who we are, we usually don't listen to the request to not be companions. We try to comfort them anyway. I go to them and ask what they need. I offer to have them walked to the boat or another area if it is too much. They want to stay. They worked there so long and have lost friends and co-workers. Too much to bear. They huddle and we wrap a bit around them as well—I send my tissue brigade to do some wiping and they comply nicely, forming a cocoon for them. One of the hardest criers approaches me and asks for a teddy. I explain that they were handed out to the families on the boat, and any extra that we might have are back on the boat. "Tell you what, see me at the terminal when we get back; I'll snag you one." That brings a smile to her pretty face. Pretty red-nosed leaking smile.

A few people arrive behind us. One is the Prime Minister of Israel who stands quietly and acts like just anybody off the street. Where is Rabbi Ron when this happens?

Jack whispers in my ear on the boat: "Hey, baby, that guy with the dreads that you were talking to wants a bear. What do you want me to do?"

"I'll take care of him."

There are only a couple of extra bears on the boat. As we are leaving the boat, I locate my guy and sneak a bear to him. He erupts in a *huge* grin and immediately wraps his arms around it and stuffs it into his coat. Apparently he was spotted by a co-worker. A loud female voice yells, "Hey, I thought the bears were for *family members only!*" in a really mocking tone. Apparently someone had told her she couldn't have one.

"But he's my brother!"—as I wrap my arms around him and give him a big hug.

He laughs out loud and says, loud enough for her to hear, "Don't worry about her; she's just one of those really rotten people who likes to make everybody around her miserable." I go to her and offer her a teddy. She laughs and says, "No, thanks. That was pretty funny, you know."

"Sure you don't want it?"

"I'm sure. Thanks. Just busting on you."

I locate my crying woman in the departing crowd. She looks much better now. Really a beauty. She is in a long line of people leaving the boat. I run forward and jump to the side so she has to pass me. I hand her the teddy as she goes by, and say to her, "Hey, do me a favor. Hold this for me for a second, will you?" She laughs and whispers, "Thank you so much." Hey, girlfriend, no sweat. A companion next to me laughs out loud, because she knows what I'm up to. My girl hugs her teddy tight, for dear life. I turn to go inside and begin the process of dragging out coolers, collecting equipment, and cleaning up.

Back at the terminal we have a couple of families that want extra teddy bears. We still have some with the messages from school kids, but are running so low that only about five are left. I hand out a couple and receive beautiful smiles in return. A guy comes up to me and says, "My girlfriend left her bear over there and now says she wishes that she didn't. Do you have any extra? She's in the bathroom, and I thought since I see you here, I'd ask for her."

"Sure. Wait right here for me so I can find you; I'll be back in two minutes." I go behind Mass Care to the storeroom and find that all of the message bears but one are gone. *Wow!!* I grab him up and start back out to deliver him to his new owner when I see the tag that was written by a well-meaning ten-year-old boy: I'M SO SORRY YOUR LIFE IS SUCH A MESS.

Oh crap. And it's the last one. The guy sees me walking and comes to intercept me. She just went outside for a smoke.

"I have good news and bad news. The good news is you got the last one of the really *nice* bears with the messages on them. The bad news is you may want to pull this message off his collar before you let her see it." He looks at the card and cracks up. He shows it to his friend and he cracks up. "No *way*. I think it's perfect. Her life *is* a mess. Trust me, she'll like it. It was meant for her."

"I'll trust your judgment." They wander off toward the door still laughing, tossing the bear in the air as they go.

Sergeant Tom is doing a PowerPoint presentation for the state police. He wants to know how my pictures came out. I promise to bring them in for him to choose from.

On the way home the local talk radio is doing a bit about New Jersey State Police behavior: call in if you ever had any dealings with them that were *good*. I can't wait to get in the house and dial the phone. I call in and tell them how wonderful the troopers are with the families. I describe how they even help us to carry people who can't walk, and how the families are always describing them as professional, polite, and wonderful to deal with. Couldn't resist.

Within ten more minutes, I'm off to join my husband—late—at a late night hockey game.

November 15

A fatal accident on the turnpike this morning has traffic stopped. I sit in front of the sign for exit 8 in the third lane for an hour. Stopped. *Ohhhh Lord.* It takes me one and a half more hours to get from exit 8 to 8A. Could have walked it faster. Maybe I should ditch the car and jog to work. . . . I'm in real trouble here. The news reports say three have died in the accident. So sad that they will not make it to their destinations this morning.

By the time I get to the accident area they are still sweeping up car parts. Pieces of car are everywhere. Bloody EMT intervention evidence is everywhere. They are loading car parts into a pickup truck bed. Splat. I am now three and a half hours later than I want to be. Unbelievable! I'm going to be late for orientation. I get out the cell phone and begin calling. I can't get through to anyone. *Unbelievable.* I am bordering on panic when I finally get through to Jack's message service. He calls me back and agrees to cover orientation for me.

I pull up to the tollbooth; my wonderful laughing, joking toll man, whom I *love* to see each day, looks at me and says sternly, "You are *really* late."

"Yeah, I know."

"I hope you have a good excuse."

"Accident at 8A. Sat there for *hours*."

"Glad you're okay. Want the paper?" He offers the morning news.

"Thanks, but I'm late—no time to read today. Have a great one, love." He waves.

I enter the gate checkpoint at the FAC. Ant'ny says: "You're really late."

"I know. Accident at 8A."

"No, you're *really* late. Do you know what time it is?"

"Yeah, I know, I know. It took me five hours to get here. Don't rub it in, okay?"

"Man, if yer gonna be *dat* late you shoulda stayed home. . . . Wanna doughnut?"

"No thanks; gotta get to work."

"'Bout time."

I run upstairs to check with the troopers to see if there is anything I need to know before going to catch the end of orientation. Sergeant Tom looks up, frowns at me, and asks, "You just getting here?" Jesus do they *all* have to rub it in?

"Yeah."

"Stuck at exit eight? You should have called—we would have sent somebody out to get you and ride you in."

"I never would have thought of that. That could have been fun!"

"Hey, any time. Call us, we'll get you here. Especially after last night." Which he says with a slow grin. Say what? Sounds almost dirty . . .

I must be obviously racking my brain, because I hear, "The radio. That was you on the radio last night wasn't it?"

"Oh, wow—you heard it? I forgot. I'm so frazzled I forgot all about that!"

"You should know that quite a few of the guys heard it. I got a few calls. It really means a lot to us. The guys were really touched by what you said."

"Well, Tom, it's true. You guys are absolutely the best. The families are always saying how respectful you are, how surprised they are about the way the guys behave and interact with them. The guys deserve a lot of praise. I try to tell them all the time when I hear compliments."

"Thank you. Really. It means a lot that you would do that for them. A couple of the guys wanted to thank you personally. I told them that would be okay, so don't be surprised if they say something to you."

"Thanks, Tom." I dash off downstairs and catch the tail end of orientation.

I have decided that today, since it is blown to hell anyway, is a day for taking pictures. I ask Sergeant Tom if he wants any specific pictures for his upcoming presentation. He wants some of his guys in action. I ride with my equipment team, who fold me up on the cooler in the back of the van and laugh as Jack drives like a crazed person to throw me off. We load the boxes of equipment and the snack coolers onto the boat, and have a few minutes to spare until the families arrive. I snap pictures of the troopers doing their thing—checking the boat for bombs. I try to line up the first shot. The trooper says, "Ready?" Yup—"Go ahead." My trooper turns around and bends over to look under the bus seat with his ass facing the camera just as I snap the picture. I didn't expect that. And I don't think he intended it that way; I was simply at the wrong angle. "Great buns, dude, but not really what I had in mind. I think the sarge wants a frontal view." He does it the other way around, grinning all the while.

There is a locked room on the ferry. A trooper asks one of the kids working on the boat to open the door for him. "No. I can't." The trooper patiently explains that they have to check the boat completely, and that we can't leave until all areas are checked. "No. I can't. I don't have the key."

"How about you go and get the key, then, so we can finish up."

"No. I can't."

"Why not?"

"The key is over there." The guy points to the marina trailer, across the parking lot where their office is located.

The trooper is running out of patience, and asks one more time for him to go to get the key. "Told you I can't."

"Okay pal"—as he reaches for his gun—"I got your key right here."

"No, no—I'll get it!" He takes off running to the trailer.

I run up front to the ferry captain's seat. "I have a favor to ask. My husband volunteers here sometimes, and he's always saying that he wants to drive the boat. Would you let me sit here like I'm driving the boat, and take my picture? I want to play a joke on him and tell him that you let *me* drive the boat." The captain laughs. "Of course. Sit." He shows me where to put my hands on the controls so it will look real, then steps back to snap a couple of photos. I can see out of the corner of my eye, as he fiddles with my camera that the boat is swinging sideways. I tell the captain, "The boat is moving."

"No, it's okay."

"No, really. I think the boat is moving." He is still fiddling with the camera.

"It's okay." One of the boat staff comes running up the steps. "Where's the boat going?"

The captain looks up and says, "The stick—move it right." I move it left. Ooops. He laughs, walks over, and calmly straightens the boat once again.

"I told you it was moving." Apparently, all the while it is at the dock, the ferry is not stopped. They actually leave it in gear so it is continually running forward into the dock. I had very slightly moved the stick so the boat was desperately trying to turn with the dock in its way.

Once again the captain steps back, laughing at me. "Now don't *move!*" and takes the picture. "You should have one from the dock as well. Stay there." He hands the camera to his staff who runs it down to Jack on the dock.

Jack can't figure out how the camera works. I'm yelling through the thick glass to try to help him, and he can't hear me. The captain hands me the loudspeaker. My voice goes *booming* across the dock, *"It's the little black button on the right."* He searches, turns the camera around and gives an exaggerated shrug. *"The right. The little black button on the right."* I swear they can hear me in New Brunswick. He takes the picture. The ferry staff run the camera back up to me and I take a great one of Jack, his arms spread wide. Just being Jack—hugging the world.

I am surprised to see national guardsmen back on the street, standing near the gate. The guard really hasn't been around much lately. There is one who has many stripes and a couple of others milling around. As we approach they stand still out of respect, but unlike the beginning, they do not salute or stand in formation. We have to wait about fifteen minutes in the street for Nelson Mandela to exit the area. He has come like so many others to use the new platform and view the ceremonial wall erected for the president's visit. I approach the one with the most stripes and explain to him that in the early days the guard used to salute the families, and that the families had always been so appreciative of that. "Do you think that you could get the guys to salute them on the way out?" He asks if I want them to salute now. "No—you know, that might look rehearsed or something. But if you'll still be here when we're done, and you don't mind, I know that the families will really appreciate that."

"Little lady, you've got it."

"Thank you *so* much." I put a flower in his pocket. He smiles.

As we exit the platform and step through the gate there is a *battalion* of National Guard in full formation, holding their guns at formal attention. *Tons* of them. They must have run around the whole city rounding them up. It's downright scary. All of a sudden the street is full of stiffly standing military in full formation on either side of our pathway, with guns held diagonally across their chests. They are absolutely beautiful, but almost a horror movie. It sets us all back a second.

As the first family member steps from the curb, the order *"Ten hut!"* barks through the air like a gunshot. We jump. They snap their guns to their sides and salute. A few of the guard have tears running down their faces. We walk through the formation, some of us turning around as we walk, looking in awe, mouths open. I feel like laughing out loud and skipping. The families are looking, smiling, whispering to each other. A companion says to me, "What did you say to that guy?" I shrug and act innocent. Another says, "I know you were behind this. How in the hell did you do it?" I laugh. At the very end of the formation is the guy in charge, in full salute with my flower still in his pocket. He looks directly at me as I stop in front of him. Although the families have all passed, he never lowers his arm. He is saluting me as well. Tears are running down my face.

He winks and gives me a devil's grin. "Well, how'd we do?"

"Beautifully. Thank you *so* much." I say as I hug him through tears. He breaks his salute to hug me back.

"Take care of them, little lady. And yourself." Oh God, I love these people. Families are going on and on about what an amazing sight that was, how uplifting it felt to have the military salute them. I wish for a moment the guardsmen could hear those words, see the emotion they created with that simple act.

The SOGs stay behind with me to take pictures at the Wall of Remembrance after our families clear the area. Trying to protect as always. I make small talk, which we don't usually get to do. I ask the one who is usually our lead escort, "You been working long days?"

"Sometimes sixteen or seventeen hours."

"Since the beginning too. You've been here on a long haul."

"Yeah. I get real tired sometimes. You too?"

I nod. "Beats a prison riot, though, I'll bet."

"Hell, yeah!"

A moment later, I offer to race him back to the group; he shakes his head.

"Come on!"

He laughs. "Homey don't run no mo'."

"*Awww,* come on, I need a good workout. Haven't had a good workout since I came here. You don't want me to get fat, do you?"

"Told ya. Homey ain't runnin'!"

On the way back in the van, Jack laughs as he tries even harder to dethrone me from my perch on the cooler. I am prepared, and hold on extra tight. Our troopers—running interference with traffic—are really in the mood to hot dog it and are putting on a show for the families. I hear when we get back that the families voiced appreciation for the light and siren show. The families have always said how much they appreciate that we stop traffic for them, give them a royal police escort. They get a kick out of the fuss and importance of it all. Anything for the families . . .

Today when I do debriefing it feels very special; we have a priest who has never gone with us before. He is a local guy, Hispanic with some limits on his English, but he is very chatty. Those limits make him just that much more profound. We talk of the best and the worst parts of the day. His best and worst are the same thing: seeing mortality. He talks of being reminded to live every day, every moment fully because there may not be any more. *Amen,* brother. I hope that is something I take with me from this experience—appreciation for each moment.

A companion speaks of beauty in people and compassion without limits. *Amen* again. I hope that the compassion vampire inside of me never dies. I hope it blooms in freedom.

This is such a precious privilege that 99.9 percent of the world will never know. This beauty, strength, compassion, and wisdom that I now witness each day of my existence. The land of extremes has but one level of wisdom—no opposite for that. Simply there. Ancient and unchangeable knowing of one another, and knowing what and how to do for others. I think I could die now and know that my destiny has been fulfilled. My reason for having the right to walk on this planet has been done. But—what next? If this is it, then what next? I am in awe of what I see and experience . . . and I am also very afraid of what will come . .

We engage in this futile effort called debriefing. But we do it anyway. At the end we have a different perspective. Not better, just different.

After debriefing we demonstrate how futile the effort is by all heading to the snacks. I reach for Oreos, my old friends, my drug of choice. Like one more Oreo could kill the pain. My new priest is next to me, reaching for cookies. Our eyes meet and he laughs as he says, "I guess we have to eat to make ourselves grow. That over there. So big. It makes us know how small we really are." *Amen.* I look at my Oreos and put them back. "Thank you again for your wisdom. And for putting words to what you see." He laughs, hugs me, and tears into his cookies. Bless these people. Please, God, let this stay with me forever.

November 16

As we arrive near the gate, a siren sounds. The siren blows when they have found bodies. Inside on the platform is a large group of Japanese firemen. We wait about fifteen minutes. Right after this group leaves, we shepherd the families up to the platform. Within seconds, Blaze approaches me. He has that look. I had heard the siren, and know that they will suspend work until families leave the area, so I fear the worst. I look at him over the rim of my sunglasses. All of a sudden he can't keep a straight face. "Now don't tell me to kiss your ass or anything. I'm not going to tell you we have to leave." I'm still looking. "You heard the siren?" I nod. "They have found five bodies. They will wait until we leave to begin to bring them out. When it's time to go today, it's really time to go. Okay?" I nod.

"Really. They have to blast to get the bodies out. They're trapped. They're setting the charges now. We have to move *fast* when it's time." I nod.

"No problem. If they get slow on us, I may ask you guys to come up and be authoritarian and loud." He nods.

The families notice a group of firemen gathering near one spot on the pile. A family member says, "Oh, look at all of those flags. Where are they going with all of those flags?" I silently pray that this person's companion is possessed with wisdom when he or she answers that question. Most people aren't aware of what the siren means. Most don't know that firemen carrying flags means that one more soul is coming home draped with honors. I hold my breath. I hear a loud voice:

"Hey, Kat, what do they do with all of those flags they're taking in there?"

Suddenly a large group of people on the platform is looking at me as if I'm possessed with wisdom and truth. They want me to answer for them. I blurt out, "They have flags everywhere; see them hanging on the equipment and the huts?" The families nod. They seem to accept that nonanswer for now. Was it wrong? Should I have told the truth?—that they *just found five more?* God, I hope You spoke through my mouth. . . . Another companion says loudly, "They use flags everywhere to boost morale." A couple of more families nod. They are very tearful today. Vulnerable. The companion who spoke last comes up to me and asks, "What *do* all those flags mean?"

"They carry one for each of the bodies that they will be taking out as soon as we leave. They drape the stretchers in American flags." He nods as he looks down at his feet. He says, "I thought so." And then looks back at me—"Is it right to lie?"

"I don't know. But it feels right at this moment. Do you think so?"

He nods. "I would want you to lie to me if I were here waiting for my wife."

I nod. "Me too."

At the end of our prayer the companions are stubborn about moving; the families always are understandably reluctant to go. They always want to linger, to look, suspended in their own space. Sometimes they get halfway to the stairs and return to have just one more look. Just one more glimpse—to connect, to absorb, to try to answer that question that has no answer: *Why?!* Sometimes I wonder if they even see anything. I don't think I would.

Our outside consultant is on grounds today, surfing the 'Net and talking on the phone. From her conversation I know that she is speaking to a newspaper reporter. I snottily point out to her that at 3:45 she should be worried about debriefing staff, since that's her job, not talking on the phone to a reporter. She wraps up her call quickly and runs to the terminal. I decide to skip debriefing. At 5:00, I go into the terminal on my way upstairs. A NOVA worker comes running up to me and grabs my arm, asking me to do another debriefing. "I swear to you I feel *worse* now. She did nothing but aggravate me. All she did was talk about herself and she doesn't even work here. I mean who is she, anyway? *Please.*" I agree to debrief them again. She scurries off to get some others who she claims were also upset during and after debriefing.

I keep thinking about a training workshop on spirituality that I once attended, where the trainer drew a representation of a spiral of life and death on the chalkboard. Our rehearsal for the ultimate death is to die and be reborn continually throughout our lives, through all of the little pains and losses.

I think I have died 100,000 times here.

I know I have been reborn here. And I have to really think about how to end this—how to make *over* be bearable—for others as well. I feel like I owe them something for their hard work—something to take the pain away. Judy and I talk a lot about leaving it behind. This is really going to hurt. A painful death.

November 17

A sweet father arrives, a smiling and warm older gent. He has lost Christopher, his son. Christopher's wife has the urn. He asks me if he can have one of his own. I run back to the trailer to see the deputy AGs on urn duty. They readily agree that he can have one. Who says lawyers suck? I retrieve the dad, walk him over. He fills out a form, is handed a flag and an urn. He asks me on the way back, "Is it always that easy? I heard that you can only have one per family."

"It is sometimes easier than others. I would have gotten something for you."

He laughs. "And I'll bet you've done it before."

I wink at him. "I'd never admit to it, but *just one more little rock* would never be missed." He gives me a hug and a smile. So little to make people so happy. . . .

A young woman is with us today who has a dying mom in a hospital in New York. She wants to stay there, not return with the group. We can't leave people; if you go with us—you stay with us. We bring her back and work out ground transportation back to New York for her. I supply her with a bunch of flowers for Mom, and a teddy. We chat until the transportation comes. She is appreciative of how we worked for her today.

I am again climbing frantically into flower beds to assist in the task of headstone building. We are taping and tying and arranging. I am hanging upside down and accidentally put a spot of tape over a portion of the person's face in the photo. *Ouch*—the worst. I apologize profusely and gently pull the tape back, holding my breath. The picture remains intact and unharmed. *Thank you, God.* I make a silent mental note to be *very, very* careful when taping. Being upside down hanging from a ledge is no excuse for taping a loved one's face.

A Buddhist family is arranging bundles of lit incense and fruit and candy with their teddies. Their incense is *dangerously* close to the teddies. I stand with Judy, watching. One of the New York policemen comes up to me and says, "That's a fire hazard. We can't let that stay."

"I know. We have our eye on it now. We were just talking about moving the incense as soon as they walk away." He nods and goes back to the corner. Suddenly a *huge,* thick chunk of wire falls at Jude's feet. We just look at each other—struck speechless. It came from nowhere, appearing to fall straight down, but there is no building here that is open to the weather. We both look up, like something is there. "Did you *see* that? It almost hit me." I just look at her.

"Where did it come from?"

"God?"

"Makes more sense than anything I can see. . . ." She picks it up and puts it in her pocket. Forced souvenir collecting.

I see another family struggling to arrange their items. I ask Judy to "Watch the flaming teddies; I'll be over there." She nods. I teeter on the edge of the wall, five feet up, helping to write and leave a note. The family directs and steers my actions on their behalf. I have someone's father's hand on my butt, holding me up so I don't fall, and I realize I would do anything for these people, anything for the families. Can I kiss it and make it better? *Can't I do something to make it better? What?!* People I don't know, never knew their names, never will see again. Will they remember us? Does any of this really help? But give me *just one more minute* here to help you fix this picture, these flags, this flower, this teddy.

Just one more . . .

A woman on the boat (one of the members of the family that I was helping at the Wall of Remembrance) remarks about a pin I have with the Towers and a flag. She wants to buy one. I take it from my jacket and pin it on her lapel. *"Oh no, no,* I didn't mean for you to do that."

"No. It's all right. I buy them at the turnpike rest stops. I can get another on the way home."

"At least let me pay you."

"No way. Just wear it in health."
She is the wife of one of the pilots.

During debriefing, as I ask them to describe their rocks, I am suddenly struck by an inspiration: a real need to have a good-bye party—a termination ceremony. I have to get enough rocks for my frequent flyers. To invite and assemble them as a special crew. I'll get Major Fred to give a sermon, a closing blessing. . . .

A young woman arrived this morning so fragile, so tearful, so weak from crying. She had not been eating and was supported by two friends. She didn't want us near her. She had not been out of her home since September 11. I asked the companions to give her space, respect her wishes—but watch her like a hawk. She held up like a trouper.

About five o'clock she approached me and told me that she really appreciated the fact that we didn't hover over her, fuss at her, or try to get her to talk. "I just didn't want anyone I didn't know to be close. But I noticed on the platform that all of you were there, just standing there behind me. I could feel your strength. I knew that you were there for me. I knew then that what you said in orientation was true; that if I couldn't walk for myself, you would pick me up and carry me. Have you done that? Carried people in because they didn't have the strength to do it alone?"

"Yes. Several times."

"Thank you so much for letting me do it my way. Having you all there was so comforting. It made me feel like I was wrapped in a big blanket. Thank you."

What a gift. . . .

November 18

We have many more families now. Many want to go and we have precious little time left to get them there. When New York opens the World Trade Center complex to the public in December, we can no longer have appointments; if they want to go they can take themselves is the philosophy in New York. Bob fights with the powers in charge about how we need to work on quality and remember who we are there for. Doesn't work. He is far better than I am at swallowing his anger, at tolerance and acceptance. I rant and rave and he lets me. I try to make the best of a bad thing, but I don't do it quietly.

Still they are uncovering bodies and we are hustled away quickly so that they can do their work. Tom Ridge waits in his limo for us to depart. They will remove bodies in front of Tom Ridge, never in front of families.

At the Wall of Remembrance the families begin their work and al-most immediately, our attorney Jake wants to leave. He sends one of his staff over to tell me that we should move the families. "If that were his momma hanging up his picture would he want me to rush her?"

"No. But he wants to go."

"Then let him tell these people that they can't have *one more minute. I can't do it.*"

"I'm only following orders." I nod. I don't ask anyone to hurry up. Neither does anyone else.

Sergeant Barry is here today. I approach him with my plan to get rubble and ask his help. I can't go running in there alone and start stuffing rocks in a bag—I wouldn't feel right about it. "Today is bad. They have bodies to deal with. How much are we talking about?"

"Couple of dozen little rocks."

He goes over and talks to the New York troopers inside. "They'll get it for you. Just today is a bad day." I nod and thank him.

Catching up to the Major, I tell him my plans for a closing ceremony, and ask if he will do a final sermon for us. He agrees. "I'll come up with something special." The final trip out will be filled with my frequent fly-ers; with honor, joy, and terrible sadness. We will get to do what the fami-lies always do—say good-bye to a piece of ourselves that will forever re-main in Manhattan. And take a piece of this terrible thing to hold forever as a reminder of how in two heartbeats our lives were forever changed. We will have our funerals and mourn and cry. God help us.

EMT Carrie has a secret. "Did you know that your husband wants that little rubber ducky that the Baptists have in child care?"

"What?"

"He saw that ducky and told us all about how he has one at home that's bigger, and he wants that little one to go with it." I had given him a big yellow rubber ducky as a joke. He keeps it on the edge of the tub.

"I had no idea."

"I'm going to get that ducky for him. I already asked. Don't tell him."

What a devil! She has worked out a deal to get the duck with the child care people, to tease him. Apparently he has been coveting this duck for a while now, and looks for it every day. Carrie is going to give it to him as a good-bye present. I really had no idea. You think you know somebody . . . She is giggling and enjoying the hell out of her secret plot.

EMT Sharon is troubled about her Chihuahua, who needs a C-section. Knocked up by a dachshund. Ned launches into a philosophical talk about sharing spirits. How have we all come to be with one another so easily, so well that we know one another's nuances and habits and little quirks? In the few stolen minutes of down time that we get together we live a lifetime in conversation. The familiarity of so many of us is so intense, so easy, so obviously from another point in time . . .

When I see Sergeant Barry again, I tell him the story about Sam trying to find out where I got the state police hat. He takes great delight in it. He tells the other guys who are all sitting around in the food tent over lunch. Another of the troopers gives me a hat; this is a tie-dyed one. My husband immediately steals it. I go to the trooper who gave it to me and sit with him at the table. I say loud enough for Fred to hear, "See that guy? He thinks that that is *his* hat. I want you to shoot him."

"Who—that guy?" He nods at Fred and uses his best tough guy voice.

"Yeah. If he mistreats my hat, I want you to shoot him. I'll split the insurance money with you."

"No problem, little lady!" We laugh and joke and tease. They make fun of Sam: one of the troopers says he's going to bring about fifty hats and hand them out to everybody. Really drive the boy over the edge. Now *that* would be fun. . . .

November 19

The weather is warm. Almost hot. We have had such amazing weather. A few cold ones but it's been bearable cold.

We have a strange NOVA companion today. She latches onto her family both physically and in mannerisms. She is holding their arms and standing so close to their space that she is invasive. One of them tells her to go away. I see Judy approach her and speak to her, so I let it be. A few seconds later she is back, hanging on them. Her NOVA site supervisor asks her to let them alone and go to the back of the platform. As we are leaving she runs back up and clings again. Disaster wackos—Is she one of those people whom they told me about early on? Are her own pain and needs getting in the way? Is this what happens—the people who should be the support system become the needy?

I see Judy approach, asking her to go down to street level. She says "No." I am moving a family group. Jack walks by and asks her to go to street level so we can move the families down to them.

"No." I go up to her and say quietly, "It's time for us to go. Please go down to street level; we'll bring the families to you." She is clutching a family member's arm for dear life, and *yells* at me: *"No. I'm with this family."* The woman she is holding reacts with a twitch and pulls away from her. I put my arm around her shoulders, wrap my other hand around her arm, and say quietly, "I need you to come with me now," as I walk her away toward the stairs. She opens her mouth and closes it without saying anything. I stop at the stairs and say to her, "You have to realize that they have found bodies out there again. In orientation we say to you that they stop work to wait until we leave so that the families don't see the bodies. This is *serious.* When they ask us to go we *really* have to go. We need you to help us with this. It's hard on all of us. Please go down to the street; we'll bring the families down for you. I need you to do that now." She goes with some encouragement from the hand that I have on her back.

It seems that the more the workers in there need us to leave, the more resistance we have to leaving. The family and companions don't even know when they have found bodies. We never tell the families that we have to hustle. They just seem to know somehow . . . and they hang back as if they are waiting. . . . The stages of where they are in grief? Are they picking up something that tells them that bodies are waiting to come home? Maybe the news reports of them locating more people have led to some unconscious need to linger and see if the person found belongs to them. I don't know. Coincidence? I don't believe in coincidence.

Bob helps us to move people. Trying to move 100 people who don't want to go is futile; they become what we call "rubber-band people" because as soon as you get them to walk away a couple of steps and you let them go, or turn around, they double back to where you found them. They linger, cry, and make my heart break, because I want more than anything to let them stand there as long as they want, but I can't. Somehow placing my hand on someone's shoulder and saying softly, "I'm so sorry, but we have to go now" seems like an unbearably cruel thing to do. I bite the bullet and Bob and I work with the same rubber-band families over and over. (We see this phenomenon with many people—we get them to move toward the stairway and street level, and assume that they will continue to exit. BUT—as soon as we turn our backs to begin to move someone else, we find our people right back where we left them.) We finally both get smart and walk them all the way to the stairs, waiting for them to start down before turning around to retrieve more.

As we are leaving I see a lone fireman. Haven't seen one in ages. Except for those who are far off carrying flags . . . I go up to him and take off my New Jersey pin, which I pin on his overalls. He looks at it and says, "Oh shit. Thanks!"

"You're welcome, sweet thing."

Our troopers are becoming twitchy from the effort of keeping the shutterbugs away and under control. As we walk you can hear the sound of shutters clicking and film advancing everywhere. An angry companion says to one persistent man, "Hey, would you want your *mother* to be treated that way? Have some *respect*."

The guy responds with a loud, "Fuck you, pal." I fear a confrontation, so I run over and touch the companion's arm. "Breathe deep. Let the troopers handle it."

"I know. This sucks. He was right in this family's face with that camera."

"I know. But they take it differently from the troopers. Don't fuss. Let them do their job. Don't want you getting punched." He nods. We continue to walk on through the noise of shutters. It has gotten to the point that the troopers can't even chase them down and take the film. There are too many of them. I wonder how many rolls of film I appear in. . . .

We have many little ones today and are boosting them up onto chairs to see. One guy who is really quite tall has stopped in the back of the group to let the shorter people see. He's looking left out and I have an empty chair. I wave him forward: "Want to step up on the chair to see?"

"It's okay."

"Aww come on up. I'll hold you so you don't fall." He does, leaning on my shoulder as he stands, now a tower in and of himself. He looks down at me and starts to say, "I worked here ten years myself. . ." He begins to slap his leg with a flower. Angry slaps. He bites his lip, shakes his head, and steps down to join his family in the front. I want to say, "Pisses me off too," but I keep quiet. He nods and says "Thanks." Yup.

Judy and I flop together into seats on the bus. We get into a discussion about the amazing things that we see and hear and encounter.

"Ever think about writing a book?"

"Jude, you know, people keep saying that to me—why? What is it about me that makes people think I can write a book? Why am I elected as the writer?"

She shrugs. "People should hear about this."

"Only one problem, Jude. I work in a disaster site; by now I've lost my memory. By the time I get home, I'll forget where I've been."

She laughs. "No *really* . . ."

"Why don't you, then?"

"No, I couldn't. I can't write." I don't know what makes her so sure *I* can write. Maybe . . .

"I think I know what I would call it if I ever did write a book: *Just One More.* It's all we ever say—all of us. The guys over there, everyone at the FAC, all of us. We always want one more: one more rescue, one more day, one more chance. We're never satisfied that it's good enough, you know? It's that sense that we want to do it better that binds us all." She tears up and nods.

A woman asks me about my Towers pin with the flag. I take it off and give it to her. She smiles, protests, and I hold my finger to my lips to shush her: "There's many more where that came from." I reach into my pocket and pull out my stash from the turnpike store. She smiles again and admires it now pinned on her coat lapel.

Bob is troubled because a family wants to bring a reporter tomorrow. He is so protective of the families. He begins to rub in the fact that two people have now written an article about all of the good work they have done here, taking credit for all of their work on arranging the ferry visits.

Collectively they have been here three times. Not a mention of me. To get back at his ribbing I say, "Hey, Bob, give that reporter to me—maybe I can get credit for my work for a change."

He growls, "Not a chance. My day will be bad enough. You just sit there and stew about how the people who have caused us the most grief around here by not doing *any* work have taken credit for all of *your* hard work." He laughs.

"Bob, you really are somebody's frustrated older brother, aren't you?" He is sweet the way he teases and sticks up for me. It feels like having a big brother. In spite of the fact that he was trying to tease me out of worrying about the article, I do read it and stew on it. I would really like to push people like that in the river. As I hit maximum self-pity, our nun comes in and tells me what a great job I'm doing. For me, fame will be a private and personal thing. I obviously need a *big* lesson on being humble, or I wouldn't get so many chances to practice it.

November 20

We have Port Authority survivors again today. The family (only one) that we have consists of two little girls, one with her broken leg in a cast, and their grandmother, mother, and another woman. Only a family of five. I brief them alone in the chapel and explain about how the Port Authority folks have really different needs. They are understanding and comfortable. They have many questions, especially about the cross. I let them know that we will be sure to get them a good view. We actually got to chat—a nice change to orientation.

We learn that one of our bus drivers lost a brother in the Towers. She actually takes a cut in pay to drive the bus for us almost every day because it makes her feel close to him. We insist that she come with us on the ferry, and treat her as a family member. She is a shy, quiet, pleasant lady who is tearful and grateful. We provide her with a teddy and flowers just as we do all the other family members.

Despite warnings from their supervisors and us, three of the Port Authority people are busted with cameras. The New York State Police take their cameras. They will not be returned.

I hoist the shorter Port Authority people onto chairs so they can see. I help them to locate buildings and put names on places long gone. They cry when they see their Towers gone. When our time is done, the Port Authority staff are not willing to leave. They double back. They stand and ignore our attempts to steer them off the platform. I go down to the street and enlist help from a New York State Trooper who comes up and booms at them: "Time to leave!" They move. I thank him. Twice.

On the way back on the bus a Port Authority man tells me his story about 9/11: It was the first time he had *ever* been late for work. He worked on the eighty-seventh floor of Tower One. As he walked into the office several people told him his wife was becoming frantic because she had called him and he was not there. She kept calling all through the office because it was so unlike him to be late. They tease him. He calls home and explains that there was an accident on the turnpike and he was delayed. He explains to his worried wife that he is fine.

"I'm telling her, 'honey, I'm okay, I promise.' Just as I say that to her, I swivel my chair around and look out the window and see an airliner coming at my face."

My heart stops. "Oh my God."

He continues without stopping: "I'm not sure if I said anything or screamed or what. All I know is that I'm holding this phone in my hand and I hear my wife's voice screaming in my ear saying over and over, 'Oh my God, what's wrong? What's *wrong?*' and I'm watching this plane coming at my face. Then I hear this choking sound and I look over to see this guy I work with looking at the plane and turning blue. He was having a heart attack."

"What did you do?"

"I drop the phone, grab a co-worker, we grab the guy who is turning blue and we run like hell, falling down and dragging him all the way and we don't stop until we hit the street. Then I run some more."

How does a person *live* through that? How do you see a plane coming at your face and *live* through that?

I discuss my plans for a termination ceremony with Bob. He agrees so easily that I think he must be yessing me and ignoring the content of what I ask. The sun is going down beautifully; I see tinges of pink through the back door. I go out front and see an amazing sight—the New York skyline is breathtakingly beautiful in pink and purple. So beautiful it looks fake, like an artist playing with colors. I run back to the trailer and grab my camera, running full speed back out front to the water to take the picture. I want the Statue as well. I find Fred talking with Judy and some others in the dayroom. "We have to go *now*." Puzzled looks. "The sunset is really *gorgeous*. We have to get to the Statue before the light goes." They run to look. I literally drag Fred by the arm running to the car. We pile in and he jumps the curb to get through the field to the water. In the distance I see the corrections van that patrols the area start up and begin to drive slowly toward us. The light has faded, but I try the shot anyway. I had lucked out and gotten a shot of a red sky one late night. I didn't think it would come out but it did. Maybe I'll be lucky again. The van slowly rolls toward us, and I dash back to the car, saying, "They're going to be really pissed at us; let's get out of here." Fred drives over walkways and more curbs to the parking lot. We get away without getting yelled at.

We talk about changes on the two-and-a-half-hour ride home in traffic. We are tired, grumpy, and hungry before we get home. I don't know what I'd do if we weren't able to share this work with each other. . . .

November 21

Somehow that huge group yesterday went smoothly overall. Today we have only eighty-five (only has become relative). That is still an unmanageable group logistics-wise, especially when you add on about forty more of us, but somehow they end up being manageable. We pack our rapidly disappearing equipment into our sad little caravan.

The only explanation for this working so well for so long is that we are in God's hands. Gotta be:

> Teddy bears—always *just enough* turn up in the storeroom;
> Hard hats always just make it,
> We always *just make it*.

Someone is definitely looking out for us. As hard as we try to mess this up by letting personalities, stress, and other agenda sneak in, it still works. Families never see the struggles, the messy arguments, the "hustle these people along" comments. The families get what they need, and we keep our acting out to ourselves.

Anything for the families.

Bob goes off in the golf cart cruising to Meditation Point (without me!). Oh, the drag of having to pay attention to my details . . . He returns with a new pin for me. "Ohooooo thanks!" I gush at him, hug him, and give him a big kiss. He secretly loves getting gushed at. Me too.

The reporter shows up out front. They will not let her in. Bob is suddenly missing, and the reporter is growing impatient and snippy. Ant'ny could care less that she is out there trying to be important. He shrugs and says, "Sorry. Not on the list. No clearance. . . ." I finally locate Bob on his cell phone, which he answers, *"What?"*

"Your reporter is at the gate and she is really ticked."

We have three elderly ladies. Two of them look like twins. They are tiny, plump, and cute. We hoist them up onto chairs and hold them tight so they can have a good view. They become pink nosed and teary. Jack flirts with them, and they immediately fall in love with him. I think he was put on earth to make women happy. He does it so well. I tell him that and he cracks up. I watch him as he hugs these tiny dears, fusses with their hard hats, jokes away their tears.

But he has become almost frantic. His movements are twitchy and nervous, feverish. Jack, what is happening in your head? You can't fix it. We don't have enough time to fix it. Maybe that's it—he sees time running away just as I do. His energy has changed and he is showing signs of stress really getting to him. Hang on, love. There are more tiny ladies for you. . . .

Trooper Sam comes up to the platform to hustle us down. Bob doesn't take it well, and they go down to the street, out of sight of the families to yell at each other. It works; Bob buys us time by arguing.

Bill, one of Bob's staff, has been making CDs of his pictures, setting them to music as slide shows. They are beautiful. I watch the one about the urn ceremony and immediately cry. He has set the pictures to "Amazing Grace." I think I will never hear that hymn again without crying. They think it's funny that I tear up immediately upon hearing it, and lots of "Hey—play 'Amazing Grace'" gets thrown around the trailer.

Bob decides that he wants a closing ceremony for everyone. He doesn't think that a "special" group ceremony is a good idea. I *knew* he was just yessing me. . . . "You'll piss somebody off unless you can set clear criteria for why certain people can go and others can't." I understand the need to not leave people out.

"Bob—I can. I counted up the sign-in sheets. And I was meticulous about keeping records of who showed—if they didn't sign in themselves, *I* signed them in. If you look at the frequent flyers, the lowest number of times that a person came in was twenty-three. That's almost half of the days that we went all together. The difference in attendance between frequent flyers and the next most frequent person is eight visits. There is a difference between someone who has been here twenty-three times and someone who has been here eight times. It's not that eight isn't significant, but some of them worked so hard. They have given so much; don't you think they deserve recognition for that?"

"If you set criteria you have to stick to it. Don't make trouble for yourself. If you get soft and let one person in who doesn't meet the criteria you will pay for it."

"I understand. Really. But I want to do *something* for these people. They gave so much."

He nods and looks grumpy. "I don't think I like it. I want you and Judy to get with [Red Cross] Jack and plan something for *everybody*. I want singing. Lots of singing."

"Okay. We're going out in style."

The rubber ducky has disappeared. They even write it up in morning report, and an announcement is made in morning meeting: the theft of one rubber duck. I ask Carrie about it. She laughs and takes me over to the Baptists' Child Care area—"Tell her about the ducky."

Bill and Betty fold their arms and look really serious, then say, "It's in protective custody." Carrie laughs. She has plans to wrap it as a gift. Sharon says, "Be sure that you put air holes in the box."

November 24

Thanksgiving is over and I am feeling really crappy with a sore throat and chills. I want to bitch. I stop on the way to buy zinc and overdose myself. I can't afford to be sick. We have *just one more week*! I have to make it!

We have ninety-five family members today. Equipment has been disappearing, and we are at a critical level with the hard hats. May not have enough. Bob gives me the "Bite-the-bullet-it's-almost-over" talk. I do. I'm learning to make the best out of just about anything, and allow the world to take its course. If fear is a lack of faith, then I'm becoming a believer. . . . We find some additional hard hats in the back of a trailer. We always just make it.

We have a friendly crew of troopers today, and Sergeant Barry arrives in a devilish mood. They are teasing and joking with one another and us. Those boys have really learned to lighten up around us, and look so much more at ease since they have learned that we love messing with them. I have declared this to be *Mess with Troopers Day*.

Sergeant Barry says that it's a good day to get rocks for our goodbye ceremony. We go in search of a bag. All we can find are clear plastic bags of all sizes and shapes. No paper bags, no opaque bags, and no boxes small enough to not arouse suspicion.

We continue our search until finally I hear, "Hey, I know what we can give you!" and the guy goes rummaging through a box and comes up with a tightly rolled piece of gray plastic. "Here. We have a couple of these, and never really found a use for them." Strange thing to say. . . .

I begin to unroll the bag. It is unrolling and unfolding to about three feet wide and is becoming taller than I am—about six or more feet long. Just the right size for a . . . all of a sudden I realize . . . *"Oh no. Is this what I think it is?"*

"We call it a scraper bag. It's a disposable one. They don't put parts in the zipper bags. When they have a really bad one and they have to be scraped off the road . . ." They gave me a *body bag*.

"A body bag?"

"Yeah. It's all we got."

"Oh man . . ."

They are all standing around laughing at me. "Guys, this is a bit gory, don't you think?"

"Yeah. But fitting for what you want it for." Ouch.

I roll it back up and stuff it in my helmet under the straps.

I find Sergeant Barry out back in the sun, chewing on one of those cigars of his. I stop for a bit to chat. Barry is telling me about his son. "I like him to know what I do for a living and I take him with me on the job whenever I can." A perfectly serious conversation about a sweet, caring father, as I drink a bottle of water, listening. "Like last weekend for instance, I took him out and we blew up a boat." He says it like people do that every day, and it's perfectly natural. I almost spit my water on him.

"You what?"

"Yeah, we were playing with a bunch of C4 plastic explosives. Practicing blowing up a drug dealer boat. I took him with us on the exercise. He loved it."

"Barry, can I play with you next weekend?"

He shrugs at me, still serious. "Yeah, I guess." He has no idea how funny he is.

On the boat a trooper comes up to me and volunteers, "Need anything?"

"I could use a hat; can I have yours?"

He stutters, "It's part of my uniform. I'll get in trouble."

"I'm teasing you." He smiles. "But don't leave it around; it might grow legs. . . ."

"And I'll know just where it walked to."

I see him in a few minutes with his hat in his pocket. I walk past him and lift it. Every time we really mess with them, they get a look like: *Should I be stern or laugh?* My victim follows me, looking at his hat on my head. "Please?" he begs in a scared little voice. They aren't allowed to be forceful with people who aren't breaking the law. I guess that taking a trooper's hat and refusing to give it back is actually breaking a law. . . . They know when we're playing with them, and they seem to love being played with, but at the same time they don't seem to know what the boundaries are to play back. The ones who are newer to the job especially seem to have trouble deciding how to act when we tease them, and they fluster easily. I can imagine him thinking *"Is it okay for me to just snatch my hat back?"*

"Oh, but I really like it." He still hasn't figured out if I'm totally kidding.

"I can get you one and bring it next time I come." He is beginning to think I'm *not* kidding. He now looks really concerned. I take the hat off and give it back. "I would never do anything that would get you in trouble. Just playing."

"We're not used to that. We don't get to play with the public, you know."

Four troopers are standing at parade rest, looking very imposing at the front of the boat, just inside the doors. We got in a shipment of pit bull Beanie Babies last night. Jack says, "We should just give these to the troopers. They look like pit bulls today." A couple of us take the dolls and begin to snap open the many pockets on the troopers' field uniforms, and stuff them with Beanie pits. They begin to crack up, but they don't change their stance. If they aren't already grinning, the corners of their mouths are twitching. The families are laughing and egging us on. Four huge guys looking scary with pit bulls poking out of their pants pockets, boots, shirt pockets, and gun belts. They leave them there. One is my guy with the hat. He says with a wink, "Don't try this with troopers at home; they might bite you!"

We have now hit critical mass with teddy bears. After this weekend there are no more. We have used every Red Cross teddy bear on the East Coast and out past Ohio. They have been sending out emergency calls for teddies everywhere. No one is willing to feed our habit any more; we have burned all of our bridges. The Baptist child care workers think that they may have a connection through another avenue and are calling around also. The closest stash of bears is too far away to make it by the next trip. We are calling stores begging donations—but everyone local has donated already, some more than once. It does not look good. . . . As I said, I'm running on faith.

Once in New York, Barry asks for the bag. We go way in, behind Tower One. We can no longer see the platform. We locate a fireman, and tell him what we're after. He simply asks how much we need. I tell him enough for a couple of dozen people to have a decent-sized rock. He takes the bag and scoops in a few handfuls. He chooses a couple of large cement chunks so that they can be broken up. "Be really careful with them, though. I'm not sure how they will break. They've been in a couple of thousand degrees for a long time. That may have changed the composition of the cement and made it fragile." We have quite a load. This rubble comes from Tower One. Barry twists the bag around the stones and tucks it under his arm. "No one will look at me twice, or notice if I'm carrying something. I'll give it to you when we get back." As we are leaving he hands it to me near the golf cart. I stuff it in the back under the seat. Ned is sitting in the cart, in the backseat. He looks at me: "What are you up to now?" I simply shake my head and grin. I now have a secret that I can't wait to share.

When we get back, I enlist Jude and tell her my plan. I show her the bag full of rocks and let her know my thoughts about the ceremony. She tears up. "Will you help me to plan?" We talk about putting some of our favorite prayers on paper, getting some photos copied, finding little boxes for souvenirs. And little cloth bags to put the rocks in. We have work to do. . . .

November 25

I'm tired. Ready to go—let go, come home. Today is chilly, wet, and dismal. We have Port Authority survivors with the families again. Lots of them.

We stand in a huddle at the gate before entering. A state government official from North Dakota and members of the Lakota Nation are praying on the platform. As they leave, the official walks up to a family member and shakes her hand, thanking her for her strength. One of the tribesmen is in full headdress; feathers billow as he walks.

Beautiful. From behind them comes a tribe member who pushes through the crowd looking right at me. He continues toward me like a man on a mission. He comes right in front of me and stops, never taking his eyes off of me. He pushes a dream catcher into my hands: "For bad dream prevention." Before I realize it he is gone. I stand there with my mouth open. I look at it stupidly for a second, then shove it into my pocket.

One very tall, pretty woman from the Port Authority climbs onto the chair I'm holding. I steady her with my arm on her back. Her eyes change to wide terror as she looks. God only knows what she saw, what she heard and endured to get out of those buildings. She is frozen with her hands held at strange angles. Her pupils widen even more. Fear response. She begins to cry and says, apparently to herself, "No. I have to look." She doubles and begins holding her stomach. Repeating, "No. I have to look." I wonder if she has intentions of throwing up on me.

I tell her, "Breathe; just try to breathe."

"I can't."

"Yes. Deep breaths in . . ." She tries.

A man describes to me nightmares that he has: he is looking up, and all he can see is a spiral of hands. "That's what I saw in the stairwell. Just hands on the railing. I wake up screaming and all I see are thousands of hands spiraling up into darkness."

Jude is happy and bubbling all day. She found out that Fred is a hairdresser in his "real" life. He's going to do her hair.

I am simply too tired.

November 26

Today is another slow day. Everyone is moving in reverse, dragging feet and droopy: family members, companions, everyone. We are late getting to the buses because no one is moving. We have a straggler, who I finally locate by the back door. I walk with her to the bus and right at the bus door she stops suddenly, looks at me, and says, "I have to let the dog out!" and turns and *runs* back to the terminal. Rich, who was standing at the door to the bus offering a helping hand, looks at me and says, "Sometimes it's just better that we don't know," and runs after her.

We are just leaving the dock when I notice Bob on the other side of the boat, standing holding onto the pole, his knuckles white. He looks gray. I cross over to his side and the closer I get, the worse he looks. He is sweating and his eyes are not seeing.

"Hey, did you eat lunch?"

"No, I forgot."

He is really clammy. I know that this stress has taken a toll on his health, which was a bit fragile to begin with. He isn't breathing well. His eyes are not focusing. I say quietly, "Come with me. Let's get you something to eat." I lead him, holding him under the arm to the back of the boat, reaching out and grabbing an EMT by the sleeve as I go. We sit him in the back, where he begins to pop nitro tablets. I grab his arms, and get right in front of his face: "Bob, don't you die here in front of these families. They couldn't take that. Don't you dare die on this boat!" He manages something that almost resembles a smile. He nods.

"I'm serious. You cannot die on this boat." I look up at EMT Ned: "Is he okay?" He shakes his head no. "What do you need me to do?" They send me for peanut butter crackers and juice. Bob eats. He pops more nitro. The EMTs watch him like a hawk. Sharon whispers to me, "He's getting a little color back. I think he's coming back a little. Get more crackers and bring them with you in your pocket. You know how he is; he won't listen and stay put here on the boat." When we reach the other side, I insist that he stays on the boat to rest. He doesn't.

We have a young man of about seventeen who lost his dad—his only parent. He came with his granny, who doesn't want to go with us at the last minute. She asks me to be with him. I promise to take care of him, and give him my arm as we walk. He is soft-spoken, sweet, dressed in a long, oversized brown sweater. I wonder if it was his dad's. Good-looking, polite. Everything going for him. But he also has heavy, heavy pain. . . . I get him a chair, which he climbs on without hesitation. He holds his map and asks me to help him to identify all of the buildings. We go through them all one by one. He thanks me and simply looks. I cannot find words for the look on his face as he simply stands there quietly. This boy must suddenly be a man. His energy is heavy, dignified, and so sad. But he stands solid, looking, without tears. I have my hand on his back to test his steadiness. He raises his hand as if he is about to point at something and simply freezes. God— what hell is he in . . . ? After a few minutes he drops his hand, looks at me, and says, "I'm through now." I help him down.

"Are you all right?"

"I am. I really am." He nods.

"I'm here if you need anything. I promised your grandma I would take care of you, you know."

"Thanks."

We have been watching one woman closely. I suddenly find myself standing directly behind her. She has been saying all morning that she knew that her husband was safe in the basement of Tower Two, that they had access to food from vending machines, and water from the bathrooms. We are very worried about her; they are digging in the subfloors of Tower Two—there are no more bathrooms. On the platform she turns around suddenly with tears rolling down her face, looks me in the eye and says, "Where did it go?" Oh dear God, don't make me have to answer that question! Fortunately she keeps talking and I don't have to answer.

"Where was Tower One?" I put my arm across her shoulders, turn her around and show her Tower One and 7 World Trade. I point, and explain the location where they are digging in the subfloors of Tower Two, where she thinks her husband is safe. I am holding my breath. I think her world is about to completely fall in on her. Oh dear God, why did you choose me? She looks at me again.

"Where did they go—the Towers?"

Oh please, no.

"They were so big. I've seen them. I had lunch here with him a lot. Where did they go?"

And she begins to talk very fast and the tears are rolling down her face with a vengeance and she has grabbed both of my arms like she wants to shake the life out of me. . . . Somewhere in the back of my head I hope she does. . . .

"Where is it all? The cement? They were so *big*. Those dust clouds. I saw the videotapes of those dust clouds just rolling through the streets.

Was that the walls, the ceilings, the floors?" She is looking into my eyes. This time she wants an answer. She's digging her fingers into my arms.

"Yes."

"And it was like this? No *stuff*? This is *all*?"

She wants to know. Oh God, what should I tell her? Talk through my mouth *please*!

I take a deep breath and quiet my voice. "When we arrived it was deep. . . ." I turn her around and show her how high it was in the beginning, using a reference point on one of the buildings. Oh God, am I doing this right? Please be talking through my mouth—please. She continues to stare where I pointed. "Still, they were so big. Where did they go—just dust?" I don't answer. I can hardly breathe. I want to be struck dead. Now. Here. Please. I can't figure out how I am choking back these tears, but something tells me not to cry. . . .

She turns back to look at me. Big eyes. Big, teary, five-year-old eyes. "He isn't coming home is he?" OH GOD!

"No."

She nods and turns back to look, still holding one of my arms. She is younger than I, or my age. I can't for a moment imagine. . . . I dissociate, and feel the weight of all of those souls. I don't remember leaving the platform.

As we return to the terminal, I am standing at a bus door to help people step down. I find myself offering a hand to the young husband from Pakistan who had gone with us the first week. He is here again—people are really not supposed to go more than once. He smiles when he sees that I recognize him. I smile back and ask, "Don't I know you from somewhere?" He laughs.

Later, in the terminal, I walk past the walls and hear, "Hey, wait up, please." I turn to see the woman from the platform. She is writing on a wall. She has color in her cheeks and a *smile*. She walks to me and holds her arms out saying, "Please, can I give you a hug?" She does. "Thank you so much. I can go on with my life now." *Oh, yes. I believe!*

"I think I can let him go."

"I am so glad." I return her hug. "If you need us . . ."

"I know. Thank you so much."

I have two pictures of unrecognizable troopers:

1. Derby saluting as the urns went by; his hand obliterated his face, and
2. The one of Hitchcock's butt from when I took the pictures on the boat.

I tape them to a paper and write on it: GUESS THE TROOPER AND WIN A FREE LUNCH. I hang it behind the food servers where everyone will see it in the chow lines. The Red Cross lunch people come up to me and say, "You know, we don't charge for lunch."
And I was told I had no sense of humor.
"I know. It's a joke." *Oh.* All day people are saying to the troopers, "Bend over; let me see your ass." They love the attention.

Mysteriously, a truck arrived last night with teddy bears. We used them all today. Again we are out of teddies . . .

Fred is talking to Ant'ny. Anthony asks, "Wots wid dat hat?" Fred is wearing the tie-dyed state police hat that one of the troopers gave me.
"Kinda sissy-fied, innit?"

Out back, around the administrative trailer, we have a lake forming. They have had to jack up the trailer already because it was sinking, but now we have water coming from somewhere—seems to be bubbling up from the ground. You have to jump over it to get to the stairs sometimes. It's getting deep toward the back section of the trailer. Judy, my favorite Red Cross person says, "Oh God, don't tell the Red Cross; they'll send in their flood team."

November 27

Last night was strange.
I slept, but woke up about 1 a.m. with a sentence in my head:

So many miles we walked together as separate spirits.

It nagged at me. I ran it over and over in my head for several minutes, thinking I should remember this. . . . I fell back to sleep. At 1:30 I wake up with a second sentence in my head:

> Through moments that seemed like a lifetime.

Okay. I run this sentence over and over in my head. Something is going on here and I guess I should remember this. I fall asleep. *Again,* at 2 a.m., *another* sentence:

> And lifetimes that were but a moment.

It's almost as if someone is whispering in my ear. All I know is that this is strange, and I need to remember it. I turn it over in my head as one complete thing and eventually fall asleep. At 2:30 a.m. my eyes open with another one:

> Together we walk for miles, spirits hand in hand.

This is plain nuts. My hair is standing up and I'm goose bumping like crazy. I go to the bathroom, memorizing this one as well. Back to bed and sleep. At 3 a.m.:

> Collecting tears like souvenirs of our journey through Courage,
> Strength, and Hope.

Now I have to write this down. It's way out of hand, and I'll never remember it. I get pen and paper, and write in the dark. I think that maybe if I wait awhile it will finish. I vaguely wonder if I'm really asleep and dreaming this. . . . Nothing else comes. Maybe it's done. I put down the pad of paper and go to sleep. Then, at 3:30, another one:

> We stand together as spirits United.

I write it down. Obviously whatever is going on isn't finished with me yet. At 4 a.m., again my eyes pop open.

> In one eternal, fleeting moment Separate became One.

God how long is this going to keep going? Apparently there's just one more line to go—sleep ends again at 4:20 as I hear in my brain:

What God has joined together, let no man put asunder.

I sleep, for ten minutes. The alarm goes off.

After opening my eyes at the alarm clock, I lie there remembering and thinking *No way is there anything on that paper. I dreamed it all.* I can't even recall one shred of the verse, so it was just a freaky dream. I sit up in bed, reach over to pick up the pad of paper, and read:

So many miles we walked together
                            as separate spirits;
Through moments that seemed like a lifetime,
and lifetimes that were but a moment.

Together we walk for miles
spirits hand in hand collecting tears
                            like souvenirs of our journey
through Courage,
                  Strength,
                            and Hope.
We stand together
 as spirits United: in one eternal fleeting moment
                            Separate became One.
What God has joined together, let no man put asunder.

I don't know what to do with this. . .

As we pull into the checkpoint, Ant'ny invites us over to the corrections van for doughnuts and coffee. He is upset because a little girl who had lost her daddy arrived late last night. She had made a card for a fireman and was crying, desperate to give it to a fireman. NOVA brought her to Anthony. He's wearing a uniform. She can't read. They let her think he's a fireman. He speaks to the little girl. God, what a terrible situation to put that poor man in—he's a sergeant in the Department of Corrections Special Operations unit. He is beside himself at absorbing that little girl's pain. She had apologized for the card not being perfect. She asked him to take it to his firehouse and hang it up for others to see. He makes the promise to her. He took it on the way home to a local firehouse where it found a home. The firemen cried when he told them the story.

I tell him what an important thing he did for her, and how he did it right. I tell him we're going to take him on the boat today so he can see for himself how important that simple act was. He tears up.

Our attorneys have a couple of guests today. They wander down on the street with Sam to stand on the other side of West Street. A New York trooper runs up to them and yells: "If you want to be here, get on the platform with everybody else. And next time don't come in here without a hard hat." Someone is talking to him. "I don't care *who* you think you are. Get on the platform or get out." We can hear it all. A couple of family members mumble things like "good for them." A couple of companions snicker.

As we are leaving the platform today, the Chicago Bulls are arriving.

In the food tent troopers are gathered. There is a big brass one there with them—lots of stripes and in dress blues. He is talking to the one whose hat I was pretending to snitch the other day. I walk past them, say good morning, and they nod hello. I say to the trooper, "Can I have your hat?"

He laughs and says "No." The big brass says casually, "Do you want his hat?" I think he's playing, so I nod. "Trooper, give this little lady your hat!" comes from him in an obvious order. Ooooops!

"Uh—Sir—is that an order?" He has a look on his face like somebody just punched him in the stomach.

"*Yes, it's an order.* Now give her your hat." I'm feeling bad, and I'm about to interrupt and say, "*I was kidding for Christsakes,*" but this guy is scary and I don't think interrupting is a good idea. . . .

"But sir, it's the only one I have. I'll get demerits tomorrow."

I'm getting really uncomfortable. . . .

"You should be better prepared with a spare. Take your demerits, trooper. You deserve them."

Oh shit.

"*Sir! Yes, Sir!*" He takes off his hat and hands it to me. He has sad eyes.

"Now, take that hat as compliments of the New Jersey State Police and please enjoy it."

I put the hat on my head and say "Thanks!" and walk away. And watch. As soon as the big meanie leaves, I'll give it back.

About ten minutes later, I pass the big meanie again. Without the hat.

"Where's your hat?"

"I gave it back to him. I actually have one at home, anyway. I just like teasing him. I didn't mean to get him in trouble."

He laughs a real belly laugh and takes my arm. "You know, something about you told me you wouldn't keep it. They *are* fun to mess with, aren't they—those new ones?" He winks. I agree.

"Oh, they're great. So serious. We like to decorate them and poke at them and steal from them because they get all flustered. They know we're playing and they like it, but they don't know what to do about it."

"These guys need that. They need to be treated like people. They need to be with the public in an environment where they can lighten up a little. They love it here."

"And we love them. They really are great. And by the way—you're *bad*." He laughs. "I know. Ain't it great?"

An early departure. I want to stop by the store on the way home to get little bags for the rocks. We drive home through the most beautiful sunset ever: orange, tangerine, blue, purple, red, everything. It lasts most of the way home. I don't have the energy to take a picture. Man, I am wearing out.

We select little gold bags with drawstrings at the store. Jude will be proud. Once home, I sit at the computer and scan in some photos for the background for Mychal's Prayer and others. I do some laundry and straighten up with my stolen extra two hours of home time before bed. This has been too much for too long. . . .

November 28

This is the first time I see Judy's new haircut—I drag her into the bathroom with some hair gel and spike her hair. As I turn her upside down under the hand dryer to fluff her up she giggles so loud that I think she'll draw a crowd. I'm shushing her and people are running in to see what's wrong. She keeps shrieking giggles.

We have mostly Port Authority survivors for today and a couple of families. Staff complain because they don't appreciate the angry and demonstrative behavior of Port Authority staff. I try to make them understand during orientation that as survivors, they just express their grief differently than families do, that they have a right to be angry. "Don't personalize it. They aren't being rude to *you*. They are just dealing with a really hard thing." They still don't like it. Can't blame them. It's hard to be bitched at all day and just smile.

One family has a young man of about sixteen, who was talking to his dad on a cell phone as he stood across the street from Tower Two. He knew the exact spot where his father was standing when he died—that's gotta be brutal. The boy wants to know if I can get him a rock from that spot. "Show me where on the map." He points to a spot. It was actually where they had started clearing debris first. There was nothing there even when we first went. It is flat and full of trucks and equipment, and I probably can't get to it. I explain that to him. "Would a rock from any other place be acceptable?" He considers it and says, "No. It's okay. I just thought that if there was a piece of that building left I would like it."

"I understand. But if you change your mind, let me know before we leave there, okay?" He agrees.

Once inside, I get a chair and say to him, "Come with me, love. Let me help you to see better." He climbs up and stares at one spot: where his father died. Studies it, like he is making an imprint on his brain. I have one. So will he. . . . He looks for a long time, then jumps down. "Change your mind about the rock?"

"No. There really isn't anything there. You were right. I have an urn; that's good." I let it be.

The Wall of Remembrance is being cleaned up. Our headstones are disappearing—the newer ones first. I had recently thought that we had lost a couple, but told myself I was wrong—that my eyes were playing tricks. . . . Behind the fence are men in white gas masks and Hazmat suits raking and cleaning. They stop, lean on their rakes, and watch us. I say to Jude, "God, what a photo that is—they don't realize that we can see them. What a horror movie scene." They look like ghosts back there just staring at us.

"Yes. A shame you can't take a picture of that one." We stand together and watch them watching us. Monsters on one side of the fence, us on the other. Both sides of a chain-link fence believing themselves to be invisible. This is a land of extremes, where normal just simply does not exist.

I can see the dumpster that has been moved to just behind the fence where the men are working. That is where the teddies and cards and mementos are going. I hope that the families don't see and realize what is happening. Our dollar teddy still lives on. I fret about his fate. I fret about all of our squishy dolls that were there for comfort in such dark moments. We all knew they wouldn't last, but now that they are leaving . . . I think about the guys behind the fence. I couldn't do it— clean up someone's headstone and throw it in a dumpster. What kind of karma do you collect for that job? It must hurt.

The flood waters around the administrative trailer are getting wider and deeper. Canada geese flew in last week. Ducks have joined the geese in the "lake." We name the lake after Bob. The water is getting pretty deep. The ducks are actually floating.

The young father whose in-laws went back to Pakistan is here again today. It's at least the third time he has been back with us. The in-laws took the urn representing his wife with them. He is faced with raising a young son alone: a five-year-old genius. The man now has a load of grief, no wife, and no body. He asks his companion if he can possibly get another urn—for himself and his son. His companion comes up to me and tells me his request. Those on duty are strict today, so I worry that asking up front will probably result in rules being enforced rather than sympathy being extended. When I approach him I ask, "I *know* you from somewhere, right?" He laughs. "Me again, yes," and explains to me about wanting so much to have an urn. I tell him that he may have to do something he doesn't want to do to get the urn—we are supposed to give out only one per family. I show him the section on the urn request form where they ask about whether anyone in the family received one. "Should I lie?"

"That is up to you. They will ask the question."

I get the sergeant on duty to come down, to go through the forms with him. When they get to the part on the form about another family member getting the urn, the man answers it "I don't know." The sarge looks up at him, then me, and smiles, shaking his head as he continues to write—he knows a manipulation when he sees one, and he asks no more questions. They finish the form; the trooper says, "Okay, let me go upstairs and get it for you. I'll be right back."

"So when he returns, I should shut up, take it, and go, right?"

"I would."

He winks at me and smiles.

The companion tells me later, "You don't know how important it is for him. In the Hindu religion it is so important." I knew—from his face. Religion aside, it was his wife.

November 29

Today we have an author with us—Gail Sheehy. She is writing about the families from Middletown, New Jersey, a town that lost thirty-five people. Bob is nervous about having an author running around with a tape recorder and a notebook, fearing that she will intrude on other family members. The governor's wife is also here, and we have a few Port Authority survivors with us.

On the boat *everyone* goes straight to the upper deck. Weird. . . . Now we have to fit all of those hard hats and deliver equipment to the upper deck. We run stuff up the stairs.

Trooper Hitchcock works today and is getting a kick out of seeing his rear end facing the chow line.

"Any body guess me yet?"

"No, but we're having fun looking for who that butt belongs to!" I give him copies of all of his pictures, which he tucks away into his pocket. Our troopers are happy today. Very verbal.

On the platform Ned overhears two Port Authority women discussing how they can get into the mall section with their Port Authority ID cards. "We should boost sweaters and stuff. All we have to do is clean them up in the washer. There's lots of stuff still there." One of those women is not leaving her hard hat on. Three people have asked her to put it on, and the last time she told the companion who made the request to "Go to hell" and walked away. I approach her and say—quietly and nicely, "Please put your hard hat on. There is still some debris falling from the buildings and we don't want you to get hurt." She looks at me and says, *"Bitch,"* then walks away with her hard hat still in her hand. I'm sure I twitched. A priest who is with us leans over to me and says, "How do you keep your sanity?" I think to myself—*by plotting the deaths of people like that*—but I say, "I roll with it, Father."

Somehow I am suddenly and unofficially appointed as the person in charge of urns. Everyone has been bringing their families to me. I run for Sergeant Tom who does the official duties of form completion and urn delivery today.

Judy and I do staff debriefing together today. It is so nice to work with her. Gail Sheehy has asked to attend staff debriefing, and Bob is fretting about it. We tell Bob she has to participate if she goes—no sitting and taking notes. We ask the group for their consent to have her stay, so that no one feels hesitant to talk. She does participate.

I am so tired. Wanna go home. Headache. Splitting headache. We talk about the gifts that we receive, and I see a face light up in the front row. Nice. . . .

Bob is growing tired. I find him in the trailer with his head in his hands. "Bob, you okay? What is it?"

"I'm *really* ready." He has been looking bad—gray in color, circles deepening under his eyes; he has had frequent bouts of blood sugar problems. This has taken its toll on him. Hang in, love. Please hang in.

I drive toward home, a hockey game and a normal future. . .

November 30

Today the dollar teddy is gone. He was left on our first visit, and he is no more. The dumpster. I look at the spot where he so proudly sat with his dollar for so long and cry. My heart breaks. *Over* is coming too fast.

Just one more day . . .

Jude sees my distress and says, "Fitting. So many of their lives are in the dumpster." At first I think *how cruel,* and am about to yell at her when I realize—she is right.

Carrie arrives with the ducky tucked in her bag. Bill and Betty have kept him safe in the child care area, hidden away. He is now being transported home with her for wrapping.

My life is coming back to haunt me. Fast. I'm not sure how I feel about that.

When I get home I call two of my friends, Cecily and Steve. Steve surprises me by being *really* enthusiastic about hearing from me. Guess I've been so busy being gone that I never realized that people missed me. "Guys, I'm okay, I'm coming home soon."

Yes, life seems to be calling me . . .

I go out back in the dark with a hammer to break rocks for the ceremony. As I open the bag that smell wafts up. . . . I remember the warning from the fireman—about the cement being potentially fragile from being hot for so long. I set the bag on the sidewalk so I have a hard surface. I tap the biggest one lightly through the bag, so I don't lose any pieces. Doesn't move. I hit it harder. Then harder. Then as hard as I can. It simply looks at me without a single crack.

I get a bigger hammer and really wale on it. Nothing. I go to the garage and get the ten-pound sledgehammer. I hit it *hard.* Good thing this bag is tough. . . . The chunk of cement looks at me as if it's saying "Is that all you've got?" I think I broke the sidewalk.

Okay. Not fragile. I get the twenty-pound sledgehammer, which I can barely carry. I heft it over my head, bringing it down as hard as I can. The cement chips a tiny bit on one corner, just a flake. I bring the hammer back over my head as fast and as hard as I can swing twenty pounds. I end up airborne on the upswing, and fall in the dirt once I make contact. Finally. I have about six two-inch pieces. I don't even mess with being gentle any more—just bang on the others as hard as I can.

When I'm satisfied that I have enough for everyone, I gather the small rocks into another bag, and pick up my "body bag" full of teeny chips and dust, and begin to throw the remnants into the flower bed, but at the last second I stop. I can't do it. People are in that dust, and I can't toss them away. I can't just throw them into the garden and leave them out there. I locate a bottle with a cork and gently pour the dust into the bottle, put it in the kitchen on the counter, then return outside to put away every hammer that we own. As I come back into the house, I find Fred bending down looking at the bottle on the counter, poking at it a bit, like a kid studying a bug.

"Is that what I think it is?"

"Yes. It was left in the bag after I broke the big ones. I couldn't throw it away."

"Good." He nods his approval.

December 1

I have lost a day and I don't know how.

All I remember about yesterday is that after coming back to the terminal, Jack came up to me and just leaned on me. I put my arms around his neck and sagged. Hung myself on him. We were hanging on each other. I buried my face in his chest and just wanted to cry.

"I know, baby; I feel it too."

I could have stayed there forever. Slept there. Died there. Maybe I did. Maybe that's how I lost a day.

There has been so much fighting lately around here. Everyone wants to be in charge. Every one of them knows best, but they have lost touch with the families, the compassion, the real reason we are here. We are all way too tired, and have been here way too long. Too many people have come in here to grab a piece of this place—to use it to stroke their egos rather than to give strength to others. In a way I'm glad that I have absolutely no real memory of yesterday, but—it does mean that some of the magic has been lost. . . .

MJ, our NOVA supervisor, is ending her rotation and is leaving to-night, so she will miss closing ceremony for the ferry visits. I give her a tearful hug and a rock. She cries her eyes out. I remember way back 1,000 years ago to the first tearful hug as my Red Cross angel left. The very first rotation of people gone. And here goes one more . . .

How many have come here from all over the world? So many special people. . . . Nameless faces in my memories—for how long? Some in my pictures. All in my heart. Especially sweet George whom I spent many a sunset with, simply breathing it in, standing together until the light faded, marveling at the beauty God sent us every night to calm our crazed hearts. George Donnelly, wherever you have gone—thank you.

As we are leaving Ground Zero, blasting charges are being set inside of one of the buildings that needs to be taken down and removed. I watch as they are running the electric fuses from a bucket—a cherry picker thing. They wait until we are well out of the area before they blast. I wish we could watch. . . .

I busy myself gathering items for the ceremony. The Major has furnished "Amazing Grace"—the words—for me to copy so that we can all sing along. I have physically let go. I can feel the bone-crunching tiredness hanging on me. My body is just too heavy to carry around.

I chat with a departing NOVA worker from the Midwest outside near the administrative trailer—as the sun is setting. "I love those beautiful geese. Wish I could take them home."

"Oh please, take a bunch! I'll drive you around the corner to Mail Boxes Etc., and they'll box those suckers up for you, get you some packing peanuts, and you're good to go!" Living in a place like New Jersey which is overrun with these nasty birds, I can't imagine the attraction. They are evil-tempered, smelly, noisy things that pollute small lakes and leave slimy goose cookies everywhere. We have been telling everyone who leaves that they have to take a goose with them. They are infesting "Bob's Lake." The water is now so deep around the trailer that I saw a duck butt sticking out of the water—they can feed in there!

Fred has presented me with a big, fat, white rose. A florist apparently had delivered a couple of them with our carnations, so he snagged me one. I put it in my half-empty water bottle and put it on my desk. I have heard that white roses signify death in Asian culture. Fitting in many ways . . . I have a sweet-smelling reminder now perched on my desk. I want to take it with me tomorrow on our last boat over, to leave at the Wall of Remembrance. . . .

Tomorrow is our last. We have eighty family members.

December 2

I groan out of the covers to sit up in the dark after not really sleeping. Has it really been almost three months? I am tired, beginning to feel my nerves wanting to twitch. I think even my bones are tired. Every day I have left in the dark. Well past darkness I am just beginning to think about that long drive home.

Is it really over?

The day dawns red, purple, and blue out the back door. It is cold. It is over. I look forward, with nervous jitters, to seeing my crew arrive. I don't know how I am going to hold it together today. I feel like a piece of roadkill—dried up, used, crappy, useless, nothing left. Nothing but jitters.

I ask Bob to do the final orientations for family and staff. He resists only to a point, probably to give me a chance to take it back. It is much more important to me to have him do it: he did the first one; he should take it out as well.

My final crew arrives one by one—hugs, greetings, and nervous faces. We cram as many people as we can (staff) on the boat to give them this last chance. Many fresh ones are with my frequent flyers, but they will not be "working" today—not really. The families will be watched by the veterans among us—the newbies are just going with us to say good-bye. One extreme to another . . . new people—old people. I pass out postcards to the fresh ones, and tell them to be sure to look at them again when they return so they have a perspective to understand the loss.

My favorite trooper, Sergeant Barry, arrives. I see him walking in, and run to him for a big bear hug. "I'm *so* glad you could be here!" We have about twelve blue men today. Barry thanks me for posting the *Name the Trooper* contest in the lunch line. "The little things like that that you did really made us feel part of everything here." We talk about how hard it was for them to loosen up with us and how important it was to them to be teased and messed with all the time. I tell Barry about a trooper whom Fred and I saw at a turnpike rest stop on the way home a couple of weeks ago: I told Fred how I just had the urge to go poke at him and try to make him laugh, but I knew it wouldn't go over too well. I'm going to miss that.

"Yeah, you would have just scared the pants off him and he would have probably arrested you. Don't mess with them out there. They won't take it well. We really aren't used to that."

It is sad that they have no time to get to know people. . . . They really are so *good* with people. I hope that the guys who have been with us can take that as a memory.

They post the lunch menu: chili. Chili, grief, and boat rides; gonna be a rough day. The Tums are already out on the counter in anticipation.

Scheming and plotting for custody of the ducky has finally paid off. After morning orientation the EMTs give us presents. Fred gets his ducky and no longer has to wonder where it went. He gets teary eyed and mushy. I get a little teddy with a dollar under his ribbon and a key chain that reads: I MIGHT BE A BITCH, BUT I'M THE PICK OF THE LITTER. Sweet, sweet people. We hug and wipe a few tears.
This is really gonna hurt.

During orientations for both families and staff we let them know that because this was the last day they can keep their hard hats and goggles.

The last boxes of teddies don't match at all—they are radically different: big ones, tiny ones, colored ones. . . . We worry some about it—wondering if it will cause problems, because if someone gets one that another one wants . . . The families become interested in choosing and trading with each other. And they smile. It could be a *nightmare* to have teddies that are all so different and have 100 people all want what you can't give them. They are having a great time trading and bartering. They are fun to watch, and I join in with an auction: "Okay, who wants a blue teddy? What will you give me for this little brown one?" as I stroll through the boat with armloads of mismatched bears.

Some choose, rechoose, and then choose another—it is great fun, and a lighthearted trip over what generally feels like the River Styx.

As we get to New York I hear the bad news that our SOGs have to pack up and go. They can't come to closing ceremony. Bummer.

We just get everyone settled on the platform, when a New York trooper comes running up to tell me that a fire has just broken out in the American Express building. A welder has touched off a spark in the wrong place. It isn't safe; we have to go. Just as the words leave his mouth, huge black clouds of smoke come billowing out of the building. Sirens begin to sound. We slowly leave. There is a big difference in appearance since yesterday, following the blasting. The whole north wall of the building has gone.

I wander to the front of the platform as the group slowly files off. Orange smoke is pouring from the pit. Black smoke is coming from the American Express building. Steam rises from the hoses that continue to pour water into the pit. Still it burns. After so long it still burns. . . . My mind goes back to a conversation with a Port Authority woman who told me about "Her Tower." Her Tower was Tower Two.

"They carved it into the bedrock. I watched it being built. We'd go stand and watch at lunch as they dug this big hole that looked like a bathtub. They called the hole "the bathtub." It has come full circle. My Tower is now a bathtub again. Ready to be reborn."

I look at the bathtub for the last time.

I look at the horror for the last time.

No more smoke, twisted metal, and dust. No more feeling the weight of all of those souls.

I take *just one more long deep breath* of this hallowed, horrible place.

Just one more look.

Just one more time of running my hand over the railing where so many have written so much. Where so many tears have fallen.

The landscape is new; a building that was burned into my mind has been blasted to bits and has disappeared overnight.

Oh God, just one more day, please? Just one more day to burn it into my brain to be sure it never leaves . . .

I want time to stand and look. I want to say good-bye. Or do I . . . ? Yes, one has been too many, and a thousand would never be enough. I want to fix this *so* badly, but there is no hope for fixing, no way to make it better, nothing that will help. Ever. And no more chances to even try. I feel the grief of letting go. Mine and theirs. My hands are balled into fists inside my sleeves and I'm chewing on my thumb. I suddenly find myself next to Bob. We have come full circle, he and I. But unlike that first time we were in that spot next to each other, I look at him and put my arm around him. "Bob, we leave as we came. In flames." He nods. "I told you: it never gets any easier." We stand with arms linked for a few seconds more after the group has left. He asks, "Ready?" *NO.* But I nod and follow him down to the group.

Rabbi Ron and Major Barb's husband, who is also a Salvation Army chaplain, provide us with eloquent prayers at the Wall of Remembrance, now bare of our families' traces. I stand in the alcove by the bushes and cry as I look at my feet. They didn't get their time. It is so unfair. At least they have this. We are told we can stay as long as we want in this area—we are safe from the smoke and danger of flames. As the prayers are said I see the spot next to me where the dollar teddy was. There is a dent in the bushes where he sat for so many days. I touch the dent softly and leave one of my flowers there for him, a red one, as always. I wander to the fence in the back, and leave a blue and white flower for the Penn State family where their Penn State baseball hat hung on the chain link fence, as I always did when Rich wasn't there to handle it for them. He's here today, but I keep with tradition. I lay a flower and prayer for all the lost souls: the dead ones, the living, and my own.

I say a prayer of thanks, and ask for protection for my crew in the days ahead—for some relief from their pain, and leave a flower for them at the steps. Finally, I pull out the Beanie Baby dog from my pocket. So long ago, Red Cross Mary had asked me to promise her that I would leave him from the two of us on the last trip. Mary had never made it over. He perched on my car seat each day since that conversation took place. I write on him "Mary and Kathi wish you peace," and settle him near where the dollar teddy lived. He will join his fellow stuffies in the dumpster by tomorrow. . . . I wonder, Mary, do you remember? Can you feel it happen from wherever you are? I did as I promised. . . . Tears come again.

I find Fred in the alcove, standing with a white carnation. I match it with a white carnation of my own—the last flower I had. We hold each other and cry, then set our flowers together. We walk back to the group. I can't care for them now—Mother Hen can only think of herself, and she feels very, very bad.

On the way back we remind the families again that they can keep their hats. A big guy says to me, "Hey, got any blue ones?" We only had about three blue ones in total, and I see one now on someone's head. I go to the box to look and come back with a blue one. The *only* blue one left in the box.

He says, "Oh God, you have no idea. Blue was Jennifer's favorite color. Oh, thank you so much. You have no idea." Yeah, I do.

I hear a voice: "Got another blue one?"

"I'll look."

As if by magic one will appear. I was just in the box and there were about four hats—no more blue ones. BUT, yup, right there on top is another blue one. I look skyward and say "Thank you." I get a big broad smile as a reward when I return with the prize.

I go to the back of the boat and begin rummaging in the cooler to hand out juice. I feel a hand on my shoulder. "Hey, baby, I'm gonna deep-six this helmet off the back of the boat. Come with me."

"Jack, I can't. I have to hand out juice."

"Somebody will do it. They always do. Come with."

"Wait." I run to the front. One pink teddy is left from way back when. *Everybody* hated the pink teddies. *Everybody.* No one wanted to take them home when we had pink ones. Blue, green, orange, yeah. It seems pink teddies were the most hated things on earth. I run back and we stuff him into the helmet and tie his little arms and legs in with the straps. We wrap the goggles around him, and I put a red flower under his ribbon. We have finally built our own headstone.

Like two kids we run together out the back door of the boat. We exchange evil grins and Jack says, "On the count of three . . ." Together we count *"one—two—three . . ."* and we heave him off of the back of the boat into the wake. He bobs on the water and floats amazingly well. My brain wants to pull out my camera and take a picture, but my body decides to wrap my arms around Jack's neck instead, and I cry. We hold each other for what seemed like forever.

"Jack, it's been so long."

"Yes."

"This is so hard."

"Yes. But I couldn't have done any of it if it weren't for you."

I look up at him. "The reason we knew each other so well when we met all those years ago is because we were meant to be here?"

"Yes. I knew when I met you we had work to do together. I sure never knew it would be this big."

I bury my face again and continue to cry.

"Oh, crap. I got so emotional I didn't get a picture." We share a wet laugh, wipe our faces, and go back inside. As we walk in, EMT Pete says, "You should have weighted it."

"Nahhh. Wanted it to float on."

Wonder how long it bobbed around. Will it ever be found? My only regret is that we didn't have an OFFICIAL sticker to put on him. Would have been perfect.

The frequent flyers have all gathered in the storeroom behind Mass Care for our private ceremony. I give the Major a nod, and he begins with his booming preacher voice to shepherd us together in a circle. I hand Judy a bag and we divide the circle between us. We know our cues because we schemed together and discussed it in advance. I am having a real hard time holding myself together. I would like very much to hide somewhere and cry until I simply dry up and blow away. We had painstakingly worked out cues to do things, but I can't hear, can't think, and can't concentrate anymore.

I force my mind back to the room to hear the sermon begin:

> September eleventh is going to be one of those special dates in history that everyone will recall where they were between the hours of 8:30 and 11 a.m. At 8:30 Inspector Anthony Infante was driving on the Boulevard in Jersey City. It was going to be just another day of meetings for the commanding officer of the Port Authority Forces at Kennedy Airport. The first call came in reporting that there had been an accident at the World Trade Towers. He rushed to Manhattan in time to calm other people as they made their way from the upper floors. . . ."

Judy and I begin to circle the room as the Major lists the lost heroes and their contributions. He talks of Joshua and the symbolic stones that we gathered and now hold in our hearts—of the need to lay down those heavy stones to build a memorial of hope. . . .

In one hand Jude and I both hold a plastic bag to reach into, in our other hands a little gold silk bag for each person. They look at us, not comprehending—one by one. They look at the reaction of the others who have their gift already, without comprehending.

Faces turn from shock to awe as flesh touches stone. Fingers curl around the stones and the faces register what looks like amazement as Tower One comes to life in front of their eyes, within their hands. Then one by one they look down. Stones are slipped into little gold bags in an almost secretive way—as if to not let others see; this is a very personal and private moment. Little gold bags are held gingerly, dearly. These are very precious stones indeed. When the circle is complete, we take our places again.

The timing has been perfect. I hear the Major say, ". . . Listen. Can you hear the voices of the heroes through the flames? They are singing 'God Bless America.' Let us lift our voices and join with them." His voice wavers with tears. I cannot even choke out a sound.

The Major invites us to speak at the conclusion of the song. Many do. I can no longer think. I stutter out "If I could speak I would say something. I can't. Just thank you." We sing "Amazing Grace." Bob says sweet things to me that run in my ears, tweak my heart, and immediately leave my brain. His little flicker of anger at my disobedience is gone. I can't retain any of the sweet things they all say as they give their good-byes to one another, and I feel a twinge of jealousy for not being able to do anything other than look at my feet. I have short-circuited *big time.*

Outside the others are gathering at the dock for the *real, official* closing ceremony for everyone. The chill is creeping in. The light is leaving fast. Movement unglues my brain a bit. We go out to join them. Major Fred does it again, leading prayer and song. Bob gives a speech. We take everyone inside for bags of goodies and teddy bears to keep.

A tap on my shoulder from behind is Sergeant Tom, who gives me a hug. He is grinning like a fool. "Did you get that stuff out on *my watch?*"

"Actually, yes."
"*How?*"
I laugh.

Beth hugs me and cries. "I had no idea that this was how it was for you." I hold her. "This is *hard*." Yes, Beth, so hard. I think "hard" is just beginning . . . I give Mabel, my favorite therapy dog, a final hug and pet good-bye. "Thank you, Mabes, for always being there for me. You saw me through a *lot*." She kisses me.

My desk is now clean. My cell phone is handed in. A NOVA worker comes up to me and gives me the final participant attendance roster for the day. I cry. She laughs.

It is hard to leave. Many of us linger a bit. Eat one last nasty dinner together. . . . I find Bob, Jude, and Vic and we sit down for our last meal.

Fred and I go upstairs to give a final good-bye to Sergeant Tom.

Fred, Jude, and I walk to the walls and leave a final message. Still nothing profound will come from this fried brain of mine. It is very dark. Time. *Over.*

We can linger no longer; we must leave for home. I burst into tears as we reach the back of the terminal. Fred pulls me through the dark backyard to the skyline, to the water. From God knows where he produces the white rose that he had given me yesterday. *"My rose!"* I had wanted to leave it in New York. I had forgotten it, and in the running around since, I didn't remember it again. He puts his arm around me and we lean at the dock railing. I pull off the petals and give him half. Together we toss them into the water. I fling the stem. The Empire State Building's decorative lighting has changed tonight from red, white, and blue to red and green for the holidays.
Good-bye.
"Why is this so *hard?*" We cry.
I watch the skyline. Broken buildings still have their lights on, still standing there trying to be buildings after all that they have been

through, still trying to pretend that they are not forming a ring around a big smoking hole. That ghostly halogen glow still rises up like fog. *Oh God,* why should it be so hard to leave this place?

There is no good-bye; this is forever. It will never leave me.

On the way home a trooper car pulls in behind us in traffic. We pull over. He begins to pass us, then pauses, riding with us, shining his light into the car. He flips the overhead lights on and off quickly as a greeting and then flies away. Haven't got a clue which one it was; couldn't see his face in the dark.

Good-bye.

Oh God, please:

> just one more boat,
> one more family,
> one more day,
> . . . one more chance.

Just one more . . .
But *over* is now.
Now it is time to cry.

The Victorian clock towers above the U.S. flag that hangs from the catwalk in the terminal building.

Exterior of the 1860s railroad terminal building in Liberty State Park that housed the FAC.

A RISING NATION

DEAR, VOLENTER
THANK YOU
FOR YOUR
HELP CLEAN-
ING UP
THE MESS IN
NEW YORK.

Cards sent by schoolchildren to cheer up the workers at the FAC. One first grade class raised $4,000 for the World Trade Center victims.

The Wall of Remembrance as it looked in October 2001, piled high with teddies and mementos . . .

. . . and as it looked in December 2002—green again.

The Penn State hat. The last family visit occurred on December 2, 2001.

The dollar teddy, left on October 6 during the first family visit. He was removed on November 30 with his dollar still intact.

Memorial walls at the FAC. "Look at those two chairs, alone and empty in front of the walls. Take that picture—it's amazing," said the nurses over lunch.

Close-up of inscription on a memorial wall.

Buses lined up to take family members to the ferries.

Ferry approaching the dock.

Families boarding for the seven-minute trip to NYC.

Families, companions, and FAC personnel walking down Liberty Street toward Ground Zero.

The iron cross which fell intact from one of the buildings at Ground Zero.

The Pile: Tower One as viewed from West Street, October 2001.

The Pit: Looking toward the Verizon building, where Tower One would have been—2002.

View of the Family Assistance Center from the catwalk that encircled the perimeter of the interior, October 2001.

Dismanteling the Family Assistance Center, March 2002.

Tributes to a husband and father guarded by teddies: Two cans of his favorite beer, a half-eaten Oreo cookie from the baby, a juice box from the son, and a dog discuit from Jake, the family dog.

Kathi cutting angels from the Memorial Christmas tree, 2002. January 2002. (Photo by Fred Bedard)

Epilogue

Everyone who read these pages before they were "officially" a manuscript said, "Tell about what it's like now—looking back. . . ."

It's hard to tell about any of it.

Not because it hurts.

Or because with the exposure to trauma, "telling" brings a person *back there.*

Those things are true, but that isn't why it's hard. I hope that I will never be able to adequately describe any of it to you: that would imply that I have accepted it enough, that *we* have accepted it enough to have language for it. I never want to *accept* what happened on September 11, 2001. It is simply not acceptable.

People ask, "What was it like?" "How have you changed?" "What did it *do* to you?", questions that I never know how to respond to. It was the most horrible and the most beautiful event I have ever witnessed or experienced. It was intense to the point that it hurt—still does, and always will. It was extreme. It was something that no one on this earth should ever have to see or do—yet—it is something that everyone should have seen and done. So you see my dilemma. Any method that I use to try to describe what it was like doesn't work because something so big is beyond my ability.

Simply being there and serving others was the highest honor I think I could ever receive. It is so intimate, so personal, and so highly privileged. Telling about it one or two years later is no easier. If you ask me again in forty years, I'll bet I can't explain it then, either . . . so I will tell you about some of the things that have happened since then in an effort to tie up loose ends. . . .

The Aftermath

March 22, 2002, was the official closing day of the FAC—the end of service delivery at a centralized location. Services for the families were to be picked up locally by many different agencies. The state police took us over to Ground Zero in state police boats to say good-bye, and to obtain some closure on the experience. It was the first time I had been back to New York since the last family visit. We went in tiny cutters (tiny when you have about twenty passengers). It was brutally cold, windy, with a coating of ice on just about everything. The spray from the boats had frozen over the decks and rails. We were ordered to stay below deck where we would have stood shoulder to shoulder, filling it completely. They fussed and worried over us, cajoled and begged because we would not stay below deck, preferring to be out in the freezing cold and wind. They feared we would slip from the icy decks and fall overboard.

It was so cold on the platform that my fingers cramped and I could barely hold my camera, even with gloves on. The experience left me feeling raw, cold, lonely, and bleeding inside. I didn't feel like I had closure. I felt like someone ripped me open and packed me full of dry ice. I was very appreciative of the experience—it was a sweet, humane gesture. I felt comfort at being with old familiar faces in that all-too-familiar place. But deep down I wished I had not gone.

When we returned to the FAC, we gathered as a group in the chapel for one last meeting. Bob and the New Jersey State Police gave speeches and presented the Governor's Resolution that officially terminated the FAC services. When Bob spoke he read one of the messages from the memorial walls that had particularly touched him. It was unsigned, so we didn't know who had left it. It was titled "ONE":

As the soot and ash rained down,
We became one color.
As we carried each other down the stairs of the burning building,
We became one class.
As we lit candles of waiting and hope,
We became one generation.
As the firefighters and police officers fought their way into the inferno,
We became one gender.
As we fell onto our knees in prayers for strength,
We became one faith.
As we whispered or shouted words of encouragement,
We spoke one language.

As we gave our blood in lines miles long,
We became one body.
As we mourned together the great loss,
We became one family.
As we cried tears of grief and loss,
We became one soul.
As we retell with pride the sacrifice of heroes,
We became one people.

We are
One color,
One class,
One generation,
One faith,
One gender,
One language,
One family.

We are the power of ONE.
We are united.
We are America!

To close the ceremony, Major Fred gave a sermon. He speaks with passion and conviction, but it is his words that always touch me the most. He could have whispered them and had the same impact on my heart.

The story of Joshua and the collection of stones was a theme that ran under the surface of many things that we did: in the Major's blessings to us in the morning meetings, my debriefings with staff, the good-bye "gift" that I gave to my frequent flyers.

During closing ceremony the Major began by telling of living in a small fishing village where all of the townspeople had collected stones to build a memorial for those they had lost at sea. Once the stones had been piled together, they put a light at the top: a shining beacon to welcome their lost loved ones home. He continued:

It is somehow so fitting that we should be here, associated with liberty and freedom: Lady Liberty with her great light shining in the harbor to welcome us home.

On October 11, 2001, we met for a memorial service on the docks, facing the World Trade Center complex where we had been taking the families by boat each day.

The sermon that day was from Joshua 4, where God instructs the Israelites to gather stones from the riverbed to build a memorial. The Lord said to Joshua, ". . . take up twelve stones . . . carry them over with you and put them down at the place where you will stay tonight. In the future when your children ask you, "What do these stones mean?" tell them, "These stones are to be a memorial to the people . . . forever."

They took up twelve stones . . . and they carried them over with them to their camp, where they put them down.

During that service on the docks, we talked about the kinds of stones that we all picked up on the visits to Ground Zero: not the ones you can touch, but the stones that we now hold in our hearts. Stones of anger, fear, and hate. Stones of revenge. Stones of grief. Now, as we are leaving, is the time to lay down those stones . . . use them to build a memorial of hope, not fear. Let us leave behind a memorial to the strength and beauty of humanity, with a beautiful shining beacon at the top.

And as we leave this place and the people behind always remember: *the light shining at the top is YOU.*

He looked right at me as he finished. He was watching the effect that his words had on me. He knew I would cry—as I did almost every morning that he gave us our blessing before we left for New York. He frequently told me that he enjoyed the fact that I would get all choked up over his sermons. In my typical fashion, I choked up and felt like my insides were dissolving. Major Barb wrapped her arms around me—laughing—and she held me tight while I sniffled and wiped my tears. And, as always there was singing. We stood with our arms around each other for one last group sing. After the ceremony, we went to the water and tossed red carnations into the river as a symbolic good-bye.

But we will carry our stones in our hearts forever.

I went upstairs to see the FEMA guys one last time, and one of the sergeants, who was beginning to pack up the state police belongings.

He asked if there was anything around that I wanted as a souvenir. Teasing, I said, "An urn would be nice."

He laughed. "Can't do that. You got a flag, though, didn't you?"

"No." Suddenly I felt left out.

"Really? Hope we have some left." He digs in a box. "Last one." He smiled as he handed me a trifold American flag. I clutched it to my chest and thought that I never wanted to let it go. I can't describe the feeling of being handed one of those. To me it was more than a flag. It felt somehow like all of my heritage crashing in on me. The weight of it, the texture, the symbolism was simply profound to me, and beyond words. I thought of all of those long gone in my family—they had struggled to make a home here in this country—so amazingly alien from their own. I thought of my brother going to Vietnam. And of those who died across the river. And those who died in the Pentagon and Shanksville. And of their loved ones who had clutched their flags in the same way as I did in that moment.

Because it was the last one, he asked me to take it out to my car. I stuffed it under my shirt as I walked through the terminal. I was conspicuously lumpy and pointed. I probably would have attracted less attention had I just walked out with it. It lives now in a little wooden case in my living room.

Three days later, on March 25, 2002, I had the pleasure of being included in the group that dismantled the FAC, returning it once again to a park and ferry terminal. Fred went with me. I took great delight in taking it all apart, carrying it out the door, and loading it onto trucks. We gathered together the final paperwork, took down the flags, the banners, and the signs, liberated the plants that were still hanging on by a thread. The last official sign-in sheet is in my possession. Bob thought I should have it.

At the end of the day, when we were down to dust bunnies, I felt lighter; as if I had closed the door without regrets. I am a person who has always appreciated the benefits of demolishing something to relieve stress. Fred did not feel better. He found it to be a sad experience and said he wished he had not gone. He wanted to remember it bustling with people.

At this writing, I still have a potted plant that used to be in the chapel. It is a painful, prickly thing that isn't a cactus. It sat by the altar and used to stab me in the leg even through heavy jeans. I remember one occasion that it actually drew blood. Looks prehistoric. During those packing activities in March we were adopting the remaining plants. Someone pushed it into my arms and said, "Here, it needs a good home." It stabbed me again. I looked at this pathetic, yellow, dying thing in my arms. It had scale bugs all over it. A shadow of its former bloodthirsty self. I looked at the person who decided I should have it and said, "I think it's dead."

"No. Just needs love. Take it home and water it. It needs you."

It lives. It has a baby one living in the pot with it (God help me!). It still stabs me when I get near it, which is every day when I feed my dogs. I have no idea what kind of plant it is, how to care for it, or even if I like it. But it is now happy and green again, so I try to admire its fierce determination to live whenever it stabs me.

I have had many occasions to be with and talk to many of my "crew," my frequent flyers. Sometimes they find me. Sometimes I find them. Sometimes when we find each other it snowballs into a group visit. I treasure those moments with them. We share an intimacy and level of intensity that many people never reach—even with their spouses and family. We can pick up as if we never left off in conversation. Being with one another is lighthearted and pretty easy—after all, we all went to the FAC and became bonded through good intentions. What's that saying about the pathway to hell?

During the end of August 2002, I remember a vague, growing sensation inside me of something dark and nasty rummaging around in my brain. I was becoming irritable, and wanted to run away and hide. Then the frantic late-night phone calls and e-mails started. My crew were feeling it too. Being able to rationally tie it to the upcoming anniversary in our minds and to understand our reactions as normal (considering) did not help it go away. Those feelings really began to blossom as the anniversary approached. A couple of times I got calls as late as midnight and after. Many times we were on the phone for *hours*. We are still companioning each other.

During that time period, Judy and I were playing phone tag and not connecting with each other, probably unconsciously on purpose. On September 11, I called her in the morning, really wanting to hear her voice. I was restless and pacing. I left a voice-mail message that I was thinking of her. I knew instinctively that it was just too hard for her to respond, and after leaving that message, I decided to just let it be. In December, out of the blue, she called: we connected again, chattering and laughing and catching up as if it were yesterday . . . so—it took her two months to call back—no biggie. She told me I was right. It was just too hard.

I have noticed that over the past three years, I frequently wake up at 4:30 in the morning. I am definitely not a morning person. During my lifetime I have never had difficulty sleeping. I'm the type who can sleep through thunder, explosions, anything. About three to four times a week my eyes pop open at exactly 4:30. There seems to be no causal factor: no noise in the house, no planes flying overhead, traffic noise, no symptoms of stress, nothing unusual. I wondered about it, but didn't dwell on it because I couldn't connect it to anything. Very recently, I asked Fred to set the alarm clock for me, as I had to get up early for a meeting out of town. He asked me about where I was going and we chatted for a bit, then he laughed and said, "Remember all those days when that alarm was set for 4:30, and you would roll out of bed and hit the road for the FAC? You were gone before the sun came up. I don't know how you did that every day for so long." The piece of the puzzle fell into place and I suddenly realized: *I'm still doing it.*

We all have varying degrees of stress symptoms that are typical of people who have been exposed to traumatic events. We have in common things such as

- Some experience recurring "flashes" of Ground Zero that look as real as a photograph, and arrive with smells and emotional responses. These flashbacks actually feel like the event is being relived.
- Hyperarousal is manifested by inability to fall asleep or remain asleep, irritability or inappropriate outbursts of anger or sadness, difficulty with concentration, always feeling watchful or on guard, unable to relax, and exaggerated startle responses (jumping more than is indicated when someone sneaks up behind and says *"boo"*).
- Some of us feel restless, anxious, and irritable when there are associations to that place. Reminders like the smell of rain on hot cement bring some of us back in time; we feel suspended in time and space.

- Talking about the experience or reading about it can bring a variety of reactions: dizziness, dilated pupils, perspiration, racing heart, muscle tension, shortness of breath, sadness, tearfulness, irritability—you name it. We have experienced this horrific event for prolonged time, with all of our senses: taste, touch, smell, sight, thoughts. We have been imprinted.
- Some of us have obsessions with looking at pictures, reading about the disaster, and talking about it. Others avoid it completely.
- Depersonalization—the sense of being outside of one's self—occurs with some of us.

Something else we all have in common is the comfort that comes from contact with one another and those who have worked there, because we share understanding. And we share the knowledge that this will be with us always. I know a man who was an early responder to the disaster, an EMT. He sometimes says to me, "I *really* need to talk." We get together and sit. "I'm here—talk. Get it out." At that point he shakes his head, lowers his eyes, tears run down his face and all he can manage is "Oh, shit." So I wrap my arms around him and let him cry. He has told me that just being with someone who knows what it was like is healing, because he can't find the words, doesn't know what to say. But with someone who has been there, words are not needed. He can watch the pictures in his head, feel the terror, feel the sadness, but not have to struggle to find an explanation because he knows that I'm back there with him. And everyone whom I know who has been to that place feels contact with other responders as comfort. Kinship. Support by just being there.

Sadly, for many of my crew, their loved ones apparently can't understand why the experience stays with us. We have accepted that it will go with us to our graves, like some demon that has possessed us. Because we don't need words with one another, we have that silent knowing—loved ones apparently feel left out and cannot relate to our experience and the way that it stays alive in our minds and hearts. Some family members apparently don't even want to understand. Reactions many get from spouses and family include:

> "Enough already."
> "Get on with your life."
> "I'm sick of hearing about this."
> "*You did this to yourself,* so shut up about it."
> "You aren't special, you know."

When I hear these things I feel so sorry. Sorry for my crew who have to deal with their pain and confusion without benefit of family support. I am fortunate—I took my husband with me. He knows.

I also feel sorry for the family members who will not give understanding to those who are in pain, having symptoms, needing support. They are missing out on being close to a beautiful person. They are denying compassion to someone who would give until they bleed. They are holding back a hug from someone who needs one. But I am also angry with them: How can you be so mean to someone whom you love? We should have learned one thing from this horrific event: life is precious and can be taken from us in a heartbeat. I would like to sit them all down and yell at them about selfishness, having consideration, respect, and most of all, showing patience and love in a relationship.

Yes, I am still a Mother Hen.

But I have also learned about the flip side. There are extremes in spousal reactions as well. I was gifted with insight from a wife of one of the FAC staff. She described to me what it was like to live with one of us afterward and to try to help with the pain without having seen it or being able to understand it: "I imagined it was bad. He told me what he could, at times just a half a sentence that I wouldn't hear the rest of for weeks. He relayed anecdotes, sometimes just phrases—then his head would drop. He would shake his head. I'd just tell him, 'Hey, whenever you're ready.' It hurt me to see him so hurt. I found it near impossible to straddle those two worlds. . . . Being Mom, friend, PTA volunteer, neighbor, while also being wife was the hardest thing I have ever done. If other people learned what he was doing, it was like it was a disease. They would physically back away from me. I knew then that I was in this alone with him. They don't get it. What should I call it? Innocent ignorance? Denial? I don't know. I feel the need to apologize for them, yet it angers me." She offered a laugh (but not because it was funny): "It really hurts to be married to one of you guys. . . ."

I'll bet it does.

I feel sorry for my crew—my angels. How can we ever convey what we carry inside?

Yes, we did it to ourselves. We walked beside grieving families and victims willingly. We lifted them up and carried them when we had to. And we took on their pain. And with every sunset we have felt it again. It never gets any easier. It will never go away.

I have no doubt what I will see with my dying breath, as I close my eyes that last time. I am sure that the vision of that devastation will appear. And with it will come the smells, the pain, and the desire to scream until I can't scream anymore.

I am not alone with that vision.

How can we ever convey to you what we carry inside? How can I explain the trauma that we have all received as a result of that work?

We are tortured souls.

But most important, how can I ever explain the way that pain is connected to purpose, to honor, to compassion, to strength?

Our souls have been touched by extraordinary beauty.

I can tell you that it hurts beyond any broken love affair, any loss, anything in my life I have grieved over. It hurts every day. It hurts so deep inside that sometimes I wonder if I might just spontaneously combust from it, even years later. But if you were to come to me with a magic wand and tell me that you could wave it all away I would not let you.

When the pain starts it is immediately followed by connections to

- purpose
- the pure and simple act of being allowed to serve others
- the honor of being permitted to share the most intimate moments of strangers, and to hope we have somehow eased their pain
- visions of dirt-covered men with bloody, dirty rags tied around their wounded hands—removing their hard hats to cover their hearts as families walked past: American pride and humanity at its shiniest and most beautiful
- walking past men as big as trees—young and strong and brave with tears silently pouring down their faces
- so many faces of family members and glimpses into the lives of the young, vibrant, beautiful people who were taken from them
- people who would do "anything for the families . . ."
- the honor of walking beside people who are angels. Anyone who served as they did is an angel.

So I take deep breaths and try to stay verbal when people question me about the experience, because I want others to understand. I can paint you a picture, give you a glimpse. (I hope that I have done that here.) I will never be able to convey the magnitude. It's a bit like giving birth: you can watch the movie to show you what it's like but you will not know how much it's going to hurt until you try it. Recently when about a dozen of us were together we were discussing the bond that we share. Fred said, "I would take a bullet for most of you, but I really don't even know you." Many of us nodded "yes." I wondered, were we agreeing that we would all take that bullet, or was it because we already had?

None of us are the same as we were on September 10, 2001. Some of the people I met at the FAC have made wonderful changes in their lives; some have received promotions and recognition for their contributions. I love to see them smile and talk of their new lives.

I had a conversation with one individual who returned home and immediately filed for divorce. "Life is too short to live with a bitch" was his simple explanation. Cold? Maybe not—maybe enough is enough. He has seen a lot of pain. He is happy now. We all learned extraordinary lessons. We have all changed. Forever.

Bob retired from his state position with New Jersey Human Services and took a consulting position in toxic waste management. He's happy and healthy again. He remains a teasing, insufferable, wonderful, warm man. Bob is not and never was close to being a beast, but I'm sure that he wouldn't want word of that to get out and ruin his reputation. Bob is still involved in the process that will determine what and where a permanent memorial is built for the New Jersey families and victims.

Jack retired from his state position in New Jersey Addictions Services and eventually chose work in the field of domestic violence. I was really feeling abandoned when he told me he was leaving. When he left, he didn't have anything lined up yet. I asked him what he was going to do. He replied, "Watch Court TV and become a greeter at Wal-Mart." He actually did the Court TV part for a while, but a personality that big cannot be contained for long.

Judy decided to end her Red Cross career in disaster work and be a person with a husband and a "normal" life in Virginia. She has always worked at disasters. She is now with a private therapy agency, providing outpatient services. The marriage has not occurred yet, but I recently accompanied her on a wedding dress shopping hunt. We had a conversation about how hard it has been for her to settle down to a normal life after 9/11. She didn't seem to realize that she has never *had* a normal life. She has always run all over the world helping others deal with pain and loss and devastation. I felt compelled to explain to her that she has to know what normal is before she can settle into it.

Rich has had ups and downs, like any sensitive person who really cares about the people in his life. Like me, he returned to his former life, work, etc., and attempted to just fit right back in. It isn't always that easy. He provides training for police, does work in safety management and in mental health. Sometimes when we speak, he appears to be very sad. He sometimes looks nervous. He is a reminder to me of how fragile humans really are, and of how incredibly strong we all are. When I look at Rich, I see a decent, wonderful human who would still give just about anyone the shirt off his back. He is still in touch with the family who lost the young man who attended Penn State. Since Rich continues to be a proud Penn State alumnus, he gladly carries that symbol for them.

Beth, the owner of Mabel, my favorite therapy dog, has changed careers: she now teaches phys ed in a high school. She also coaches basketball. She is *so* happy. Mabel continues her therapy work, healing others by wagging and licking.

Fred had a midlife crisis, and developed some insight into the fact that (1) we really have no control over the universe, and (2) worry is a waste of time. He is finding gratitude. He went through a frightening but successful bout with cancer. Fred celebrated his new lease on life by buying a motorcycle. (I was not happy about the motorcycle. New Jersey drivers are not known for politeness.) For the past eight years a yellow rubber ducky sat on the edge of the bathtub. I had given it to him as a joke. Now there are two, looking like a momma and baby. He tells me that the duck reminds him of extraordinary experiences, how wonderful people are and how lucky he is. Every day he stops for a moment and remembers. . . .

One of my frequent flyers, George, really didn't make it into the journal except in a very fleeting way. Not because he was unimportant by any means. Most likely because he was always just there, being strong and steady and doing what he needed to do without comment or incident. But because I'm telling you about changes, I want you to know about him now: George lived in South Jersey—more than a three-hour drive from the FAC. He sacrificed family, friends, work to be at the FAC for at least half of the boat visits and to volunteer for additional work in the trailer. George is quiet and reserved, but he has a very expressive face. Initially, when I was doing something annoying like following him around and telling him that he really needed to eat lunch before 3 p.m., and that other people could see the families while he took a little break to care for himself, he gave me a few looks that were a little standoffish. I approached Rich, who knew him, and asked what was going on. Rich explained simply that George didn't like authority figures. At some point, George apparently decided that I meant no harm because he began to reward me with the most amazing smiles. George has a smile that belongs in magazines. Immediately after working that long stretch at the FAC, George had a rough time dealing with the aftermath and the stress. Things were very dark for him for a while, but he came through it and completely turned his life around. He has a new and better job, a new and better place to live, and a new girlfriend he seems to be very, very happy with. I have watched him step outside of his comfort zone and try things that he would not have done before. He talks about the wonderful blessings he now has. He is truly radiant. George is proof to me that no good deed goes unrewarded. He is proof that out of something really evil, blessings come. I believe that the life that he has now is his gift for the sacrifices he made, and the pain he felt as a result of giving to others so selflessly. For me, he clearly illustrates transformation and gratitude.

Since December 2001, four FAC staff (that we know of) died of heart attacks. So much left to give and do. Vital, giving, wonderful people—not yet old enough to die. Veteran disaster workers tell me that disasters screw up your electrical system. I'm not really sure of the exact way that it happens, but apparently it is common for people to have heart attacks in relationship to disasters. Certainly seeing so many people in pain simply hurts your heart. The work is stressful. One of my fellow sunset worshippers, George Donnelly, was one of them. He was well loved. I hung his picture on one of the memory boards at the request of some of his NOVA staff. He was an angel when I stood beside him here on earth. I know that he still is and is still smiling.

Yes, we did it to ourselves.

I know that I would do it again in a heartbeat.

The memorial walls from the FAC were removed from the terminal building, shrink wrapped, and taken to the New Jersey State Museum for display. There are over 250 panels in all. They have been in other locations in New Jersey since. Bob invited me to join him in providing information to museum staff so that they could understand the reactions of people who would view the display. I was amazed at how I teared up and had trouble describing the walls. The museum staff had not yet seen them.

It was funny to watch the reactions of the museum staff when we explained that these walls belong *to the families*. If the families wanted to come and write on them some more, or add things to the walls, they should let them. These staff members were used to strict rules: "Don't touch the display." They wanted to set rules for the walls, protect them, preserve them as they were when they came in the door—this was blasphemy. Every fiber of museum conduct was now turned upside down. (The first rule of disasters is that there are no rules.) The staff were beside themselves that we should *want* them to give markers to the families so they could write on the display. I really felt for their distress. After about a forty-minute orientation and discussion, Bob and I accompanied them in to see the display and pointed out some of the messages that were special to us. We told them stories about the families who left the messages. The energy and power of that place clings to everything related to it. Its power is indescribably huge. They understood.

I volunteered for a few days at the museum, to be available for people who came in to see the exhibit, to answer questions. We had a special viewing just for the families. I walked around the corner of a wall and directly into the gent from Pakistan who went with us to Ground Zero on that first day. (His in-laws had taken the urn back to Pakistan with them.) He just keeps popping up—I couldn't resist: "Don't I know you from somewhere?" He laughed. He had his son with him, now six years old. The child really is a prodigy—he writes articles for a magazine in India. I shook the boy's hand and explained to him how I knew his father, then said to him, "I hear that you are very bright. Is that true?"

"Oh, *yes!*" he answered in a very adult and authoritarian voice.

"And a handful?"

"Oh, *yes!*" The father nodded his head, smiling.

"Do you know which one is my momma?"

"No, I don't. Would you like to show me?" He took my hand, walked me to a wall, where he provided me with a very formal introduction to her picture, explaining to her how I accompanied his father to New York.

I have seen the walls in a couple of their locations. They are a "wandering" display until a decision can be made and construction completed on a permanent place to house them. For me, the walls are a constant reminder that the effects of such a horrendous act live on forever. The trauma will never end—it may evolve over time, but it will speak to us and nag in the back of our brains forever. When the walls are moved, they are always settled into place in a different order. Originally, at the FAC, one family wrote a continuous message that spanned the top of twelve separate boards, which at that time were all on the perimeter. It has become disjointed. Interestingly, if you see the fragments without the knowledge that they once fit together, they stand alone. They make sense to the reader.

One wall has an orange teddy bear stapled to it, arms spread wide as if to offer a hug. When that teddy arrived Jack picked it up and threw it away in disgust: "Orange. It's ugly. Who would make an orange teddy bear? It's hideous! *No one* would want an orange teddy bear. Look at that thing. *Ugh!*" His reaction was both funny and strange to me. Strange because it was so negative and intense. He *really* didn't like that bear. The next morning I entered the terminal building from the back door and there was that teddy: arms spread, stapled on the wall. A family had found him, saved him from the garbage can, and used him as their memorial on the most visible board there. You *had* to pass by it. You had to see that bear. I cracked up. I grabbed Jack and dragged him over. I was doubled over laughing at his shocked face as he backed away, shaking his head, whispering, "Oh God, no . . ." When I see that wall, I smile.

When I see the rest of the walls, I engage in rituals: I first hunt for the three messages that I left and the one from my husband. Strangely, they usually jump right out at me. I find myself right in front of each one without even looking—as if they call to me, and pull me near. In a way it is almost a need to check to be sure that I really was a part of this thing, that it wasn't a dream. When the familiar is done, I look for the families with whom I had opportunity to become acquainted: the beautiful woman who has her name on a bomb, the woman from Pakistan, the note left by a young pregnant woman to her husband—on behalf of Jake the dog. There is a photo of a man whose wife turned to me on the platform in horror to ask, "Is this all that is left?" One woman always left scented candles for her husband. The first thing we smelled each morning as we came to work was Christopher. I look for him. I then look for the oldest messages—the ones I saw first at the FAC: those from the little ones who couldn't talk, couldn't write, but could make the tears run down my face uncontrollably.

I really can't stand and read the walls. Still. But I find my hands drawn out to touch them, like a moth to a flame. The heavy, heavy boulders in my chest return, my stomach tightens, a lump comes to my throat. The edges of my vision blur out and I go back through time as if I'm actually there, and I feel it, hear it, smell it, and taste it all over again. I can feel on my skin the chill of the air inside the terminal. The memories flood back with such intensity that I feel like someone has smacked me in the face. I want to scream. But I don't. As Bob said, "It never gets any easier." Instead of fighting it, I let the sadness squash down on my shoulders and wrap around me. I reach out my hand and touch my past. I simply let my fingertips rest there on the plastic shield that now protects the walls, and I experience the weight of it. In some strange way it feels like coming home.

My work involves dealing with staff of mental health agencies in New Jersey. I frequently run into people who volunteered to work at the FAC. I have found that some people worked there "only" once or twice and feel upset because they didn't do more. Not just mildly troubled, *really* upset. They seem angry with themselves, and strangely, talking about feeling jealousy toward people who went repeatedly.

I had many conversations at the FAC with people who were not assigned to companion a family, but were simply "warm bodies"—people to watch for tripping hazards, hand out equipment, or some other task. They rarely understood the impact of simply standing beside someone. And they couldn't, because they had the perspective of only that day, that experience. So I would tell them about a young widow who was in so much grief that she couldn't deal with others talking to her, hovering near her. We stepped back, didn't speak, offer, or touch. We stood, and we watched. Later she told me how wonderful it was to just *know* we were there, that we were strong, capable, and simply there. Just in case . . .

I had an interesting conversation with a therapist from one of our agencies near the two-year anniversary. He said he wished that he had the strength to go more than once, but once had almost broken him: it pushed him past his limit and he couldn't bring himself to go back. He told me that he wished he was as healthy as I was. I told him that I thought he had it backward: that people like him knew their limits and were probably much healthier and more courageous, because they set boundaries for what was good for them and they didn't exceed those boundaries. I'm not sure that my decision to be there so much came from being healthy. In retrospect, I think that healthy people should run screaming from such a thing. . . . He responded by laughing and saying, "You're crazy; you know that?"

Yup.

To have served the families this way for "only" one day is a wonderful and amazing show of strength, courage, and compassion. Really. If you are a person who did not go there, step back, and objectively look at the face value. Remember those burning buildings. Remember the film clips and the photos. Consider the horror of it burning for *months*. And imagine the fear and impact of walking around the corner in New York City to see that, let alone putting your feelings aside to deal with the pain of someone else. What do you think you would feel if you saw America blasted and burning? If you could smell it?

In October 2002, author Gail Sheehy asked me to gather a group of frequent flyers to participate in an interview. Gail's book on the Middletown families was almost completed. She wanted to include a section in her book about what happens to disaster workers afterward. Jack came up with the idea to meet in the chapel of the terminal: the old crowd back at the FAC together. I called the state park staff, who were more than compassionate and understanding about giving us time in the chapel together. The questions centered around the hardest part of the experience and how we have changed as a result. Bob and a couple of others spoke. It was my turn, and the question about the hardest thing came up. Bob was seated behind me. "Tell about the first trip over." I felt like I physically dropped through the floor. My heart stopped. I turned to look at him. "How did you know?"

"It's the same for me. Go on. You'll do a good job at telling it." I was amazed that we shared the same experience as being the hardest, mostly because at that moment I realized that although I would feel comfortable sharing anything with Bob, we had never discussed our experiences there. I was also amazed that he *knew* what was the most difficult for me. We had shared so much, but that sharing wasn't with words.

Fred and I sleep in a Victorian-style iron bed that is made to use as a canopy: with rails that run around the perimeter of the top of the bed. From the rail directly over our heads hangs a large, bright blue dream catcher that was thrust into my hands on the sidewalk outside Ground Zero by a member of the Lakota Nation: ". . . for bad dream prevention." The man who handed it to me walked through our group with his eyes glued to me, as if I were a target. I saw his eyes light on me as he walked down the steps from the platform, and during the minute that it took to reach the spot where I stood, he never took his eyes off of me. I remember thinking *"Why is he looking at me that way?"* As he pushed the dream catcher into my hands, I wondered: what made him choose me? Out of all of the people he walked past—what made him look right to me in the middle of that crowd, push his way through, and give me this gift? The whole encounter was so odd that I found myself speechless and unable to ask. It has a bear fetish tied in the middle and a small silver feather. I have not noticed bad dreams in our house over the past three years. But there is no need for nightmares: I can close my eyes in waking moments and find myself back there. A bright blue dream catcher is oddly out of character mixed with Victorian oak in our bedroom. It matches nothing we own. I sometimes stop and look at it and think about fate, and faith; why we choose to take certain paths, and the not-so-random selection that seems to occur in life. I don't believe in coincidences.

One evening in early November 2002, I had just finished printing out what I thought was a version of this work that may be coherent enough for someone else to read. I still resist the thought that I should release these pages to anyone. Those around me encourage it, so I moved at a snail's pace in that direction (mostly for those who were there with me; it is their thoughts I want to respect).

As I carried the pages downstairs, the phone began to ring. I cursed under my breath because I was about to leave to meet someone and was not in the mood for telemarketers. I almost didn't pick up, but something told me to answer the phone. A deep voice on the other end said, "Hi. I'm Bill, from the Port Authority . . ."

All of my hair stood on end.

". . . got your phone number from Gail Sheehy . . . thought that you might be willing to work with us and lend us a hand with getting the families down into the Pit for the upcoming holidays."

I looked down at the pile of papers in my hand, and wondered what strange energy surrounds these pages—that every time I have them in my hand and think of doing something with them, the phone rings. And somehow I get catapulted into a new chapter of my life.

It goes without saying. The compassion vampire awakes from her slumber in the back of my brain, and I hear her use my voice to say, "Of course, anything I can do, Bill. Anything for the families."

We chat a bit about the details, about the place that was once named the "Pile," and is now known as the "Pit." We shared stories about our work there, and about the powerful energy that the place gives off—regardless of the name it has, or the stage it is in.

Several retired Port Authority police have apparently gotten together as volunteers, wanting to take the families down inside the Pit on Sundays, Christmas Eve, New Year's Eve, and on both holidays. No pay. They have an area where they will wait for the families to arrive, and they will provide escort down the long ramp into the Pit. The time for families to take advantage of this opportunity is bureaucratically limited, with only precious few holiday weeks. They plan to finish by January 4.

I'm about to walk on the edge again.

My brain begins to spout slogans to itself. Something it does to try to make sense out of the self-inflicted and irrational behavior its owner sometimes engages in. Yes, God takes care of fools. . . . Fear is a lack of faith. . . .

I hadn't planned on it, but when I got home from my first day back at the World Trade Center complex, I realized that writing about these visits would sort it out in my mind. Seeing it in black and white always makes things look different and there is something cathartic about writing one's thoughts and feelings on paper.

Red Cross Mary said to me on my first day at the FAC "Journaling keeps you sane." (There are those slogans—I'm doing it again.) I can tell you in all certainty that writing helped me to see more clearly before, so I thought that maybe it would help me to make some sense of this part of my life. . . . So I made a few more entries into the journal. I have given you the first and last of my return visits in the remainder of these pages. The best way I can think of to "tell about what has happened since" is to go full circle.

I see life as a series of circles—all interconnected, like the links of a chain. Sometimes, when the end becomes the beginning and I look back at where I've been, things click into place and I find that I have learned something. I have been fascinated to look back over my life and see how apparently random coincidences brought events and people together. Sometimes the people who came into my life had been within an arm's reach, but I didn't know they were there because the circle they were in had not yet linked with my own. I did say before—I don't believe in coincidence . . .

I'd like to explain myself by letting you step behind my eyes just one more time, see how things have changed for me, and meet the new angels whom I have met. If I have learned anything from this experience, I now know that the world is filled with angels. Everywhere. All you need to do to find them is open your heart, hold your arms wide, and let them into yours. . . .

December 22, 2002

I wake up in the dark, with butterflies in my stomach. My mind flashes back to last December. Oh God, here we go again—the crying, the heavy sadness—*What am I—nuts????* Why did I ever agree to do this, feel that grief again, open all of those old scars and go back there to that place? What made me think that this was a good idea: that I had the strength or the ability to do this again? I pull the blankets over my head. I picture the New York skyline in my mind: when I was a kid, the first day I saw it smoking and hazy with devastation, and the last time I saw it. I can never decide—do I never want to see it again, or do I never want to leave it?

I have been back there since December 2, our last family visit from the FAC. On March 22, the closing day of the FAC, the New Jersey State Police took everyone over for one last look, for us: a sweet and humane gesture. It did not help me. I had no sense of closure, no final anything. It left me feeling raw. It left the beast that now lives in my chest feeling restless and craving, wanting something, but not knowing what—chewing on me from the inside out. I was glad for the opportunity to go—to be there with those I worked with one last time. It was amazing to see the amount of progress that was made in the removal of debris in only three months.

This morning I lay in bed in the dark and brood over the fact that I am actually afraid of what may come from today, going back in there with families. I think back over the past year. At times when I was alone I sat in the middle of an empty room and screamed.

Because it just hurt so much.

It was too big to hold, too bad to face, too ugly to talk about, and held me so tight that I couldn't let it go if I tried. So I screamed. And cried. And it didn't help. So I practiced acceptance. I focused on the beauty.

So why am I going back there to do it again? Why would I stand in a line miles long for the chance to do it *just one more time*? Because I can't *not* go. Just like the first time, it pulls at me so strongly that I am beyond reason. I have this strange sense of compulsion—a lack of choice almost. So I climb out of bed, and take the butterflies in my insides downstairs to feed them coffee—lots of coffee.

We have planned to meet Chuck and his wife, Lee, at Liberty State Park and cross over the river by ferry to walk those familiar streets into the family viewing area on the corner of Liberty and Church streets. Chuck is from my office and worked at the FAC, mostly in the trailer, but went with us on the ferry visits a few times. He has friends who were early responders who had dug for bodies in the rubble. He has tried to help them with their pain. Lee is a dear woman, who put up with him weeding the yard at 3 a.m., and similar strange coping behaviors as he tried to sort out what he saw and heard. She stood beside his silence and waited for the tears to come. Lee will now share some of his experience firsthand.

Somehow, on the way up the New Jersey Turnpike I manage to convince Fred that it's exit 13A that we should get off at for Liberty State Park. It isn't. It's exit 14B. Okay—I drove there every day for *months*. And that was not even the first time I had been to New York City. I know the exit with my eyes closed. Not today. We get off, and then immediately back on the turnpike. My psychology professors would have told me about resistance, denial, and several other defense mechanisms that were telling me I didn't want to go there . . . and about self-sabotage.

Any other time and place maybe I could laugh. Not yet.

We arrive at the Liberty State Park Terminal Building, now back to being the spot to purchase tickets for the ferry to Ellis Island and the Lady in the harbor and a museum with a gift shop. Looks familiar, feels familiar, but the energy is so different—gone are the food tents, the people, the intake area, the snack stations, the smiles. It is cold and empty of people except those in the long line for the ferries out. Today no one hands me breakfast: my Rice Krispies bar and bottle of water as I yawn out a sleepy "morning!" on my way out back to the trailer. There are no trailers.

We are preoccupied with looking for Chuck and Lee so that we can jump on a boat over. *But*—the water taxi station has a hand-scrawled note taped to it: "The water taxi is not running this weekend. Sorry for the inconvenience." Off to a great start. We finally meet up with one another. Chuck apparently also insisted on taking the wrong turnpike exit. What are the odds of *that*? I take comfort in the fact that I'm not the only one having a hard time with this. . . . We decide to leave one car parked at the terminal and drive the other over to the city.

On the sidewalk of Church Street, we pass the chain-link fence and the barricade fencing that holds the public back. At street level, we look across from in front of the Millennium Hotel, now with windows and a shiny façade, toward the American Express building.

"Look—there's our corner without the platform."

From the sidewalk you really can't see into the pit because a chain-link fence surrounds the perimeter of the hole, and quite a distance past that is the high steel barricade that keeps the public away. From the sidewalk on Church Street, it is just too far back to see *into*, only across from. Thousands of people are there: looking, trying to take pictures through the fence, and pointing. Many are foreign, speaking other languages, looking touristy. We reach our destination, and as I stand explaining myself to the Port Authority cops on the other side, with my fingers wound through the chain link, I am struck by the smiles and the welcoming response that is almost immediate. They offer, "Whatever we can do for you."

Oh no—the other way around. "Please—put us to work!" We chat and get acquainted.

I ask one of the Port Authority cops, Jim, if we can go down inside the Pit for a while, since it is early and no families have arrived yet. We walk down the long ramp, seven stories down. Before us are the remnants of the parking garage, to the right the remnants of the train station, currently being reconstructed. I am having a hard time conjuring up the Towers in my mind, placing them where they need to be. My mind flashes back to the disorientation of some of those people on the platform who had worked here for years, but could not remember where things were. Now I'm the one who is disoriented. I hear myself asking Jim the most frequently asked question: "Where's the Burger King?" Now I can't find it either.

Jim points out the locations and the angles for me, and the scene comes back to life in my head: first as rubble, then as the Towers standing. I realize that I am slowly beginning to see. My eyes had been shut down from the returning shock as I entered, but now details begin to emerge—a flag hanging, a tiny Christmas tree near a union trailer, signs, objects. Details. My senses are beginning to work. Suddenly:

"Oh God. Chuck—I can smell it."

"Yeah, me too."

It was as if a breeze came every few seconds and carried with it that smell . . . was it just memories wafting in and out—or is it still there?

I sit on a concrete barricade and just look. As I let my eyes wander around I begin to feel heavy sadness settling around me again. But quiet. Just quiet. If I close my eyes, my brain substitutes the pile of rubble for me. I open my eyes and close them to just absorb the sensations running through me. Memory mixes with reality. My brain ponders the changes. But I am processing in photographs, not in words . . .

There is a sense of sacredness here—like walking into a huge cathedral—quiet, like God touching your face. It was always quiet here, but in a strange way. We always had to yell at each other to speak. A tractor trailer an inch from your shoulder would be unheard over the machinery and the noise of the work happening all around. But you could hear a sniffle from a family member across the platform. When it was time to leave you could hear the prayer from the fringes of the group. A place so loud that it became silent. Extremes. It was always sacred here as well: a hush that is almost peaceful, spiritual, holy. I don't know the word to place on it, but the feeling of its power is undeniable for those of us who have been here.

This time the horror has changed, but I don't know how to form it into words to be able to even think about it. I feel the change and accept it as different—violent and ugly still, but different somehow. I allow the photographs piling up in my head to simply sort it out for me; I'll feel it later when I get home and can maybe think about it a bit.

We take pictures. Chuck and I touch base with each other—checking in on reactions. "No, it never does get any easier" comes from my mouth in response to nothing, and I think of Bob that first day on the platform as he spoke those same words in my ear. I think just now it was Bob I spoke to—like entering a time warp vortex on the Sci-Fi channel. I'm here, and back there, but nowhere—all at once.

As we go back up the ramp, I walk over toward the fence on the corner of West and Liberty, wanting to see the spot a little better where we stood every day with our families. On the other side of the fence, our platform has been replaced by *green grass,* shiny new windows, and functional buildings. No more plywood covering missing windows—now people are behind those windows, walking around—looking out. Dust has been scrubbed away, brass doorways have been polished. Traffic lights are on the corner and are working. Cars are in the street again. Honking. People are everywhere. I take the photo of the corner where I stood so many times looking in. Now I'm looking out at a group of people taking pictures of me—standing where a crane that was bigger than any crane should have been was moored.

There is now bustling city life where our families stood and cried, where I wandered through rubble when the platform became too heavy to bear. I feel like a ghost again—transparent and filmy, but now I'm on the other side of being the ghost.

I used to watch my life go by and not feel a part of it, being at the FAC so much. Now I stand and look at where my feet had been, and see the scene as it was—and is now—all at the same time. Movies are running in my head again. I think about how it should be frightening, the way that my brain can conjure up a hologram-type movie to play over top of reality. I know that this probably qualifies as a hallucination. But the flashbacks are not scary. They simply are.

I feel very happy about seeing life here.

Families begin arriving. In my first group a woman stops on the ramp and cries, "They will put something here on top of him." She pauses and gazes down to the footprint of Tower Two. "He's down there," she says softly as she points. Her family members comfort her, and they continue on.

Another family has a young girl who hesitates as the rest of her family begin to leave. She hangs back. I ask her if she would like to take a rock with her, thinking that it may help her to go. "Nah. It's okay." I place a hand on her shoulder as we walk fast to catch up to her family, who are now almost all of the way up the ramp. About halfway up the ramp she turns to me and says, "I need a rock."

"Let's go."

I walk back down with her, and wait as she wanders a bit and picks up a few rocks until she locates one that feels right. She tosses it in the air, pockets it, and smiles. She leaves looking much lighter.

A Hindu family arrives, seven members in all. The father explains that he lost his son in Tower One. He asks where it was. I point it out. He asks to be allowed to take his family to that spot to pray. I ask Jim if it can be done, and he gathers them together and takes them out, gently leading them around mud puddles and trailers to a spot where they can pray for their loved one and have privacy.

As they leave they offer hugs and thanks in gratitude. It strikes me how different this is. Now the families can actually interact with it—they can take a piece, spend time without being herded. It is small and individualized. I used to hear from families at the FAC that they thought that the visits were sensitive, giving. But now it is so much more so.

I have the sense that something is shifting inside me again. I remember that on the platform in October 2001 I felt myself change like a slap in the face—that strong. I feel it again—that strong. And I can no more put it into words than the last time, except that this time something is not so heavy anymore. . . . It is so hard to try to think about something that has no words, so I just absorb some more.

As soon as we come up from the bottom of the ramp, someone else is on the way down, and someone is waiting for an escort. Early responders ask to come in as well, coming for their own closure—if there is such a thing. Between our trips down as we escort families, we chat near the gate. Port Authority guys tell their stories; we tell ours. We get friendly.

A steady and heavy stream of elbow-to-elbow pilgrims moves on the other side of the fence. I was at Lourdes. It was the same as this. They come to look for and at something they can't see, seeming to have painful questions that they never ask. Some speak no English. They try to point their cameras in at an angle that will give them no picture. They stand and stare at us through the chain link, as we stare back with that question between us that nobody ever asks. . . . God, this is strange. This is the strangest thing I have been on the other side of.

One of the cops, Phil, has been running cameras from the crowd over to the edge of the pit, to take shots for them. I wonder if I think that this is tourist-offensive and I can't decide, so when he returns from taking shots I ask him his thoughts. "Doesn't bother me. They should have pictures. They come here from all over to see."

He tells me it is this way every day: a nonstop sea of people. I think about all the opinions running in a jumble in my head, and finally make a decision: yes, we should all have a picture of the horror—so we always remember it. Every person who wants to see should have that right—I did.

I hear a heavy, deep Southern drawl interrupting my thoughts:
"'Scuze me, but would yew mind?"

I look into the face of a guy on the other side of the fence, who is wearing a baseball hat and thin leather jacket, freezing, and obviously not a New Yorker. He holds his camera up, offering it. I stick my arm through the opening where the gate is and take his camera—a little throwaway.

"Sure. What would you like?"

"Anythin' I cin git, please."

I take a couple of the Pit, and one of the memorial. He grins out a big "Thank yew" as I hand him his camera and a smile.

Whenever I am near the fence waiting for families to arrive I find myself running cameras back and forth with Phil. Fred laughs and says, "Look at you. You look like a trained monkey." Yes, I feel a bit like one on this side of the zoo attraction. . . .

Just inside the gate is a long wall that is about chest high, topped with a railing. On the railing are wreaths made of ribbon, each with an American flag. There are thirty-seven wreaths in honor of the Port Authority staff who were killed in the attacks. Port Authority lost thirty-seven civilian and thirty-seven uniformed personnel. Phil opens the gate for a man and woman, who go over to stand beside the wreaths, overlooking the pit. Phil, who is standing next to me, leans over and smiles: "He's asking her to marry him." The man asks the woman for her hand, and slips a ring on her finger. She begins to cry and accepts his proposal. The friends and family that they brought with them cheer and clap on the other side of the fence, with their noses pressed up to the chain link. I can't imagine wanting to start a life in front of a spot where so many were lost. *Why?*

"I think if I were her I might toss him over the wall. I'm not sure how I feel about this one."

He finishes the story for me: ten years ago the man proposed marriage on the 110th floor, but he never married her. They wanted to renew their engagement, but their spot was gone . . .

We wish them well as they leave and are folded into hugs and congratulations on the other side of the fence. No matter where they had renewed that proposal, the loss of their spot, and all of those lives, will follow their memories forever. Now I understand why. I couldn't do it, but I understand.

A British woman hands an expensive digital through the gate to me. She wants a picture of one of the signs that covers a building behind us. I take shots of the memorial, the Pit, and tell her I can't get the whole sign in the frame unless I go down the ramp. She wants to wait the few minutes it will take. In the meantime Chuck has ended up with another camera from her group. We go down, down, down, down together, almost to the bottom before the sign is readable, and fits in the viewfinder. We take the photos and jog back to a bit of teasing from Phil about having to arrest us for running off with other people's property. The gentleness and ease of these guys is amazing—the way they interact with so many so well. I have found another group of angels. . . .

Single lens reflex cameras barely make it through the opening. My hands are freezing, and have been for hours, so I take care to wind the straps around my arm so I don't drop them seven stories. . . . People hand over everything from cameras worth hundreds of dollars to throwaways. Children have little plastic kid cameras that make my fingers feel big and clumsy. And they keep coming. Pilgrims everywhere.

Chuck has finished escorting a man who apparently recognized me from the ferry visits through the FAC. The guy asks him to, "Tell her I said 'thanks.'" So sweet. I'm a little glad he didn't tell me himself—I probably would have cried all over him. Warms my heart.

I meet Jim coming up, halfway up the ramp. He asks me if I'm okay. I ask about him. He was here digging from the beginning, picking up body parts. He has been here a lot, through all of the changes. He has those eyes that smile at you, but behind them is much pain. Through all of their hurt, guys like this can be so tender, so caring with the families, and with us. They tear up when the families cry. It must be so hard to have to be cop-tough and human at the same time. And they are *so* human, so vulnerable, so hurt. I say a little prayer for him as we go our separate directions on the ramp.

This is the kind of stuff that can make you want to suck on a shotgun.

Down in the footprint of Tower Two is a family with a little girl. They release a red Mylar balloon that floats slowly past the American Express building. The photo it would make is striking, but I can't get my hands to do it. Somewhere drifting upward with that balloon is Daddy. Husband. Although I wish I could put it on film, and could have without disrupting the family, it seems sacrilegious—I just can't do it. I burn it into my brain instead.

The day has ended. We arrive back at the terminal building. Getting ready to leave, I resort to old habits; taking shots of pink sky and the Manhattan sights. It looks so pretty in pink. We head into the building to use the bathroom before tackling the turnpike. Fred goes into the men's and I hang out in the area that used to be our "family room." I look around at where teddy bears were stored, where mass care and the nurses were, the snack station, child care, tables and chairs. The memories come rushing back, and turn into visuals; the movies are running again. A lump grows in my throat. I turn around and see the spot where Mabel, my favorite therapy dog, would curl up and ready herself for a nap when she saw me walking in with my hard hat, on my last check for stragglers needing to board the bus. I saw her begin to make doggie circles. . . .

I saw myself taking that last run through.

I saw myself walking into the chapel; sitting at chairs talking to the EMTs.

I saw myself reading cards made by children and crying at the tables and laughing with Judy and the smells of *Whatthehell are they cooking for lunch?* And the line for the Tums . . .

I actually *saw* it. Reality dimmed all around me and the movie popped out of my brain until it was almost all that I could see.

Again I get the sensation of being a ghost, watching my life as it was—now a year later—as if I see a movie. I somehow, suddenly don't belong to either one of those lives anymore. . . . I think I have never had a visual sensation with a memory like this. Everywhere I turn, I see the old me superimposed over the reality of now, like a hologram. I *actually see it—this is too creepy—too scary.* It *really* hurts, and I don't know why. The pain rushes back. The tears want to come. Instead, the image of my husband comes walking into the movie looking substantially real. The fog lifts.

"This really hurts being here." He folds me into his arms and hugs me tight. Fred likes it back to normal, being what it is supposed to be.

"I miss the people being in it. It's lonely and empty now. And it hurts to remember." He puts his arm around me and walks me out to the train platform. The hologram movie fades, taking the ghosts with it.

As we walk to the car we talk about feeling good about today—the good people whom we met, the families we worked with, being glad that we took the risk and came back. I take a deep breath and feel it as being light. I feel feverish and windburned from being in the cold all day, and am amazed at how physically tired I am. I have a deep sense of having had the opportunity to give something back, and I have warm gratitude for it.

Somehow, it was healing.

January 4, 2003

Today is supposed to be the last, and the weather is New York bone-chilling cold. I feel like a stuffed tick in leggings, jeans, two sweaters, and a heavy coat. This time I brought gloves. They don't help.

When we arrive at the gate, I poke my camera through, and ask, "Will you please take a picture for me?" Phil, who taught me everything I know about taking pictures for strangers, laughs and opens the gate for us. We are greeted with stories about the holidays and the Christmas service; they had opened up the gates and let in anyone who wanted to partake. Apparently there were quite a few takers. There is also news that Sundays may still be available for the families. Today is possibly not the last. . . .

We brought our friend Mike with us, a firefighter with understandably mixed emotions. As soon as we get down the ramp, a woman turns around, looks at him and says, "Michael? What are you doing here?" They speak. Through the day, he meets up with two other people he knows. The world has become so small. . . . Fred laughs. "I guess we know why *you* were supposed to be here today."

The first family I meet had lost a son, a firefighter, in Tower Two. Mom proudly shares his picture. It was her first visit there since September 11. She is tearful, but so obviously proud. I think it must be the pride that sustains her and gives her strength. We talk about the lives he saved, the bravery he showed, and it seems to comfort her. As she is leaving she asks to have her picture taken with me.

The Hindu family I met on my first visit returns, this time with a son who was not able to make the first trip. Jim takes them to their spot in the footprint of Tower One to allow them quiet time to pray. He stands tall, dignified and quiet, at a distance waiting for them. I would bet if they wanted to be there all day he would wait there.

Jim is leaving a family he was speaking with. I had watched them embracing him and thanking him. He has tears in his eyes. He simply says, "I have been adopted now by so many people. . . ." He shakes his head. I wrap my arms around him, hold him, and rub his back. "It's so hard. Breathe deep, brother." Those who lost firefighters and police identify with him so quickly. I can't relate to how hard it must be to be there in uniform, to represent a loss for someone. His courage and gentle way must be so soothing.

Jim tells me about his experiences here since day one. He has been having trouble breathing. Many of the workers are having respiratory symptoms. He talks of not mentioning it to his wife because he does not want her to worry. "The only time I can really breathe is when I'm here. Working with the families helps." I worry about what will happen to him when the families don't come any more. What will he find to ease his pain? Sometimes I feel suffocated under the weight of it all too, and my work was easy in comparison. . . .

They are taking down the big Christmas tree that stands behind the cross on Church Street. On the tree are personalized ornaments and tokens from families of the victims. These are being gently removed by workers for use again next year. Also on the tree are tiny plastic angels: one for each person who died on 9/11. The Port Authority guys are discussing their feelings about the fact that the little angels are going to be thrown away with the tree. We get a box and head over to the tree, to take the angels to leave in the family room for the families.

A married couple who were on their way out hear our discussion and ask if they can accompany us to the tree to see it close up. We agree. When they hear of our mission to save the angels from the dumpster, they ask if they can help us to collect. We agree.

The tiny, fragile angels have been tied to the tree with *huge* wire— in a gauge heavy enough to hold down a house during a hurricane. I have to laugh—picturing the overkill; this was man's work: big heavy clumsy fingers, and the thought that "more is better." These angels are so tiny that the weight of trying to unwind the wire is enough to break many of them, no matter how gently I try to support them. Many have broken as they hung there—little heads suspended on huge lengths of heavy wire—looking very gory. I am nipping myself with the wire cutters, cutting myself with the wire, and stabbing myself with the pine needles. I am bleeding all over the angels. There is something amazingly creepy, but so fitting about holding a handful of bloody angels here in this spot. As we cut and collect, we pass a few angels through the fencing to onlookers, especially if they have children with them. We are cautioned by workers: "Be careful. It's like feeding stray cats. . . ."

As I put a handful of angels into the box, I look up and see a man on the other side of the fence standing stiffly straight, with tears streaming down his face. Big, solid, burly guy. He is simply looking. Hands folded behind his back, feet spread: military parade rest stance. At a quick glance, there would be no sign that he was in any distress. But pain hung on him like a heavy, black, wet blanket. If I could have climbed the fence and wrapped my arms around him I would have. I walked over and poked an angel through the fence to him. His red sad eyes looked at me and said "thanks." His shoulders slipped down just a bit. Oh, God, do I know . . . I'm without voice—I simply nod to him and go back to the tree. I glance over a couple of times and he remains rooted there like an oak, crying and dignified in his spot, but then he is gone. The pain pulls at my heart. If I could only do *something* . . .

After too many rounds of "Look—there's another one! Get that one! Just one more . . ." I am now scratched up my arms from being pricked as I climbed through the lower branches of the tree. Fortunately they tied it well in its stand: it held my weight well. We have retrieved all of the angels that we can reach. The married couple who had joined us are pleased that they were able to help us liberate the little angels, and have put some in a bag to take home to family. As they say their good-byes, the husband says, "I don't know you, but I feel close to you. I will never forget.this."

Yup. Me too.

We hang back to take some photos. The crowd on the sidewalk has thinned to almost nothing. I see a lone man poking his camera through the barricade fencing, trying to take a picture of the cross. I walk over and ask him if he wants me to take the shot for him. He is very pleased and passes the camera under the fencing. I walk closer to get a good shot. When I turn around, there is a *line* of people behind him, all holding their cameras in front of them—like offerings. Like stray cats, indeed. *What did you do—call the rest of the people on the bus?!!* Sweet Jesus, there is a line of people wanting pictures and looking for all the world like they are bearing a gift with their little cameras held out in front of them. Where did they all *come* from?

"Did you call all of these people?"

"No, I *swear!*" and he thanks me as he goes on his way, laughing.

"Please?" says the next one softly, with big eyes. I take a deep breath and commit myself to carrying through this task, all the while praying that God sends no one else to this line, or sends *me* a lightning bolt . . .

I take camera after camera, and blessedly, after a couple of dozen people, the line ends with a man who speaks no English. He holds up his camera, pantomiming three shots, saying "badda bing, badda bing, badda bing" for two horizontal and one vertical shot, ending at the cross.

No—he did *not* just say badda bing . . . I laugh my way over to the edge, and take his three photos. As I return he says, "Yes?"

"I got badda bing, badda bing, badda bing," doing an imitation of his three shots as requested.

"*San-ku!*" and thumbs up, the universal language for "good job!"

"Welcome."

As this is going on, I see Fred talking through the fence to a man who turns out to be a friend of the one that I am taking pictures for. They are talking about football. My husband is arguing about the Giants with a guy from Italy who speaks *very* little English . . . badda bing . . .

We take our own photos of the cross—it still makes my hair stand on end. A sculptor could not have created a more moving and bitter-sweet representation. I try to imagine how I would feel to be one of those who entered the destroyed Customs building to see such a thing simply standing there in the center. . . . As we are walking back toward the gate to the family viewing area we get the urge for street hot dogs, which (especially five minutes after you have finished eating one) always reminds me of the cautions that they give you during foreign travel: *never eat food that the natives cook on the street!* New York City street dogs create a special pain in the stomach, like no other indigestion. As I cross the street to the hot dog cart, I catch a familiar-looking person out of the corner of my eye—the man who was standing and crying.

"Oh *shit. It's you!*" he says as he opens both arms and walks quickly across the street. He gives me a big burly bear hug. "You can't possibly know . . . Oh God!"

Yes. I can.

We hug for a few eternal seconds, exchange a smile, and go our separate ways. Those words: "I don't know you, but I feel close to you. I will never forget this" echo through my brain.

A pretty, young girl is standing at the railing at the base of the ramp with someone who appears to be her boyfriend. She cries softly for a bit. As they prepare to go, she sees a stone that she wants and tries to reach it through the rail. He tries for her. They can't get it. Their words are too soft to hear, but her body language says to him "It's all right; never mind." She bends down where she stands, picks up a stone, brushes it off, but looks back over the rail at the one she *really* wants. I approach, and tell her to go get her stone.

"Oh, I was afraid that someone would yell at me."

"Don't worry. No one will yell at you here. Go ahead."

She wanders around, picking a couple of other stones before she claims her prize. No need to hurry anymore—the one she wants is waiting within reach and she approaches it with tantalizing slowness. I hand her tissues to wipe her hands and to wrap her stones in.

Jim and I chat about tattoos; he is also a tattoo artist. He had worked in a shop with friends of mine. Yes, the world is very small today. I think back to the FAC, and how many of us had been on the fringes of one another's lives for so long: going to the same schools, living around the corner, having mutual friends. What puts us in the same spot at the same time?

As the day ends and we are rounding ourselves up to leave, Fred approaches with his arm around Christina, the daughter of a friend of ours.

"Tina has accompanied a friend here, with his dad, who had lost a brother."

The world is getting even smaller. . . . We leave together and wander over to the Winter Garden, which now has glass, palm trees, benches, people, and smells of chocolate chip cookies inside. I close my eyes, and see in my brain the Winter Garden with fractured steel, burned and broken glass, glazed by heat and smoke. I can actually feel the smoke burning my eyes. I can smell it.

When we used to arrive at the dock and walk past the Mercantile, the blast damage to the Winter Garden was the first really visible sign of what was to come. Family members would gasp at the sight of it. I open my eyes again, and inhale chocolate-scented air deeply. I look up at the beautiful domed roof, sparkling in the late afternoon sun.

We wander outside through the back of the Winter Garden, toward the water, and walk that familiar sidewalk through to the corner of Liberty and West Streets. Remnants of cracked granite and sidewalk remain here and there—but, if you didn't know what happened those signs of damage might not even register. We pass the corner where the little alcove had housed our teddies, our flowers, our headstones. They are gone.

Without a trace. Sad, yes . . . but . . . Life is here . . .

All of a sudden I can't stop smiling.

Will I go back to those seventeen acres of New York again? Yes. As long as they are able to take the families in, and they are willing to grant me the honor and the privilege by opening the gate.

And in the future, when they build whatever it is. Eventually I will go to allow my brain to absorb "it" as well.

It will never be *over*. Not for me.

That's a good thing, because I have come to realize that *over* is the start of beginning, of new, of different.

Behind every *over*—there will always be

one more . . .

Order a copy of this book with this form or online at:
http://www.haworthpress.com/store/product.asp?sku=5464

COMPASSION AND COURAGE IN THE AFTERMATH OF TRAUMATIC LOSS
Stones in My Heart Forever

_____in hardbound at $39.95 (ISBN-13: 978-0-7890-2741-2; ISBN-10: 0-7890-2741-0)

_____in softbound at $19.95 (ISBN-13: 978-0-7890-2742-9; ISBN-10: 0-7890-2742-9)

Or order online and use special offer code HEC25 in the shopping cart.

COST OF BOOKS_____

POSTAGE & HANDLING_____
*(US: $4.00 for first book & $1.50
for each additional book)*
*(Outside US: $5.00 for first book
& $2.00 for each additional book)*

SUBTOTAL_____

IN CANADA: ADD 7% GST_____

STATE TAX_____
*(NJ, NY, OH, MN, CA, IL, IN, PA, & SD
residents, add appropriate local sales tax)*

FINAL TOTAL_____
*(If paying in Canadian funds,
convert using the current
exchange rate, UNESCO
coupons welcome)*

☐ **BILL ME LATER:** (Bill-me option is good on US/Canada/Mexico orders only; not good to jobbers, wholesalers, or subscription agencies.)

☐ Check here if billing address is different from shipping address and attach purchase order and billing address information.

Signature_____

☐ **PAYMENT ENCLOSED: $**_____

☐ **PLEASE CHARGE TO MY CREDIT CARD.**

☐ Visa ☐ MasterCard ☐ AmEx ☐ Discover
☐ Diner's Club ☐ Eurocard ☐ JCB

Account # _____

Exp. Date_____

Signature_____

Prices in US dollars and subject to change without notice.

NAME_____

INSTITUTION_____

ADDRESS_____

CITY_____

STATE/ZIP_____

COUNTRY_____ COUNTY (NY residents only)_____

TEL_____ FAX_____

E-MAIL_____

May we use your e-mail address for confirmations and other types of information? ☐ Yes ☐ No We appreciate receiving your e-mail address and fax number. Haworth would like to e-mail or fax special discount offers to you, as a preferred customer. **We will never share, rent, or exchange your e-mail address or fax number.** We regard such actions as an invasion of your privacy.

Order From Your Local Bookstore or Directly From
The Haworth Press, Inc.
10 Alice Street, Binghamton, New York 13904-1580 • USA
TELEPHONE: 1-800-HAWORTH (1-800-429-6784) / Outside US/Canada: (607) 722-5857
FAX: 1-800-895-0582 / Outside US/Canada: (607) 771-0012
E-mail to: orders@haworthpress.com

For orders outside US and Canada, you may wish to order through your local
sales representative, distributor, or bookseller.
For information, see http://haworthpress.com/distributors

(Discounts are available for individual orders in US and Canada only, not booksellers/distributors.)

PLEASE PHOTOCOPY THIS FORM FOR YOUR PERSONAL USE.
http://www.HaworthPress.com   BOF06